East German Film and the Holocaust

Film Europa: German Cinema in an International Context
Series Editors: **Hans-Michael Bock** (CineGraph Hamburg); **Tim Bergfelder** (University of Southampton); **Barbara Mennel** (University of Florida)

German cinema is normally seen as a distinct form, but this series emphasizes connections, influences and exchanges of German cinema across national borders, as well as its links with other media and art forms. Individual titles present traditional historical research (archival work, industry studies) as well as new critical approaches in film and media studies (theories of the transnational), with a special emphasis on the continuities associated with popular traditions and local perspectives.

Recent volumes:

Volume 22
East German Film and the Holocaust
Elizabeth Ward

Volume 21
Cinema of Collaboration: DEFA Coproductions and International Exchange in Cold War Europe
Mariana Ivanova

Volume 20
Screening Art: Modernist Aesthetics and the Socialist Imaginary in East German Cinema
Seán Allan

Volume 19
German Television: Historical and Theoretical Pespectives
Edited by Larson Powell and Robert R. Shandley

Volume 18
Cinema in Service of the State: Perspectives on Film Culture in the GDR and Czechoslovakia, 1945–1960
Edited by Lars Karl and Pavel Skopal

Volume 17
Imperial Projections: Screening the German Colonies
Wolfgang Fuhrmann

Volume 16
The Emergence of Film Culture: Knowledge Production, Institution Building, and the Fate of the Avant-Darde in Europe, 1919–1945
Edited by Malte Hagener

Volume 15
Homemade Men in Postwar Austrian Cinema: Nationhood, Genre and Masculinity
Maria Fritsche

Volume 14
Postwall German Cinema: History, Film History and Cinephilia
Mattias Frey

Volume 13
Turkish German Cinema in the New Millenium: Sites, Sounds, and Screens
Edited by Sabine Hake and Barbara Mennel

For a full volume listing, please see the series page on our website:
http://www.berghahnbooks.com/series/film-europa

EAST GERMAN FILM AND THE HOLOCAUST

Elizabeth Ward

berghahn
NEW YORK • OXFORD
www.berghahnbooks.com

First published in 2021 by
Berghahn Books
www.berghahnbooks.com

© 2021, 2024 Elizabeth Ward
First paperback edition published in 2024

All rights reserved. Except for the quotation of short passages for the purposes of criticism and review, no part of this book may be reproduced in any form or by any means, electronic or mechanical, including photocopying, recording, or any information storage and retrieval system now known or to be invented, without written permission of Berghahn Books.

Library of Congress Cataloging-in-Publication Data

Names: Ward, Elizabeth (Lecturer), author.
Title: East German film and the Holocaust / Elizabeth Ward.
Description: New York : Berghahn, 2021. | Includes bibliographical references, filmography, and index.
Identifiers: LCCN 2020015862 (print) | LCCN 2020015863 (ebook) | ISBN 9781789207477 (hardback) | ISBN 9781789207484 (ebook)
Subjects: LCSH: Motion pictures—Germany (East)—History. | Holocaust, Jewish (1939–1945), in motion pictures.
Classification: LCC PN1993.5.G33 W37 2020 (print) | LCC PN1993.5.G33 (ebook) | DDC 791.43/658405318—dc23
LC record available at https://lccn.loc.gov/2020015862
LC ebook record available at https://lccn.loc.gov/2020015863

British Library Cataloguing in Publication Data

A catalogue record for this book is available from the British Library

ISBN 978-1-78920-747-7 hardback
ISBN 978-1-80539-145-6 paperback
ISBN 978-1-80539-561-4 epub
ISBN 978-1-78920-748-4 web pdf

https://doi.org/10.3167/9781789207477

Contents

List of Illustrations	vii
Acknowledgements	x
List of Abbreviations and Acronyms	xii
Introduction	1
Part I. 1945–49	**15**
Chapter 1. Picking up the Pieces: Kurt Maetzig's *Ehe im Schatten*	23
Part II. 1949–61	**47**
Chapter 2. The German Democratic Republic's Ambassador of Good Will: Konrad Wolf's *Sterne*	53
Chapter 3. Reframing Victimhood: Konrad Wolf's *Professor Mamlock*	75
Part III. 1961–71	**89**
Chapter 4. Crimes of the Past and Politics of the Present: Wolfgang Luderer's *Lebende Ware*	97
Chapter 5. 'In Babelsberg, Nothing New': Gottfried Kolditz's *Das Tal der sieben Monde*	114
Part IV. 1971–80	**131**
Chapter 6. New Encounters on Well-Worn Paths: Kurt Jung-Alsen's *Die Bilder des Zeugen Schattmann*	137

Chapter 7. Returning to the Past: Frank Beyer's
    Jakob der Lügner   153

Part V. 1980–89   173

Chapter 8. Shifting Identities: Michael Kann's *Stielke, Heinz,
    fünfzehn*   179

Chapter 9. Calendar-Based Shame? Siegfried Kühn's
    Die Schauspielerin   194

Conclusion   216

Filmography   222

Bibliography   225

Index   239

Illustrations

Figure 1.1. From a position of strength to one of submission, Elisabeth's body language shifts over the course of the film in ways that reflect her loss of agency. © DEFA-Stiftung/Kurt Wunsch. 33

Figure 1.2. Prior to the coming to power of the NSDAP, Willy Prager (Dr Silbermann) was one of Germany's best-known *Kabarett* performers. After 1933 he was banned from the stage and *Ehe im Schatten* was his first film role since 1932. © DEFA-Stiftung/Kurt Wunsch. 36

Figure 1.3. *Ehe im Schatten* points the finger of responsibility at 'ordinary Germans' – and even the film's audience – for the persecution of Jews. © DEFA-Stiftung/Kurt Wunsch. 39

Figure 2.1. Walter is repeatedly positioned as an outsider in *Sterne*. © DEFA-Stiftung/Lotte Michailowa. 57

Figure 2.2. The similarities and differences between Walter and Kurt's interactions with the Jewish prisoners reflect subtle variations in each character's values. © DEFA-Stiftung/Lotte Michailowa. 59

Figure 2.3. Sketches and photographs reveal Wolf's careful use of montage to contrast Walter and Kurt's behaviour in two key sequences. © DEFA-Stiftung/Lotte Michailowa. Source: Akademie der Künste. 61

Figure 2.4. Subtle, but significant, reminders of Jewish persecution haunt the film throughout. © DEFA-Stiftung/Lotte Michailowa. 67

Figure 3.1. Hans Mamlock's victimhood may be explicitly aligned to his Jewish background, but the reasons for his persecution are less clear. © DEFA-Stiftung/Walter Ruge. 80

Figure 3.2. The symbolic use of hands as the white-gloved Inge and the black-gloved Dr Hellpach loom over Professor Mamlock. © DEFA-Stiftung/Walter Ruge.	83
Figure 3.3. Inge's voice concludes the film and points to the antifascist future. © DEFA-Stiftung/Walter Ruge.	84
Figure 4.1 Images of entrapment convey how Chorin becomes a prisoner in his own home. © DEFA-Stiftung/Dieter Jaeger, Hans-Joachim Zillmer.	102
Figure 4.2. The filmmakers' desire to present the events of Budapest in 1944 as a critique of the inequalities of capitalism leads to a visual and narrative over-emphasis on the Jewish characters' wealth. © DEFA-Stiftung/Dieter Jaeger, Hans-Joachim Zillmer.	104
Figure 4.3. The final scene suggests Kastner will be judged for his actions with Becher. © DEFA-Stiftung/Dieter Jaeger, Hans-Joachim Zillmer.	110
Figure 5.1. Martyna's attack is all the more shocking given the political and cultural 'freeze' shaping East German filmmaking in the late 1960s. © DEFA-Stiftung/Herbert Kroiss, Erich Krüllke. Source: Filmmuseum Potsdam.	120
Figure 5.2. The use of set pieces from the Indianerfilm underpins scenes of confrontation and revenge in *Das Tal der sieben Monde*. © DEFA-Stiftung/Herbert Kroiss, Erich Krüllke. Source: Filmmuseum Potsdam.	123
Figure 5.3. Rudek's attempts to prove he is a 'decent German' are contingent upon his acceptance into the antifascist communion. © DEFA-Stiftung/Herbert Kroiss, Erich Krüllke. Source: Filmmuseum Potsdam.	126
Figure 6.1. The point-of-view shot forces the spectator to witness the murder of Dr Marcus from the perspective of the perpetrator. © Foundation Deutsches Rundfunkarchiv (DRA)/rbb media.	145
Figure 6.2. A poster by the communist resistance is pinned to Frank's shirt, on top of which Koberschulte pins Frank's 'Judenstern'. © Foundation Deutsches Rundfunkarchiv (DRA)/rbb media.	146

Figure 6.3. Frank Schattmann and Andrea Wohlfahrt visit Auschwitz so that future generations can see the past through Frank's eyes. © Foundation Deutsches Rundfunkarchiv (DRA)/rbb media.   150

Figure 7.1. In the screenplay, Herschel and Roman Schtamm are actually described as twin brothers, although this is not made explicit in the film. © DEFA-Stiftung/Herbert Kroiss.   163

Figure 7.2. Erwin Geschonneck's star quality complicates readings of Jewish victimhood in *Jakob der Lügner*. © DEFA-Stiftung/Herbert Kroiss.   164

Figure 7.3. Even in her fanciful daydreams, Lina wears the 'Judenstern'. © DEFA-Stiftung/Herbert Kroiss.   167

Figure 8.1. The film's inability to transcend stereotypes ultimately renders its treatment of antisemitism superficial. © DEFA-Stiftung/Herbert Kroiss. Source: Filmmuseum Potsdam.   184

Figure 8.2. At the end of the film, Heinz runs off into the distance to be reunited with Gabi – still carrying the uniform that he wore when he was inculpated in crimes against civilians. © DEFA-Stiftung/Herbert Kroiss.   185

Figure 8.3. In *Stielke, Heinz, fünfzehn*, the victimhood of Jews is visually appropriated, but narratively absent. © DEFA-Stiftung/Herbert Kroiss.   187

Figure 9.1. Maria's unreflexive appropriation of the body language of the leader of the Bund Deutscher Mädel appears out of place against the backdrop of antisemitism. © DEFA-Stiftung/Norbert Kuhröber.   203

Figure 9.2. The depiction of Maria/Manja is incongruous with both character and setting. © DEFA-Stiftung/Norbert Kuhröber.   208

Figure 9.3. The antisemitism in *Die Schauspielerin* is so 'everyday' that it is difficult to apply the term perpetrator at all. © DEFA-Stiftung/Norbert Kuhröber.   210

Acknowledgements

The publication of this book marks the end of a research and writing process that has lasted several years. This journey has been underpinned by the collegial generosity, personal support and academic insights of so many brilliant people.

I am most grateful to Bill Niven and Erica Carter who have not only been the most wonderful mentors, but also incredibly supportive friends. Their support for the next generation of scholars is unparalleled and I thank them for all they have done and continue to do. I hope to be able to express my full gratitude by paying this forward in my career.

I would like to thank everyone who has read and commented on drafts of chapters in their different forms and whose feedback has been invaluable. The support from colleagues within the German Studies community and, in particular, the German Screen Studies Network is a wonderful source of inspiration and I look forward to our future conversations, collaborations and exchanges. I would like to express my personal thanks to Chris Homewood for his support and friendship, as well as to Kerry Dobson, Chris Harris, Eleanor Halsall, Alison Price-Moir, Helen Fenwick, Rob Miles and Catherine Baker for their generosity of spirit, enthusiasm and shared laughter.

Thank you to Berghahn Books, in particular to Chris Chappell, Mykelin Higham and Caroline Kuhtz, for their ongoing belief in this project and for all their behind-the-scenes work in bringing it to press. I am also most grateful to the readers for their insightful and constructive feedback that undoubtedly helped to develop this book further.

A considerable amount of archival work underpins this book. I would like to thank the archivists, collections specialists and reading room staff without whose knowledge, insights and support I could not have completed this book. Here in particular I would like to thank Tim Storch and the Bundesarchiv, Ute Klawitter and the Bundesarchiv-

Filmarchiv, Birgit Scholz and the Potsdam Filmmuseum, Nicky Rittmeyer and the Akademie der Künste, the Politisches Archiv des Auswärtiges Amts, Jörg-Uwe Fischer and the Deutsches Rundfunk Archiv, the archives and library of the Deutsche Kinemathek, the Press Documentation Centre of the Filmuniversität Babelsberg Konrad Wolf, the DEFA-Stiftung, the Deutsches Filminstitut & Filmmuseum and the Margaret Herrick Library.

During the writing process, I spent significant amounts of time in university libraries in Germany. The ability for anyone to walk in and make use of academic materials and benefit from the resources is a model that every scholarly institution should seek to emulate. I am also most grateful to the Arts and Humanities Research Council, the Deutscher Akademischer Austauschdienst, the German Historical Society, Women in German Studies and the German Screen Studies Network for providing generous funding that facilitated much of the research in its earlier stages, and to the University of Hull and the University of Leeds for their institutional support. Some material in this book has appeared in print previously and I wish to thank *German Life and Letters* and John Wiley & Sons Ltd, Metropol Verlag and Peter Lang for allowing this to be incorporated within this book.

On a personal note, thank you to my family and friends. Thank you to Jennifer Rushworth, Philip Chadwick, Sarah Garforth, Catherine Barnard, Daniel Wolpert, Rachel Green, Matthew Hunter, Theresa Guczogi and Giorgia Faraoni who have endured the full spectrum of emotions, have championed the successes and have been by my side during the challenges. They never once questioned my ability to undertake this project – often in spite of my quite vocal protestations to the contrary – and I could not wish for more loyal coffee companions and truer friends. Finally, to my parents for their ongoing love and support, thank you.

Abbreviations and Acronyms

AdK	Akademie der Künste (Academy of Arts)
BArch	Bundesarchiv (German Federal Archives)
BDM	Bund Deutscher Mädel (League of German Girls)
DEFA	Deutsche Film-Aktiengesellschaft (German Film Corporation)
DFF	Deutscher Fernsehfunk (German Broadcasting)
DDR-FS	Fernsehen der DDR (GDR Television)
FBW	Filmbewertungsstelle Wiesbaden (Film Evaluation Board Wiesbaden)
FRG	Federal Republic of Germany
GDR	German Democratic Republic
HV Film	Hauptverwaltung Film (Central Administration Film)
KAG	Künstlerische Arbeitsgruppen (Artistic Working Groups)
KdAW	Komitee der Antifaschistischen Widerstandskämpfer (Committee of Antifascist Resistance Fighters)
MFN	Most Favoured Nation
OMGUS	Office of Military Government, United States
NÖSPL	Neue Ökonomische System der Planung und Leitung (New Economic System of Planning and Management)
NSDAP	Nationalsozialistische Deutsche Arbeiterpartei (National Socialist German Workers' Party)

PA AA   Politisches Archiv des Auswärtigen Amts (Political Archive of the Federal Foreign Office)

SBZ   Sowjetische Besatzungszone (Soviet Occupation Zone)

SED   Sozialistische Einheitspartei Deutschlands (Socialist Unity Party of Germany)

SMAD   Sowjetische Militäradministration in Deutschland (Soviet Military Administration in Germany)

Ufa   Universum Film-Aktiengesellschaft (Universum Film AG)

VEB   Volkseigener Betrieb (People's Own Industry)

VVN   Vereinigung der Verfolgten des Naziregimes (Association of Persecutees of the National Socialist Regime)

ZK   Zentralkomitee (Central Committee)

INTRODUCTION

In 1988, the East German Ministry for Culture and the Secretary of State for Church Affairs jointly curated the exhibition 'Und lehrt sie: Gedächtnis!' ('And Teach Them: Memory!') to mark the fiftieth anniversary of the 1938 November Pogroms ('*Kristallnacht*'). The final section of the exhibition was dedicated to films about the Holocaust and Jewish persecution, a subject which, according to the accompanying catalogue, was a 'thematic constant' in East German cinema.[1] We may well approach such claims with scepticism. After all, it was only in 1990 that the East German parliament (*Volkskammer*) finally acknowledged the German Democratic Republic's (GDR) 'joint responsibility' for the 'humiliation, expulsion and murder of Jewish women, men and children' under National Socialism.[2] This statement by the Volkskammer marked a significant shift in terms of official, public statements about the National Socialist past by state representatives. Until this point, moral and criminal responsibility for the crimes of National Socialism had been firmly placed at the door of the Federal Republic of Germany (FRG). But to what extent did this belated acknowledgement of the GDR's failure to confront its 'joint responsibility' for the German National Socialist past also undermine the state's assertion that the treatment of Jewish persecution was a 'thematic constant' in East German film? This book examines the changing ways East German filmmakers approached the subject of the Holocaust and the National Socialist persecution of Jews throughout the course of the GDR's existence.

It is certainly true that prior to 1990, the ruling Socialist Unity Party of Germany (Sozialistische Einheitspartei Deutschlands or SED) never officially acknowledged any inherited responsibility for the crimes committed on its territory or by Germans during the Third Reich. Instead, it sought to recast East Germans as both the working-class victims of, and antifascist victors over, 'capitalist fascist' oppression by presenting National Socialism as the inevitable outcome of a politically and economically driven class struggle. This allowed the SED to argue that the destruction of the political and economic structures that had facilitated the rise of National Socialism meant that the GDR had 'eradicated imperialism and militarism, racism and antisemitism by its roots'.[3] By extension, the FRG was viewed as an unreformed continuation of those same structures that were still ruled by 'capitalist fascist' forces. As expedient as this realignment of responsibility undoubtedly was, this political-economic presentation of the past nevertheless left one crucial point unexplained: the specificities of Jewish persecution.

This interpretative framework served not only as an exculpation from the past, but also as a legitimization for the present. By presenting the working class and the communist resistance as the respective victims and victors of National Socialism, East Germans were largely absolved of responsibility for the crimes of the past. Meanwhile antifascist resistance members were celebrated as the heroic founding fathers of the 'first socialist state on German soil'.[4] The extent to which such claims stood up to scrutiny is dubious. While it is certainly true that the SED party leadership included several individuals who were members of the communist resistance and who had been persecuted under National Socialism, this did not extend to the population at large: only one per cent of the East German population were considered antifascist veterans.[5] As the writer Christa Wolf later reflected, it seemed that 'a small group of antifascists who governed the country extended . . . its consciousness of victory to the whole population'.[6]

In order to understand the cultural and political significance of East German Holocaust films, we must first turn our attention to the antifascist film. It should come as little surprise that the state doctrine of antifascism was a highly visible theme in East German film. Described by the Ministry for Culture as 'the first great tradition' of East German cinema,[7] the antifascist film played a key 'mediating function' in shaping collective memories of the past.[8] From biopics of leading communist figures (*Ernst Thälmann – Sohn seiner Klasse*, 1954; *Wo andere schweigen*, 1984), to war films (*Mich dürstet*, 1956; *Fünf Patronenhülsen*, 1960), resistance narratives (*Stärker als die Nacht*, 1954; *Leute mit Flügeln*, 1960) and childhood dramas (*Sie nannten ihn Amigo*, 1958; *Die Schüsse der Arche Noah*, 1983), antifascist films crossed several genres and remained a staple of East German cinema throughout the existence of the GDR.[9] According to Daniela Berghahn, antifascist films constituted roughly thirteen per cent of East German cinematic output, and annual film weeks and even month-long celebrations were programmed to showcase the scope of this 'cornerstone of East German film culture'.[10] Moreover, in light of its popular appeal and ability to be exported around the world, film always played a central role in articulations of national identity abroad. As early as 1951, the Secretary of State for Foreign Affairs, Anton Ackermann, declared that DEFA's best films were 'our most effective diplomatic emissaries abroad because they bear witness in their vital, visual and acoustic force to the fact that, in the shape of the German Democratic Republic, a new, peaceful and democratic German state has come into being'.[11]

Given the significance of antifascist films in projecting and canonizing heroic East German narratives of the National Socialist past, we could perhaps expect there to be little space afforded to alternative forms of victimhood, not least those that could not easily be situated within an antifascist framework. Angelika Timm stresses that while the Holocaust was 'not ignored' in the GDR, 'for decades it played only a minor role in the GDR's historiography and political culture'.[12] Since the Holocaust was largely subsumed under narratives of antifascist resistance, it has long been assumed that the Holocaust and Jewish persecution were topics also largely absent from East German cinema screens. It is certainly true that in the GDR there was no comparable model to the West German process and discourse of *Vergangenheitsbewältigung* ('coming to terms with the past') which created a public and scholarly space for discussions about Jewish victimhood and German perpetration.[13] Rather, the equivalent public and scholarly debates in the GDR were shaped by the parameters of the class-based victim–victor framework of commemoration. However, when we look to East German filmmakers' engagement with Jewish persecution, a very different picture emerges.

The Holocaust was a present and permissible theme in East German cinema. Films about Jewish persecution were made throughout the state's existence and were regularly marketed on an international platform. Indeed, the GDR's only Oscar nomination was for *Jakob der Lügner* (*Jacob the Liar*, 1974), a film about the persecution of Jews which does not feature a single antifascist character. We must, however, be cautious about the conclusions we draw from this, as ascertaining the simple presence of a theme offers limited insights into how that theme was presented. If we focus exclusively on release schedules, it is clear that filmmakers in the Soviet Zone of Occupation led the way in cinematic engagements with the Holocaust.[14] The very first postwar German film, *Die Mörder sind unter uns* (*The Murderers are Among Us*, 1946), was licensed by the Soviet Military Administration in Germany (SMAD) and broached the subject of the mass murder of the Jews through somewhat veiled references to concentration camps, the symbolic use of stars (intended to evoke the '*Judenstern*') and a carefully placed newspaper article with the headline, 'Two Million People Gassed!'. In the ensuing years, passing references became more integral narrative elements and the GDR's principal state-owned film studio, the Deutsche Film-Aktiengesellschaft (the German Film Corporation, DEFA), continued to produce films that dealt with Jewish persecution throughout the course of its existence.[15] However, the state's seeming willingness to permit, if not encourage, East German films that engaged with issues of Jewish victimhood is immediately complicated by its refusal to approve the release of three non-East German productions now widely considered seminal in the history of the Holocaust on film: *Nuit et brouillard* (*Night and Fog*, 1955), *Holocaust* (1978) and *Shoah* (1985).[16] In each case, political objections about how the past was (and was not) presented motivated the decision not to release or broadcast the production.[17] Thus on their own, release schedules only offer a partial insight into the relationship between East German film and the Holocaust. Rather, if we are to understand the complex and shifting relationship between film and the Holocaust in the GDR, we must interrogate how aesthetic and narrative strategies were employed in these films within the context of a state in which memories of National Socialist persecution were highly prescribed, tightly controlled and invariably politicized.

Methodology

East German Film and the Holocaust is the first dedicated study of representations of the Holocaust and Jewish persecution in East German film. To date, critical examinations of East German Holocaust films have largely been limited to individual chapters within international studies of the Holocaust or they have featured within wider discussions of antifascist film in the GDR.[18] This is not to claim that East German cultural engagements with National Socialist Jewish persecution have been completely overlooked by scholars. Paul Doherty's *The Portrayal of Jews in GDR Prose Fiction* (1997) explores the depiction of Jewish characters in both the context of the Third Reich and postwar Germany. Mark Wolfgram's study *Getting History Right: East and West German Collective Memories of the Holocaust and War* (2010) draws on empirical data and quantitative sources such as opinion polls, audience attendance figures and newspaper reviews in the course of exploring representations of Jewish persecution in East and West German television, film, radio and newspapers. Manuela Gerlof's study of East German radio plays, *Tonspuren: Erinnerungen an den Holocaust im Hörspiel der DDR* (2010), provides a particularly illuminating point of comparison with East German cinema and there are several parallels in terms of production and reception between the broadcast of radio plays and the release of feature films that deal with Jewish persecution. Finally, Elke Schieber's *Tangenten: Holocaust und jüdisches Leben im Spiegel audiovisueller Medien der SBZ und der DDR – Eine Dokumentation* (2016) provides a detailed thematic overview of East German films and television programmes that dealt with Jewish persecution and which allows scholars to trace the shifting levels of interest in engagements with the Holocaust. *East German Film and the Holocaust* builds on these studies through an interdisciplinary approach that places close readings of nine feature films alongside detailed archival research into the production and reception of the films in order to explore how East German filmmakers presented Jewish persecution on screen and how the state responded to such films. Each chapter combines close readings of the films' visual and narrative strategies with an examination of the films' production histories by drawing on a range of documents from the DEFA studio, the Ministry for Culture, press holdings and the filmmakers' archival holdings.

The analysis of the films in this book is informed by three principal concerns. Firstly, in order to examine the ways in which filmmakers addressed Jewish victimhood, it is important to establish how the characters' Jewish identity is codified. This encompasses not only the visual and linguistic means by which a character's Jewish identity is conveyed on screen, but also the narrative function and agency attributed to the characters themselves. This point is particularly important given that discussions of victimhood and persecution in the GDR were underpinned by a binary construction of National Socialist persecution: whereas political victims were presented as active 'Fighters against Fascism' (*Kämpfer gegen Faschismus*), Jewish victims were presented as passive 'Victims of Fascism' (*Opfer von Faschismus*). Consequently, it is important that we examine the Jewish characters' function in the plot and the impact of other – and, above all, antifascist – characters on this presentation. From this, we can establish the extent to which Jewish victims were reduced to passive ciphers for the demonstration of antifascist resistance or whether the films actually provided a unique space for the exploration of Jewish victimhood by placing the spotlight on a victim group frequently pushed to the margins of East German commemorative discourses.

An analysis of victimhood should not be divorced from an examination of the perpetrators. There was a clear image of the National Socialist perpetrator in the GDR that was characterized by a dual displacement. In the first instance, responsibility was displaced vertically onto political or military elites whose actions were considered symptomatic of a politically and economically motivated class struggle. Secondly (and often concurrently), responsibility was discharged horizontally through geographical displacement whereby a clear link was established between the fascist National Socialist state of the past and the capitalist Federal Republic of the present. By analysing both the types of persecution depicted and the presentation of perpetrators, we can establish the extent to which East German Holocaust films reflected or diverged from the political rhetoric which surrounded and informed discussions of responsibility in the GDR. In this way, we can examine whether East German film upheld dominant narratives of the National Socialist past or whether it challenged the audience's relationship to the National Socialist past and, in so doing, offered an alternative space for the exploration of the figures of victim and perpetrator.

Finally, this book explores how the films were marketed by DEFA and discussed in the domestic and international press. Both the domestic distributor, Progress Film, and the international distributor, DEFA-Außenhandel, sought to promote desired readings of the films through press notes, specially-designed film booklets and programmes for audiences, posters and lobby photographs. Comparing the dominant tropes used in the press materials with those employed in the films themselves exposes important points of convergence with, and divergence from, the discussion and presentation of Jewish persecution in East German culture and society more broadly, and the specific presentation of these themes in each film. Here we discover that some of the most interesting debates surrounding East German Holocaust films in the press were not only about the films themselves, but also about the dominant modes of Holocaust remembrance in the GDR. In this contested space, we repeatedly discover fascinating exchanges about East German commemorative narratives, the extent to which these were indeed representative of East Germans' own lived experiences and whether such frames of reference were still valid and relevant for younger audiences.

All the films examined in this book were released in different political, social and cultural contexts. Situating the films within their domestic release context allows us to understand the broader political, social and cultural debates unfolding at the time of the films' production and release and also avoids the danger of viewing DEFA – or even the GDR – as homogenous and unchanging. The so-called 'freezes and thaws' that characterized East German society often redrew the parameters of permissibility within a matter of months. A film could enter pre-production during a period of relative liberalization (a 'thaw'), only to encounter difficulties upon release because of the renewed political or cultural orthodoxy prevailing at the time (a 'freeze'). However, reading the films as a transparent window onto East German society also poses key challenges if we are to understand the complexities of East German Holocaust films. DEFA may have been a horizontally and vertically integrated state-owned film studio, but it would be misleading to read its output as unproblematic reflections of party positions. Seán Allan has rightly argued that to view East German cinema as little more than 'an appendage of the state ideological apparatus', is to 'ignore the often considerable tensions that existed between the filmmakers and their political masters'.[19] Rather, as the director Roland Gräf argued, 'art in the GDR always developed from friction, never from pure affirmation'.[20]

There were recurring themes in East German cinematic representations of Jewish persecution. Visually, the trope of assimilated Jewish Germans as protectors of German culture recurs in every decade of the GDR's Holocaust films. Narratively, responsibility for antisemitic persecution is repeatedly displaced onto political and military elites, and there is a consistent reluctance to consider the relationship between 'ordinary' Germans and antisemitism. Instead of grappling with widespread societal acceptance or propagation of antisemitism, the films often seek to valorize examples of antifascist solidarity and heroism, especially during the 1950s and 1960s. Although there was no explicit attempt to prescribe the limits of representation for East German cinematic engagements with the Holocaust, self-censorship undoubtedly played a role in East German filmmaking. Directors and screenwriters largely understood the parameters of aesthetic and narrative representation and the extent to which they could deviate from these dominant modes. But that does not mean that filmmakers did not seek to test, question or even challenge these boundaries. Indeed, when we study East German Holocaust films in detail, we see that it is precisely the discord between content and context that renders East German Holocaust film such valuable means of studying Holocaust memory in the GDR.

Terminology

In any study of the Holocaust and Jewish persecution, it is important to discuss terminology. The term 'Holocaust' is used here in accordance with the definition of the United States Holocaust Memorial Museum: 'The Holocaust was the systematic, bureaucratic, state-sponsored persecution and murder of six million Jews by the Nazi regime and its collaborators'.[21] It is not the assertion of this book that Jews were the only victims of National Socialist persecution. However, at the heart of this book is the question of how Jewish persecution was presented on screen within the context of a country that prescribed the primacy of communist persecution and resistance during the Third Reich. The films selected are all feature films with plots which play out between 1933 and 1945 and which feature a Jewish character as a primary figure in the film. Characters are described as Jewish in this book according to their designation as such in the films' plot. It is important to note that in several of the films studied here, the Jewish characters reject the imposition of a 'Jewish identity' upon them as defined by the National Socialist state and the films frequently show the difficulty assimilated Jewish-German citizens face when a National Socialist conceptualization of what it means to be Jewish is forced upon them.

The term 'Holocaust film' is a contentious one. Despite its frequent use in film scholarship, the term is rarely defined. There are no clear parameters that delineate what constitutes a Holocaust film and the term is frequently employed to encompass films that may or may not foreground the experiences of victims or survivors, that do or do not feature perpetrators, that can be set during the 1930s, during the Second World War or in a postwar context, and that are located in Germany, the so-called Greater German Reich or beyond. This book applies two criteria to the selection of films. Firstly, all the films examined here take place between 1933 and 1945. Secondly, Jewish victimhood or persecution is central to the plot. Using these criteria, nine East German films have been selected for detailed examination. The list of films is not exhaustive and the employment of the aforementioned selection criteria also means that familiar East German films such as *Die Mörder sind unter uns*, *Affaire Blum* (*Blum Affair*, 1948) and *Nackt unter Wölfen* (*Naked Among Wolves*, 1963) do not feature as case studies in this book. The omission of these films is not intended to question the importance of these films' discussions of Jewish persecution, but the core focus of this book remains on films that primarily foreground the Jewish experience during the Third Reich.

Chapter Overview

This book is divided into five parts that correspond to decisive shifts in East German culture, politics and society. Each part begins with a discussion of the political, social and cultural developments in the period and the key developments in East German Holocaust commemoration and film that serve to frame the case studies within the broader filmic landscape. Part I examines the challenges of addressing audiences from the immediate aftermath of the Second World War to the foundation of the GDR in 1949. Described by director Kurt Maetzig as 'a wonderful period' in which 'we were very free and could make the films we wanted to make', this chapter examines how themes of Jewish persecution were approached by filmmakers at a time when DEFA operated under the auspices of the SMAD and the influence of the SED on the studio was significantly limited.[22] Although several films during this period include Jewish characters who are victims of National Socialism, only one film places a Jewish victim at the core of the plot: Kurt Maetzig's *Ehe im Schatten* (*Marriage in the Shadows*, 1947). Upon release, *Ehe im Schatten* became one of the most successful postwar German films and was even considered by the Academy of Motion Picture Arts and Sciences for the category of Best Film. In recent years, however, Maetzig's film has been increasingly criticized for its heavy – and seemingly critically unreflexive – reliance on melodrama, a mode of filmmaking that was highly prevalent and popular in film during the Third Reich. This chapter approaches the film from a different perspective and argues that Maetzig actually seeks to appropriate and invert these familiar visual and narrative tropes in order to challenge National Socialist binary constructions of Jew and German and to rehabilitate this recently ostracized section of the population back into the nation's emotional psyche.

Part II examines the impact of celebratory antifascist conversion narratives on the depiction of Jewish victimhood in the GDR's first decade up until the construction of the Berlin Wall through Konrad Wolf's *Sterne* (*Stars*, 1959) and *Professor Mamlock* (1961). The period from the founding of the GDR in 1949 to the building of the Berlin Wall in 1961 saw the rapid politicization of DEFA and a concurrent fall in the popularity of East German films among domestic audiences. Studies of East German cinema have rightly emphasized the centrality of the *Aufbaufilm* ('construction film') in (re)shaping an inherent sense of East German identity among audiences in the 1950s and it is no coincidence that this decade should have seen an exponential rise in the number of antifascist films in an attempt to promote the newly founded state's core founding narrative. The two case studies in this section reflect the central tenets of the *Aufbau* period. Both films focus on young protagonists and their antifascist conversion as they move from a position of passive indifference to becoming committed individuals determined to act against the National Socialist state. Although the topic of the antifascist conversion may appear to situate these films firmly within familiar discourses of the primacy of antifascism, these chapters argue that *Sterne* and *Professor Mamlock* create an important space for the discussion of Jewish victimhood that exists independently of celebrations of antifascist resistance and sacrifice.

Part III examines the impact of the Eleventh Plenum on East German Holocaust film. The Eleventh Plenum of December 1965 was originally intended as a forum for the discussion of economic matters. However, by the autumn of 1965, it became increasingly clear that the New Economic System (*Neues Ökonomisches System der Planung und Leitung*) had failed to overcome the GDR's ongoing structural economic problems. At the Plenum, the SED leadership attempted to divert attention away from its own shortcomings and onto the alleged 'manifestations of immorality' and presentations of a 'lifestyle alien to socialism' in East German culture.[23] The consequences of this cast a long shadow over East German filmmaking. Twelve films – nearly the entire year's production – were banned as a result of the Plenum, but it was the long-term effects that proved to be more decisive for the future direction of the studio. The aesthetic innovation that underpinned so many of the banned productions was hastily superseded by a return to the familiar through a heavy reliance on genre films coupled with the avoidance of any topics which could be considered politically or socially controversial. Here we encounter an unexpected and surprising finding in relation to East German Holocaust film. Two of the earliest films to be released after the Eleventh Plenum and during this cultural 'freeze' address issues of Jewish persecution in ways which, while not challenging the primacy of antifascist resistance and sacrifice, certainly did not promote them. Wolfgang Luderer's 1966 film *Lebende Ware* (*Living Wares*) presents Jews as the sole victim group of National Socialist persecution and does not feature a single antifascist character. Gottfried Kolditz's *Das Tal der sieben Monde* (*The Valley of the Seven Moons*, 1967) tells the story of the star-crossed lovers of the *Volksdeutscher* ('ethnic German') Rudek and the Jewish Pole Martyna. One of the most disturbing scenes in the film is the revelation that Martyna has been raped by a German National Socialist. These chapters explore what these films reveal about the parameters of representation and remembrance in the GDR, not in spite of the cultural political climate of the period, but precisely because of the (real and perceived) restrictions in place.

Part IV analyses two DEFA productions from the 1970s, *Die Bilder des Zeugen Schattmann* (*The Pictures of Witness Schattmann*, 1972) and *Jakob der Lügner*.[24] Although both films had a television rather than a theatrical premiere and *Die Bilder des Zeugen Schattmann* was broadcast as a four-part television film, both films were made by a cast and crew composed almost entirely of DEFA employees. The 1970s was a decade of upheaval and change in the GDR. The change of leadership from Walter Ulbricht to Erich Honecker ushered in the period of reform many artists had been anticipating since the building of the Berlin Wall in 1961. Some of the most immediate changes were seen in culture. In 1972, Honecker's proclamation that there should be 'no taboos' in art was widely seen as a tacit endorsement to delve into previously unexplored stories using new artistic approaches.[25] The political developments of the early 1970s were not the only cause of this cultural 'thaw'. By the early 1970s, a new generation of filmmakers and audiences was coming of age, a generation that had only experienced the war as children and who, therefore, had limited – if any – first-hand experience of life during the Third Reich. On first viewing, *Die Bilder des Zeugen Schattmann* and *Jakob der Lügner* seem to uphold the generational shifts that underpinned this period of transition from a first-generation to a postwar-generation perspective of the National Socialist past. Kurt Jung-Alsen's *Die Bilder des Zeugen Schattmann* rehearses the familiar narratives of the 1950s and 1960s through the centrality of the film's antifascist conversion narrative. The younger director Frank Beyer offers a very different examination of Jewish victimhood in *Jakob der Lügner*, a film that is set exclusively in a ghetto and that only features Jewish victims of National Socialism. But again, we must be careful not to align the films with their wider production context without also reflecting on the content of the films themselves. It is certainly true that Jung-Alsen's film celebrates the actions of the antifascist resistance, while the Red Army was deliberately written out of Beyer's film because 'no division of the Red Army and no partisan group ever liberated a ghetto'.[26] However, closer analysis renders the films' engagement with Jewish persecution more complicated. Not only was *Die Bilder des Zeugen Schattmann* the first and only East German film to be shot on location at Auschwitz, but the graphic depiction of Jewish persecution offers the most confrontational images of any East German Holocaust film. At the same time, *Jakob der Lügner* may avoid any reference to the antifascist resistance in the plot, but the decision to cast the veteran antifascist actor Erwin Geschonneck in the role of the protagonist's best friend problematizes the primacy of Jewish victimhood in the film.

The final section, Part V, examines the GDR's last decade through the films *Stielke, Heinz, fünfzehn* (*Stielke, Heinz, Fifteen*, 1987) and *Die Schauspielerin* (*The Actress*, 1988). This decade represents by far the clearest break with first-generation narratives of the National Socialist past. This can be seen not only in the overwhelming absence of antifascist characters, but also in the choice of hero: *Stielke, Heinz, fünfzehn* presents a passionate member of the Hitler Youth as the Jewish protagonist and *Die Schauspielerin* places a strong, independent woman as the central figure of identification and persecution. The break with the traditional narratives of the National Socialist past also opened up a critically reflective space for the discussion of how the past had been, and would be, remembered. The chapters conclude with a study of the behind-the-scenes debates about the resonance of the antifascist narratives of the past for the first generation of Germans to be educated and socialized exclusively in the GDR.

East German Film and the Holocaust reveals that the partial or sole focus on Jewish persecution was not questioned by DEFA or by East German officials at any point in the GDR's history. The inclusion of Jewish victimhood was not contingent on the celebration or commemoration of antifascist resistance, although films that feature an antifascist character often complicate the depiction of Jewish victimhood. However, although the focus on Jewish victims was not contentious, the figure of the perpetrator remained problematic throughout DEFA's output. The reluctance to move beyond the recurring characters of the sadistic SS officer or corrupt 'capitalist fascists' meant that there was little space for the audience to reflect self-critically, and nor do the films invite the audience to do this. Instead, spectators largely remain onlookers and are not called upon to question their own actions – actual or hypothetical – in relation to the figure of the perpetrator. This is not to claim that East German Holocaust films are simply reflections of familiar state discourse. On the contrary, this book reveals two surprising points. Firstly, in spite of the centrality of the antifascist resistance to East German projections of national identity, both DEFA and the Ministry for Culture repeatedly sought to promote East German Holocaust films in the West rather than more familiar antifascist action adventures. Moreover, when these films were marketed in the West, plot synopses and promotional material were often altered to downplay the more conventional, ideologically inflected readings of the film used for the domestic market. Secondly, East German Holocaust films repeatedly created an alternative space for discussions not only of Holocaust memory in the GDR, but also of the cornerstones of intergenerational national identity in the past and present. Through these nine case studies, we discover that East German Holocaust films reveal a far more complex engagement with Jewish persecution than has hitherto been understood, not only within film, but also within society more broadly.

Notes

1. Grabowski and Strohschein, 'Und lehrt sie: Gedächtnis', 108.
2. Cited in Timm, Hammer, Zirkel, Davidstern, 588. See also Timm, Jewish Claims Against East Germany, 226.
3. Honecker, 'Unser Staat – eine sichere Heimstatt des Humanismus'. Cited in Gerlof, Tonspuren, 48.
4. Honecker, 'Rede Honeckers zum 40. Jahrestag der DDR'.
5. Brinks, 'Political Antifascism in the German Democratic Republic', 209.
6. Wolf, 'Das haben wir nicht gelernt'.
7. Barnert, Die Antifaschismus-Thematik der DEFA, 11.
8. Schmidt, 'Krieg und Militär im deutschen Nachkriegsfilm', 443.
9. Ernst Thälmann – Sohn seiner Klasse (Ernst Thälmann – Son of His Class), Wo andere schweigen (Where Others Keep Silent), Mich dürstet (I'm Thirsty), Fünf Patronenhülsen (Five Cartridges), Stärker als die Nacht (Stronger Than the Night), Leute mit Flügeln (People with Wings), Sie nannten ihn Amigo (They Called Him Amigo), Die Schüsse der Arche Noah (Shots from Noah's Ark).
10. Berghahn, Hollywood Behind the Wall, 64.
11. Ackermann, 'Zum 5-jährigen Bestehen der DEFA', 7.
12. Timm, 'Ideology and Realpolitik', 188.
13. The term Vergangenheitsbewältigung (also translated as 'mastering' or 'overcoming' the past) is a postwar concept used to describe efforts primarily in the Federal Republic and reunified Germany to address legal and moral legacies of the past.
14. The film studio DEFA predated and outlived the East German state. It was officially created in May 1946 and sold in 1992.
15. DEFA's final film to deal with Jewish persecution was the co-production Krücke (Crutch, 1993). Set in postwar Vienna, the film includes a number of scenes featuring Jewish characters who have survived the war.
16. Of course, the ability to receive West German television throughout most of the GDR meant that many East Germans may have watched Holocaust when it was first broadcast in the Federal Republic in January 1979.
17. See van de Knaap, 'Enlightening Procedures', 74–77; Schieber, 'Im Dämmerlicht der Perestroika 1980 bis 1989', 228; Thiele, Publizistische Kontroversen über den Holocaust im Film, 329–33.
18. For example, Barnert, Die Antifaschismus-Thematik; Möller and Horche, Die Vergangenheit in der Gegenwart; Heimann, Bilder von Buchenwald; Kannapin, Antifaschismus im Film der DDR; Kramer, Die Shoah im Bild; Thiele, Publizistische Kontroversen über den Holocaust im Film.

19. Allan and Sandford, *DEFA: East German Cinema, 1946–1992*, 1.
20. Cited in Schittly, *Zwischen Regie und Regime*, 314.
21. United States Holocaust Memorial Museum, 'Introduction to the Holocaust'.
22. Brady, 'Discussion with Kurt Maetzig', 83.
23. Honecker, 'Aus dem Bericht des Politbüros an die 11. Tagung des ZK'.
24. Both *Die Bilder des Zeugen Schattmann* and *Jakob der Lügner* were co-productions with East German television.
25. Honecker, 'Zu aktuellen Fragen bei der Verwirklichung der Beschlüsse unseres VIII Parteitages'.
26. Mark, 'Letter from Prof. Mark of the Żydowski Instytut Historyczny to DEFA'. When referencing archival material, the original German descriptor will be used if the document has an official title. If there is no official title, a description of the material will be provided in English.

PART I

1945–49

The ghosts of the National Socialist film industry knew no *Stunde Null* and clear lines of continuity bridged the purported caesura of 8 May 1945.[1] The idea that the German film industry could continue to make films in the same way as it did during the Third Reich was never entertained by any of the Allied powers who were certainly apprehensive about allowing any resurrection, let alone a continuation, of German filmmaking. Throughout 1945 and 1946, actors, directors, cinematographers and film producers continued to appear before special denazification tribunals (*Spruchkammern*) where they were required to account for their personal or professional conduct between 1933 and 1945. Punishments handed down by the tribunals ranged from employment bans, to fines and even imprisonment and within a matter of months many of the Third Reich's leading stars suddenly found themselves *personae non gratae* within what had been one of the most successful film industries in the world.[2]

By the 1950s, actors had largely been able to resume their careers on the screen and stage. Some of Germany's most successful directors of the Third Reich, however, never stepped out from the shadows of the past. Leni Riefenstahl underwent four denazification trials but never escaped the label of the 'Führer's filmmaker'. Veit Harlan was accused of crimes against humanity on account of having directed the antisemitic film *Jud Süss* (*Jew Süss*, 1940), for which he was acquitted twice. But his decision to attend the Hamburg premiere of *Ehe im Schatten*, Germany's first postwar film focusing on Jewish persecution, caused a small scandal and Harlan faced the indignity of being unceremoniously and very publicly ejected from the event. He may have been one of the most popular directors during the Third Reich, but Harlan never achieved comparable levels of success in postwar Germany.

The question of who should be allowed to make films in postwar Germany was heavily debated from the outset. Should those who benefited professionally and financially from an industry that systematically ostracized Jews and that produced films designed to mobilize the German public for the National Socialist cause be allowed to continue their careers largely undisrupted? This question was further complicated by the fact that for many of those working in the film industry in the late 1930s, emigrating was neither financially nor professionally feasible. Should carrying out one's profession in a totalitarian system therefore be understood as an unequivocal act of support for the state or rather as a reflection of pragmatic necessity? There was also no objective measure to gauge complicity. Should an actor who appeared on Hitler's infamous 'Führerliste' or Goebbels' 'Gottbegnadeten-Liste' be subject to punishment?[3] Many cast and crew members of *Jud Süss* subsequently claimed that they were employed under duress and had attempted to subvert the film's rabid antisemitic message wherever possible. Should such individuals be spared punishment?

These questions were answered differently by the Allies in ways that broadly mirrored the denazification strategies carried out in the Soviet and the Western zones of occupation. In the SMAD, denazification was part of a far broader restructuring of society which saw the structural dismantling of the political and economic scaffolding that supported the growth of National Socialism: once Germans had been liberated from 'capitalist fascist' forces, they would be free to reorientate themselves towards a new, antifascist order. This approach to denazification meant that filmmaking activities were quickly allowed to resume in the Soviet Zone. The founding of DEFA came after nine months of planning and development. Preparation for an East German film studio began in September 1945 when Herbert Volkmann, who had been tasked by the SMAD with leading the Office for Literature and the Arts, was instructed in accordance with SMAD Directive 51 to compile a list of 'all active people in the area of theatre, music, dance, film and visual arts'.[4] Over the subsequent weeks, a number of filmmakers reported to Volkmann and, by the end of the month, he had successfully formed a collective known as the *Filmaktiv*. The collective was accordingly instructed by the SMAD to prepare to form a production company and initiate plans for a German film industry in the Soviet Zone. Two months later, the *Filmaktiv* began shooting its first documentary and by May 1946 it had begun work on its first feature film, *Die Mörder sind unter uns*, even though it had yet to receive its official filmmaking licence from the SMAD. Nine days later on 17 May 1946, DEFA was formed and officially received the Soviet seal of approval.[5]

The quick resumption of filmmaking activities in the Soviet sector stood in marked contrast to the Western zones. The Western allies – in particular, the American Military Government – were highly distrustful of Germans' reliability and suitability to make their own films in light of the medium's mobilization under National Socialism. As late as 1947, the vice president of the American Motion Picture Export Association, Irving Maas, insisted that, 'Nazi propaganda poison so deeply pervaded the whole German mentality, that extreme measures must be taken to provide the necessary mental catharsis'. Consequently, he determined that Germans should be fed 'heavy doses of all pictures except those of their own making'.[6] Perhaps unsurprisingly, the American studios' insistence on an embargo on the resumption of German filmmaking activities was not solely motivated by concern about the political and ideological content of German-made films. By saturating the market of a traditionally cinephilic nation with American productions, the American studios looked to gain a long-term strategic and financial advantage over their German rivals.

The fact that the German film industry was able to resume activities in the Western zones as soon as it did owed much to the efforts of the German film producer Erich Pommer.[7] Pommer had been in exile in the United States since 1933 and returned to Germany in 1946 as the film officer for the American Military Government. As Pommer quickly discovered, the challenges facing the German film industry went far beyond the American military government's reluctance to issue production licences to German filmmakers. The decentralization of the film industry had denied filmmakers in the Western zones a fully integrated production base akin to the new DEFA studios in Babelsberg. This resulted in as many as forty production companies vying for similar, and extremely limited, funding.[8] Even when the necessary permits had been issued and the funding secured, the Western zones suffered from a chronic lack of materials: Agfa was one of the few factories producing raw film stock which had not been destroyed in the war, but it was located in the Soviet Zone.

Initial Engagements with Jewish Persecution

The shadows of the National Socialist past not only lingered over individuals and the film industry, they arguably haunted the filmic medium itself. Throughout the Third Reich, film had been employed to shape attitudes and influence normative responses to exclusive constructions of German national identity. In keeping with Goebbels' prioritization of entertainment above overt propaganda, political and ideological messages were most frequently embedded in genre-driven productions. Two of the most popular films of the Third Reich were genre films and were also considered by the Allies to be among the most politically and ideologically toxic films produced under National Socialism. Wolfgang Liebeneiner's *Ich klage an* (*I Accuse*, 1941) locates its pro-euthanasia message within a romantic melodrama and attracted an audience of almost eighteen million people. Veit Harlan's *Jud Süss* firmly embeds its antisemitic plot within a classical Hollywood realist narrative. The film drew nearly twenty million spectators, making it one of the most successful films of the Third Reich.

The harnessing of film for political and ideological purposes during the Third Reich presented postwar directors with significant challenges, especially for directors who were seeking to engage with the recent past. Firstly, despite the concerns of the American authorities, German audiences had little appetite for overtly political films. This in part helps to explain domestic audiences' lukewarm responses to the Western allies' 'atrocity films', documentaries made by the Allies using footage taken during the liberation of concentration camps. One of the core aims of the 'atrocity films' was to inculcate Germans with a sense of collective guilt, but they rarely found their desired outcome. One OMGUS post-screening report of audience responses to the atrocity film *Die Todesmühlen* (*Death Mills*, 1945) concluded that 'the local population, as seems to have been the case all over Bavaria, stayed away in droves', while one sixteen-year-old is recorded as having remarked, 'for the next propaganda performance, take Dr Goebbels as an advisor'.[9] The second challenge for postwar directors seeking to engage with the recent past was finding a way to signal clearly to the audience that a character was Jewish without reverting to the antisemitic stereotypes that were all too familiar to the German public. Twelve years of National Socialist propaganda on cinema screens had attempted to present Jewish characters as dangerous outsiders by exaggerating their supposedly 'Jewish' physiognomic features and stressing their purported cultural and emotional alterity. This representational challenge helps to explain, at least in part, why so many German films produced between 1945 and 1949 appear to offer such frustratingly elliptical engagements with Jewish persecution. Time and again in immediate postwar films, there is a clear discomfort in declaring characters' Jewish identity directly. Instead, characters merely allude to their Jewish identity or somewhat clumsily announce their Jewish background during an onscreen exchange with colleagues, neighbours or minor characters.

Even when Jewish victimhood was acknowledged in films in the immediate postwar years, it rarely formed the focus of the plot. This can be seen in the roughly fifty *Trümmerfilme* ('rubble films') that were produced across the four sectors of Germany between 1945 and 1949. In these films, we encounter physically and psychologically wounded men returning from the war and it is their suffering that forms the focus of the narrative and emotional heart of the stories. When Jewish characters do appear, their experience overwhelmingly fades into the background. Helmut Käutner's *In jenen Tagen* (*In Those Days*, 1947) features a couple in a 'mixed marriage' who are attacked during the November Pogroms, but the film eschews questions of guilt and responsibility entirely. There are no identifiable perpetrators; instead, the film presents its characters as 'innocent victims of circumstance'.[10] Harald Braun's *Zwischen gestern und morgen* (*Between Yesterday and Tomorrow*, 1947) focuses on a group of German postwar survivors in Munich. The individuals are linked through their interactions with the symbolically named Jewish woman Nelly Dreifuss (a play on the name Dreyfus), who was murdered under the National Socialist regime.[11] The strong focus on the victimhood of the postwar survivors once again relegates antisemitism to merely one social ill in a society replete with victims, but strikingly short of perpetrators.

Yet despite the manifold challenges facing filmmakers in the immediate postwar years, German films from 1945 to 1949 reveal a surprising willingness to broach the subject of National Socialist persecution. Although Jewish victims are rarely the focus of these films, antisemitic persecution is a present theme, especially before 1947. The first German postwar film, Wolfgang Staudte's *Die Mörder sind unter uns*, makes a number of elliptical references to Jewish victimhood. We first encounter the female protagonist Susanne Wallner stepping off a train carrying a suitcase and bag, and we later learn that she was sent to a camp 'because of her father'.[12] Staudte also shows how antisemitic attitudes continued after May 1945. A shot of rats in the rubble of bombed Berlin evokes memories of the virulently antisemitic film, *Der ewige Jude* (*The*

Eternal Jew, 1940). In the next scene, the intoxicated protagonist Mertens returns home and bemoans the presence of 'rats everywhere' in front of a visibly shocked Susanne. At times, the film is far more explicit in its references to Jewish persecution. Staudte pointedly includes a lingering shot of the film's perpetrator, Ferdinand Brückner, reading a newspaper with the headline, 'Two Million Gassed'. These instances hardly constitute a rigorous interrogation of Germany's recent past, but we should also be mindful of the context in which the film was released. Alongside the aforementioned representational challenges, *Die Mörder sind unter uns* premiered just two weeks after the verdicts were delivered at the Nuremberg Trials. However unsatisfactory its engagement with Jewish persecution may appear to audiences today, the film was released at a point when the facts were not yet definitive, the perpetrators were still being prosecuted and the full extent of their Jewish victims' suffering was not yet entirely clear.

Films that did place Jewish persecution at the heart of the plot overwhelmingly performed poorly at the box office. The American-licensed production *Morituri* (1948) features a group of (implicitly Jewish) prisoners who escape from a concentration camp, but the film only attracted 424,476 spectators.[13] Meanwhile, the German-American co-production *Lang ist der Weg* (*Long is the Way*, 1948) never secured a national release. Erich Engel's *Affaire Blum* works against this trend. The film explores the role of society's antisemitic prejudice through the real-life case of a German-Jewish industrialist falsely accused of murder. However, by setting the action in the Weimar Republic and revealing the protagonist's innocence to the audience from the outset, the director avoids addressing potentially difficult contemporary issues in postwar Germany.[14]

One notable exception to this pattern is Kurt Maetzig's 1947 film, *Ehe im Schatten*, which attracted 10,125,385 spectators in its first four years. The film's success has drawn considerable scholarly interest and Maetzig's film is one of the most widely discussed German productions of the immediate postwar years. As the next chapter highlights, *Ehe im Schatten* has been heavily criticized for its reliance on melodrama to the point that Robert Shandley has asked whether we can 'make the claim that this narrative actually marks any ethical transformation at all'.[15] The following chapter offers a significant revision of this reading by arguing that Maetzig does not merely use melodramatic structures and tropes, but rather appropriates and inverts familiar visual and narrative models in order to challenge National Socialist depictions of victims and perpetrators, Jews and Germans.

It is important to note that Maetzig's film predates the founding of the GDR and the SED only produced a report on the film a month after its release. While acknowledging this important distinction, *Ehe im Schatten* remains an essential case study for understanding East German filmic engagements with the Holocaust. The focus of this chapter is not a comparative examination of the internal film licensing and production structures in the Soviet Zone and GDR. Rather, this chapter seeks to explore the extent to which dominant domestic narratives in the immediate postwar years are reflected in the film's depiction of victims and perpetrators, and whether the film creates a space for discussing the recent National Socialist past beyond the dominant cultural, political and social debates.

Notes

1. *Stunde Null* or 'zero hour' is a term used to denote the end of the Third Reich and beginning of postwar Germany. The term increasingly assumed a sense of rebirth and a clear break from National Socialist to postwar Germany.
2. Emil Jannings, Werner Krauss, Paula Wessely, Eugen Klöpfer, Marianne Hoppe and Heidemarie Hatheyer were among the household names who were banned from the stage and screen for up to five years. For some, the punishment was much harsher: Gustaf Gründgens and Heinrich George were both interred in Soviet prisoner camps. Following a concerted campaign by fellow actors who clearly held Gustaf Gründgens in high regard, he was released in 1945. Heinrich George died in captivity in 1946.
3. Literally, the 'Führer's List' and the 'God-Gifted List', these lists named key actors, directors and film technicians who were to be exempted from conscription during the war. See Niven, *Hitler and Film*, 204–7.
4. Cited in Mückenberger, 'Die ersten "antifaschistischen" DEFA-Filme der Nachkriegsjahre', 12.
5. DEFA's founding members were Hans Klering, Alfred Lindemann, Willy Schiller, Karl Hans Bergmann and Kurt Maetzig.
6. *The New York Times*, 'German Film Growth Decried by US Aide', 18 January 1947. Cited in Hardt, *From Caligari to California*, 182.
7. For more on film policy in American sector, see Brockmann, *A Critical History of German Film*, 191–93.
8. Berghahn, *Hollywood Behind the Wall*, 14–15.
9. Brewster S. Chamberlain, cited in Culbert, 'American Film Policy in the Re-Education of Germany after 1945', 179.
10. Hake, *German National Cinema*, 98.
11. The Dreyfus Affair was a political scandal that exposed widespread societal antisemitism at the turn of the twentieth century in France after Alfred Dreyfus, a French Jewish army captain, was wrongfully convicted of treason.
12. Earlier drafts of the screenplay indicate that Susanne was sent to a concentration camp because her father was a communist. The final film appears to leave the cause

of her persecution intentionally ambiguous. Shandley, 'Rubble Canyons: *Die Mörder sind unter uns* and the Western', 134n7.
13. Pleyer, *Deutscher Nachkriegsfilm 1946–1948*, 156.
14. For more on *Affaire Blum*, see Shandley, *Rubble Films*, 105–8.
15. Shandley, *Rubble Films*, 84.

Chapter 1

PICKING UP THE PIECES

Kurt Maetzig's *Ehe im Schatten*

Ehe im Schatten was very much a film of firsts. The first film of director Kurt Maetzig, *Ehe im Schatten* (1947) was also the first postwar German film to achieve eight-figure box office returns. It was the first DEFA feature film to play in the British sector of the recently divided Germany and 'its great educational value' temporarily led the US Military Government to suspend its ban on non-American licensed films playing in its occupied sector of Berlin.[1] This made it the first (and only) film to premiere in all four sectors of Berlin at the same time. The popular and critical success of the film is all the more remarkable when we consider the fact that less than eighteen months after the German surrender, it was also the first postwar German film to place Jewish persecution at the heart of the plot.

Ehe im Schatten depicts the fate of two actors during the Third Reich. Elisabeth Maurer is a successful stage actress whose career is in the ascendancy. On stage, she outshines her fellow actor, Hans Wieland, and off-stage she is romantically pursued by both Hans and Herbert Blohm. Elisabeth initially pursues a relationship with Blohm, only for it to falter when she reveals her Jewish identity to the NSDAP sympathizer. Following the coming to power of Hitler, Blohm gains a position in the Propaganda Ministry and Hans' acting career flourishes. However, the concurrent introduction of antisemitic legislation marginalizes Elisabeth, who is prohibited from acting on stage. Hans proposes to Elisabeth and stresses the protection he could offer as an 'Aryan' spouse. Elisabeth accepts, but their marriage is soon put under strain. After resisting pressure to divorce Elisabeth, Hans is sent to fight at the front and Elisabeth is effectively confined to their apartment having been ostracized from all public, social and cultural events. Hans returns, but the couple's happy reunion is short-lived when Elisabeth is unwittingly introduced to the Secretary of State from the Propaganda Ministry at Hans' film premiere. When the Secretary of State learns of Elisabeth's Jewish identity, he demands her immediate deportation. Blohm informs his erstwhile friend of the decision to deport Elisabeth to a concentration camp and an argument breaks out between the two men. During their heated exchange, Hans attributes blame for Elisabeth's fate not only to Blohm's actions, but also to the passivity of all those – including himself and Elisabeth – who failed to act sooner. Hans returns home to Elisabeth and commits a murder-suicide by adding poison to their drinks. The film ends with a shot of two coffins and a superimposed dedication to the actor Joachim Gottschalk, whose fate during the Third Reich served as the basis for the screenplay.[2]

Ehe im Schatten has frequently been described as a compromised film. While its early confrontation with the recent past has been praised, it has been argued the film's heavy reliance on melodrama ultimately facilitates a superficial and unreflective engagement with Jewish persecution. Without doubt, the film eschews causal analyses of antisemitism and the argument that Maetzig ultimately 'obscures, rather than clarifies, the historical reasons for Elisabeth's persecution' is certainly valid.[3] However, this chapter offers an important re-reading of the film by demonstrating the significance of emotional responses and revealing the extent to which Maetzig not only uses, but also critically employs melodramatic tropes to challenge normative values perpetuated under National Socialism. In so doing, the film seeks to engage audiences emotionally, a strategy that was particularly significant within the original release context of 1947.

The significance of *Ehe im Schatten* resides not only in its early focus on Jewish persecution, but also in its candid assessment of German culpability. Contemporaneous productions licensed in the Soviet Zone such as *Die Mörder sind unter uns, Affaire Blum* and even Maetzig's later film *Rat der Götter* (*Council of the Gods*, 1950) predominantly focused on criminal guilt and embedded this within increasingly political and politicizing attributions of responsibility, while films licensed in the Western zones such as *In jenen Tagen* and *Morituri* overwhelmingly omitted the figure of the perpetrator altogether. *Ehe im Schatten* works against this trend by focussing on the far more ambiguous question of moral guilt. The second part of this chapter explores the extent to which the film mirrors or challenges the dominant trend to present a perpetrator as a criminally culpable individual. In so doing, it will be argued that the importance of *Ehe im Schatten* ultimately resides in its ability to engage audiences not in spite of, but because of, its reliance of affective responses.

Approaching Jewish Victimhood

The representational challenges facing directors who sought to engage with Germany's recent past in the immediate postwar years come to the fore in *Ehe im Schatten*. Elisabeth is one of three principal Jewish characters in the film along with her uncle, Dr Louis Silbermann, and her colleague and fellow actor Kurt Bernstein. Each character responds differently when confronted with antisemitic persecution: Silbermann continues to treat his patients and help other Jews evade detection by the Gestapo until he too becomes the target of their search; Bernstein attempts to emigrate to Vienna, only to return to Berlin after escaping from a deportation train; and Elisabeth agrees to marry Hans after he hears of the security an 'Aryan' spouse might afford a Jewish partner. Given the importance of Elisabeth's Jewish identity to the plot, the film has to signal her Jewish identity to the audience, while also ensuring that it does not inadvertently replicate National Socialist antisemitic tropes of physical or cultural alterity. Maetzig achieves this by employing linguistic markers of identity. Each Jewish character is required to state explicitly his or her Jewish identity for the sake of others. Bernstein is asked outright by another character if he is Jewish, Elisabeth's Jewish background comes as a shock to Blohm, who is described in the screenplay as 'speechless' at the revelation, and Silbermann is forced to place a sign outside his surgery to inform his patients that he is Jewish. Contrary to the spurious claims of National Socialist propaganda, there is nothing in the characters' physical appearance, or religious or cultural practice that would otherwise have revealed that they are Jewish.

Significantly, the announcement of the three characters' Jewish identity in the plot occurs around the time of the Reichstag fire, a decisive point in the NSDAP's seizing of power and its attempts to open up social, political and 'racial' lines of division in German society. It is at this point that the characters' friendship circle begins to break apart and, for the first time, they start to be defined by their differences rather than by their commonalities. Against the backdrop of this division, Maetzig continues to stress that his Jewish characters are highly integrated into German society and, above all, identify as German. Even Silbermann, who declares he will not leave Germany because his patients need him, appears to speak out of a belief that the democratic structures of Germany will affirm his status as a German doctor rather than out of any prosemitic allegiance. Indeed, in an earlier version of the screenplay, Silbermann's insistence on his status as a patriotic assimilated Jew was even more pronounced through the revelation that he had been awarded the Iron Cross in the First World War.[4]

In his desire to demonstrate that the Jewish characters are highly assimilated Germans, Maetzig draws on the nineteenth-century literary trope of Jewish Germans as highly fluent in classical German literature and thought. Throughout the film, the Jewish characters are strongly associated with German culture: Elisabeth cites lines from plays by Schiller, Büchner, Goethe and Heine; Bernstein's fluency with German political science and thought situates him firmly within the German intellectual tradition; and Silbermann's reaction to his marginalization in society is to console himself with the fact that 'I am becoming well acquainted with my bookshelf'. This is contrasted with the disregard the non-Jewish characters demonstrate for German cultural heritage. During the November Pogroms, Hans runs to a policeman and pleads with him to intervene, shouting 'Do your duty!'. The policeman refuses, claiming that the German rioters are assaulting police officers, are destroying property in Schillerstraße (Schiller Street) and that he has been advised to go to Goethestraße (Goethe Street) instead. The invocation of Schillerstraße and Goethestraße as sites upon which Jews and Jewish property are being attacked serves to expose the present-day violence of the erstwhile *Kulturnation* further.[5]

The representational strategies employed in *Ehe im Schatten* have nonetheless come under increasing criticism in recent years. Described as a 'compromise in aesthetic terms',[6] it has been argued that through his heavy reliance on melodramatic tropes, Maetzig not only failed to break away from dominant stylistic forms employed during the Third Reich, but that he did this within the context of a film dealing with antisemitic persecution. To understand the ways in which melodramatic tropes are employed in *Ehe im Schatten*, it is helpful to draw on Rick Altman's model of genre as a semantic and syntactic system. Following Altman's conceptual framework, genre can be broken down into semantic elements or 'building blocks' such as characters, locations and sets, and syntactic units that represent the 'structures' or 'fundamental syntax' into which the semantic elements are arranged.[7] Although melodrama should not be considered a self-supporting genre, but rather a mode which works alongside and through other genres, it is characterized by a number of recurring semantic and syntactic elements, namely the repeated use of close-ups, a reliance on emotional excess and the employment of clearly drawn characters with readily identifiable moral virtues such as innocence and villainy.[8] The 'constitutive relationships'[9] or syntactic structures into which these elements are arranged frequently revolve around 'chance happenings . . . sudden conversions, last-minute rescues [and] revelations, and *deus ex machina* endings' that serve as 'constant violations in the established direction of events'.[10]

Semantic and syntactic melodramatic tropes operate on multiple levels in *Ehe im Schatten*. Melodramas frequently explore the negotiation of female identity in the public and private spheres and the impact of 'social and racial difference' through the 'tensions between individual and community'.[11] *Ehe im Schatten* depicts a woman's marginalization and ostracism from public life and her growing frustration at being confined to the domestic sphere. She is in a 'mixed marriage' and the plot is marked by frequent episodes of emotional excess which is conveyed to the audience through repeated uses of close-up shots. The film concludes with the tragic murder-suicide of Hans and Elisabeth which is set in motion by a chance meeting with the Secretary of State. Given that the film ends with the couple's death, we could ask whether the ending does actually offer the spectator 'emotional pleasures'. However, as Steve Neale has argued, a seemingly unhappy ending can still facilitate a cathartic response and emotional satisfaction. Even if their romance is frustrated within the narrative, the couple's declarations of undying love for one another point to an unspecified point of future happiness. Consequently, 'the wish and its fantasy are not themselves lost [or] destroyed forever' and a seemingly unhappy ending can 'function as a means of postponing rather than destroying the possibility of fulfilment of a wish'.[12] Elisabeth's appeal, 'promise that they won't ever, ever separate us again', is verbally affirmed by Hans and is then sealed with a kiss that marks the couple's love within and beyond the narrative, thereby representing what Douglas Sirk famously termed the 'happy unhappy ending'.[13]

The criticisms of Maetzig's employment of melodramatic tropes in *Ehe im Schatten* can be divided into two categories. The first set of arguments attributes the stylistic continuities between *Ehe im Schatten* and German films made during the Third Reich to the difficulty in recruiting experienced technical staff in the immediate postwar years. It is certainly true that the film is a 'who's who' of Third Reich cinema.[14] Paul Klinger (Hans) would have been familiar to German audiences in 1947 from films such as *Die goldene Stadt* (*The Golden City*, 1942) and *Immensee* (1943) by Veit Harlan, who has been described as the 'chief melodramatist in the Third Reich'.[15] While some of the crew members of *Ehe im Schatten* such as Alice Ludwig (editing) and Otto Erdmann (art direction) had largely worked on light-hearted entertainment films during the Third Reich, others had worked on far more questionable films. The lead cameraman, Friedl Behn-Grund, had worked on the pro-euthanasia film *Ich klage an*, while Maetzig's assistant director, Wolfgang Schleif, and the composer, Wolfgang Zeller, had both worked on the antisemitic film *Jud Süss*, as had the actress Hilde von Stolz.[16] This has led to the impression that the melodramatic style of *Ehe im Schatten* was largely inevitable given the formative training of key cast and crew members during the Third Reich, an outcome exacerbated by Maetzig's own relative lack of experience as a director.[17] Consequently, *Ehe im Schatten* has been described as a missed opportunity to (re)define German filmmaking after the Third Reich: one that marked less of 'a new beginning' for German cinema as much as 'a resignation to the status quo garbed in emotional rhetoric'.[18]

While the first set of arguments conveys a certain sense of inevitability about the film's style, the second interpretation suggests a far more calculated approach. Robert Shandley has argued that the continuities between *Ehe im Schatten* and Ufa's melodramas should not only be understood as the 'residual influence' of Third Reich cinema, but also suggests that there were lingering doubts about whether a German audience 'would respond positively to the fate of Elisabeth Wieland, Kurt Bernstein or any other Jewish characters in the film. But to an audience raised on Ufa products, kitschy sentimentalism was a sure thing'.[19] Furthermore, it has been argued that the references to the characters' Jewish identity are so subtle and infrequent that Maetzig ultimately circumvents the fact that the characters – and in particular, the lead female protagonist, Elisabeth – are Jewish.[20] In this way, the use of melodrama allowed Maetzig to elicit the desired response because 'the sentimental tone of the film provides many opportunities for the spectator's enjoyment without having to concentrate specifically on the historical reasons for Elisabeth's persecution'.[21] Barbara Bongartz has similarly pointed to the 'depiction of tearful faces in close-up' as a means of allowing spectators 'to cry about themselves rather than go to the historic events in a detached way in order to make them realize that they shared responsibility for these events'.[22] In this way, it has been argued that *Ehe im Schatten* allows audiences to evade confrontations with the recent German past and, in so doing, avoids causal analyses of antisemitism and instead privileges the emotional impact of the plot on the audience.

It is certainly true that melodramatic tropes structure the narrative and guide audience responses in *Ehe im Schatten*. This is particularly evident in the film's emotional climax, the murder-suicide scene. The scene opens with Elisabeth sitting at the piano. While Hans sits in silence, Elisabeth recites lines from plays that they had previously performed on stage together. Hans then silently fetches a vial of Veronal and secretly pours it into their drinks. Unbeknownst to him, Elisabeth sees him do this, but she silently acquiesces to his actions by drinking the poisoned drink and then reassuring Hans that she loves him. The scene closes with Hans carrying the dying Elisabeth to the marital bed before they both fall unconscious in one another's arms. Here Maetzig seems to indulge in melodramatic tropes without reflection. The repeated use of close-up shots of Hans and Elisabeth's faces mediates the characters' heightened emotions as the couple approach their dramatic death. When Hans and Elisabeth die in one another's arms, Maetzig appears to achieve the hallmark of the melodrama: an unambiguous ending which offers audiences 'emotional pleasures equally clear-cut and extreme'.[23] The privileging of emotional and narrative excess signals to the spectator that the dramatic and cathartic climax is approaching and appears to evade any examination of the specific reasons for Elisabeth's persecution. However, if we examine how melodramatic tropes are used, rather than simply identifying which tropes are used, it becomes clear that *Ehe im Schatten* provides a far more critical engagement with Jewish persecution than has hitherto been acknowledged.

By using and appropriating melodramatic tropes, Maetzig creates an ending that seems to fulfil audience expectations of melodrama, while at the same time placing the focus on the victims of National Socialist persecution. An important narrative device in melodrama is the impact of abstract forces such as destiny, chance and fate in changing the course of characters' lives. In *Ehe im Schatten*, the chance encounter with the Secretary of State after Hans' film premiere – an event which never happened in the film's source material – initiates a series of events which leads to Elisabeth's death the following day.[24] In keeping with the conventions of the melodrama, this does indeed mark an unexpected plot twist, but when placed within the context of the whole film, it becomes clear that this is actually the fulfilment of a series of events that has been signalled from the very first scene. *Ehe im Schatten* opens in a theatre with Elisabeth and Hans playing the lead roles in Schiller's

Kabale und Liebe with Luise (Elisabeth) reacting to the news that Ferdinand (Hans) has just poisoned their drinks. Here, Elisabeth's first lines, 'I die innocent', anticipate her eventual off-stage fate. Maetzig subtly modifies Luise's line in the Schillerian text so that the line 'Heaven and earth have nothing more unfortunate than thou' becomes 'heaven and earth contain nothing more unfortunate than us'. This pronominal shift anticipates the film's ending and Maetzig thereby signals from the outset that the couple will be united in life and in death. It is also important to remember that although the meeting between Elisabeth and the Secretary of State could be attributed to abstract forces such as fate or chance, the Secretary of State's order to deport Elisabeth is not capricious; it is motivated by political and societal antisemitism. Melodrama may be reliant on dramatic irony, but the impact of the final scene in *Ehe im Schatten* is not only dependent upon the spectator's knowledge of Elisabeth's impending deportation as announced in the previous scene, rather it is also reliant on the event that is never explicitly mentioned in the film: the Holocaust.[25]

Taken in isolation, it is true that there is little evidence in the final scene to suggest that Elisabeth's death is related to her Jewish identity. However, by this point, Maetzig has established that Elisabeth is Jewish and has demonstrated how her marginalization is directly related to antisemitic legislation. From today's perspective, the relationship between the on-screen events and the off-screen context may appear peripheral, but in the immediate postwar years, the ongoing societal, media and political debates about the recent past and the circulation of images about concentration camps and Jewish victims would have actively informed the reception of the film. In order for the ending of *Ehe im Schatten* to have elicited such an emotional response among audiences in 1947, Maetzig had to undercut antisemitic prejudices potentially levelled against Elisabeth, as well as work against the dominant social and gendered narratives that played out in films of the Third Reich.[26] Although we could indeed accuse Maetzig of pushing all the right buttons to elicit an emotional response to Elisabeth's death, he did so through tropes which had just a few years earlier been imbued with strict social, political and 'racial' significance designed to condemn the very model of femininity presented by Elisabeth.

Ehe im Schatten certainly found widespread popular appeal: it was the most popular film of the immediate postwar years, with box office figures reaching 10,125,385 by 1951. When we consider other productions released during the same period, the success of Maetzig's film among domestic audiences is clear: the second most popular film during the same period was *Razzia* (8.1 million), followed by *1–2–3 Corona* (6 million), *Straßenbekanntschaft* (5.3 million) and *Die Mörder sind unter uns* (5.2 million).[27] It is certainly true that Maetzig avoids causal analyses of antisemitism and in its place privileges the emotional impact of the narrative on the spectator. However, the importance of emotional responses to a film depicting Jewish persecution in the context of 1947 should not be understated. National Socialist antisemitism was dependent on the ostracism of Jews from German society. To achieve this, Jewish citizens had to be emotionally distanced from the collective conscience of the non-Jewish, German population. It is important to remember that the overwhelming majority of audience members in 1947 would have been neither Jewish nor persecuted under the National Socialist regime. They would, however, have been exposed to a high level of antisemitic propaganda. It is, of course, impossible to ascertain with complete certainty how audiences responded to the film at the time, but if the newspaper reports about the impact of the film are indeed indicative of audiences' responses to the film's ending, they should be considered less affirmations of an expected reaction than as an indication of Maetzig's ability to rehabilitate Jewish victimhood within the nation's emotional psyche.[28] As one journalist remarked at the time, 'we can be in two minds about the correctness of this method, but one look at the audience is proof of its effectiveness'.[29]

Strategies of Absence

Correspondence to and from Kurt Maetzig strongly suggests that the director made a number of pre-production decisions designed to foreground the reasons for Elisabeth's persecution. In keeping with one of the dominant features of the melodrama, *Ehe im Schatten* focuses on the conflicted experience of Elisabeth. There is certainly evidence to suggest that Maetzig was keen to emphasize the inner conflict of his female protagonist. In October 1946, DEFA's head dramaturge published an article in the trade paper *Die Neue Filmwoche* appealing for 'films that show the fate of modern, working women with all the conflicts that arise from the discrepancy between one's private life and professional life' and in particular films that 'in the strongest, most deadly form oppose bureaucracy'.[30] In the same month as Georg Klaren's article appeared in *Die Neue Filmwoche*, Maetzig wrote to Axel Eggebrecht, who was advizing Maetzig on the screenplay, to discuss his decision to omit reference to the fact that Meta Wolff had a twelve-year-old son. In the letter, the director points to a clear dramatic advantage to making the couple childless, namely that Elisabeth's isolation and loneliness would be more powerfully conveyed in an empty apartment than if a child were present. Interestingly, Maetzig provides a second reason why Elisabeth should be childless: if she were to have a child, the audience may believe that this was 'an equivalent for her lost career'.[31] Here the decision to retell the couple's story from the perspective of Elisabeth rather than Hans gains context. Joachim Gottschalk was one of the Third Reich's most popular actors, but his wife Meta Wolff was comparatively unknown. Although Maetzig draws on the real-life couple's story, *Ehe im Schatten* traces the impact of National Socialist antisemitic legislation on Elisabeth and her transition from a powerful, professionally successful woman on stage to becoming entirely dependent on her husband.

Maetzig conveys Elisabeth's loss of power by subtly changing the shot composition of the characters' body language. When we first encounter Elisabeth and Hans on stage, Elisabeth dominates the scene. Despite the disparity in power between the eighteenth-century Schillerian couple, it is Luise who retains her composure and who comforts an emotionally wrought Ferdinand. When the curtain falls on the production, the audience cries out Elisabeth's, not Hans', name. Elisabeth initially rejects Hans' advances and, even after Hans and Elisabeth become a couple, his body continues to be subservient to hers.[32] Throughout the first third of the film, Elisabeth occupies a position of greater power in their relationship. However, as antisemitic legislation increases, Elisabeth becomes increasingly marginalized in society, confined to the domestic sphere and fully reliant on Hans. Her diminishing power is in turn signalled by the couple's embraces, in which Hans is increasingly positioned in the dominant position once occupied by Elisabeth (Figure 1.1).

When considering how the film does not simply use, but rather critically employs, melodramatic structures, it is also important to note that the couple's death does not actually mark the end of the film. The audience is first offered the typical melodramatically structured ending in which the *Liebestod* ending reaches its apex to the swelling sound of Wolfgang Zeller's soundtrack. Having declared their undying love to one another, the scene fades to black and appears to have reached its emotional climax. However, at the point of heightened emotional catharsis, the image fades back in to reveal a cemetery scene in which the lavish soundtrack is replaced by the diegetic sound of coffin bearers walking in the gravel as they carry two coffins side-by-side. The stark contrast between the two soundscapes creates a sober point of comparison. The fatal consequences of the previous scene are played out to the

Figure 1.1. From a position of strength to one of submission, Elisabeth's body language shifts over the course of the film in ways that reflect her loss of agency. © DEFA-Stiftung/Kurt Wunsch.

audience and the spectator is forced to acknowledge that the characters' dramatic proclamations of love were not followed by the postponed fulfilment of a wish, as we would expect with the melodramatic mode. Rather, the final scenes take place in the sombre setting of a cemetery. The film then closes with its third 'ending' in which a dedication to the real-life actor Joachim Gottschalk and his family is superimposed over the cemetery scene before the screen finally fades to black. The intrusion of the closing text serves as a poignant reminder to the audience that not only does Elisabeth and Hans' story have a fatal conclusion, but that their fictional story was drawn from the fate of a real-life couple.

One problematic aspect nonetheless remains, the film's closing dedication:

> This film is dedicated to the memory of the actor
> JOACHIM GOTTSCHALK
> who was driven to his death in spring 1941 with his family
> and together with him to the memory
> of all other fallen victims.

The director's decision to dedicate the film to a non-Jewish actor and to 'all other fallen victims' unquestionably marginalises Elisabeth's – and, by extension, Jewish – victimhood. It is clear from correspondence from Maetzig that he did not consider the film to be a biopic of Gottschalk's life. Indeed, in a letter dated February 1947, Maetzig stressed to DEFA's press office that *Ehe im Schatten* was not to be marketed as a 'Joachim Gottschalk film'. Not only did the storyline deviate from core facts from the actor's life but, according to the director, the film dealt with a 'collective fate' [*Massenschicksal*] rather than an 'individual case' [*Einzelfall*].[33] Nonetheless, we should be wary of concluding that the film's universalizing dedication to Jewish victimhood was a strategy of marginalizing the latter. In a letter written just a few weeks later, Maetzig privately expressed both his long-held desire to make a film about 'the terrible fate of Jewish "mixed marriages" during the Hitler period' and the 'great responsibility' he felt from such a 'great and moving film theme' towards 'all those who had suffered in these past terrible years in Germany'.[34] While such statements do not preclude criticism of the ending, they are certainly not indicative of a desire to downplay Jewish suffering. Instead, we should ask ourselves once again whether, within the context of the immediate postwar years, including Jewish victimhood within the 'collective fate' of Germans was, however problematic such a decision ultimately is, an attempt to reintegrate Jewish suffering into the national story.

The difficulty in reconciling the final title card with the film's exploration of Jewish victimhood is exacerbated by the fact that Maetzig seeks to draw attention to Jewish victimhood through a strategy of absence. The epilogue was one of the most heavily rewritten scenes. In total, Maetzig wrote four endings. The first version depicts Silbermann and Bernstein at the cemetery as Hans and Elisabeth are buried.[35] An air raid alarm sounding in the background is overlaid with Chopin's Piano Sonata No. 2 in B-Flat Minor ('The Funeral March'), while the two Jewish men lament the fate of the Wielands:

Silbermann   What a terrible end!
Bernstein   I saw it coming. But let's go. It's dangerous here. . .

Maetzig sent an early draft of the screenplay to Axel Eggebrecht, who recommended that he conclude the film with Blohm contacting the Propaganda Ministry. Maetzig, however, was resolute that 'under no circumstances' should such a scene be added as this 'would very much go against the feeling' of the film, thereby signalling that the victims' absence, rather than the perpetrators' presence, should underline the film's ending.[36]

Nevertheless, two new endings were written.[37] One version removes Silbermann's dialogue entirely. Instead the doctor 'wipes away a tear' as Bernstein insists, 'Best that we go!'.[38] The other version includes Silbermann's dialogue as he laments the loss of the Wielands, while Bernstein points to a future point of criminal reckoning:[39]

Silbermann   There they carry our friends. Talent – hope – love. So
             many – so many –
Bernstein   But one day. . .

All three drafts conclude with a forward projection. The implication is that the story will continue and, in this regard, they echo the final scene of *Die Mörder sind unter uns* through the suggestion that a sense of natural order and criminal accountability will follow in postwar Germany. However, the film's actual ending removes any sense of an appeal to the future and instead encourages the audience to reflect rather than project. Silbermann and Bernstein no longer appear, thereby removing any indication that they may survive the war or are even alive when the funeral takes place, the soundtrack of Chopin is replaced with silence and spoken dialogue is exchanged for written text. Maetzig concludes his film with a free space for audiences to reflect over an ending shaped by absence.

Figure 1.2. Prior to the coming to power of the NSDAP, Willy Prager (Dr Silbermann) was one of Germany's best-known *Kabarett* performers. After 1933 he was banned from the stage and *Ehe im Schatten* was his first film role since 1932. © DEFA-Stiftung/Kurt Wunsch.

The association of the Jewish characters with postwar absence also informs the depiction of the other Jewish characters in the film, in particular that of Silbermann. As a character who refuses to abandon his patients or his belief that as an assimilated Jewish citizen he will be protected by his compatriots, the image of the character with his back to the smouldering ruins of Berlin is particularly poignant (Figure 1.2). Silbermann appears as an almost spectral figure traversing the shell of a city which has lost its heart. The shot of Silbermann standing among the rubble can thus be read as a question to the audience that asks how postwar Germany can rebuild a city and a country which both remembers what is absent and reintegrates Jewish survivors into the postwar landscape.

Everyday Perpetrators

The perpetrator was an ever-present figure in German film in the immediate postwar years. The first cinematic engagements with Jewish persecution were in the form of 'atrocity films' that promoted the thesis of collective guilt. Given the centrality of 're-education' initiatives in the Allies' postwar reconstruction plans, it should come as little surprise that documentary films repeatedly foregrounded the culpability of the German nation in the crimes of the Third Reich. However, such overt confrontations quickly had the effect of disengaging audiences. An OMGUS report from screenings of *Die Todesmühlen* in February 1946 concluded that 87.9 per cent of those surveyed after watching the film asserted that they did not feel that they bore any personal responsibility for the events depicted.[40] By late 1946, the Allies had abandoned this approach entirely.

In contrast to the thesis of collective guilt in the 'atrocity films', German feature films in the immediate postwar years emphasized criminal guilt. *Die Mörder sind unter uns*, for example, concludes with an exchange between the two protagonists in which Susanne implores, 'We do not have the right to judge', to which Hans replies, 'No Susanne, but we have the duty to bring charges, to demand atonement in the name of the millions of innocent murdered people'. As the camera zooms out of Brückner's prison cell, images of desolate men, women and children are superimposed over the face of the former National Socialist captain. In keeping with dominant portrayals of the National Socialist period in the immediate postwar years, guilt is displaced onto selected military and political elites, thereby sparing 'ordinary Germans' from questions of complicity.

Ehe im Schatten works against this growing trend. Instead of attempting to displace responsibility for the recent crimes vertically, Maetzig demonstrates how individuals' own failure to act created a climate for the societal propagation of persecutory actions. This is most evident in the characters' diverging behaviour in their personal and professional lives. Blohm reassures Elisabeth that the party opposes 'a few unsavoury characters who came from the East, not you' and he is prepared to enter into a relationship with her, as long as his colleagues do not find out. Hans attacks this very point at the end of the film when he confronts Blohm about his misplaced belief that one's personal and professional conduct could be so easily separated. In response, Blohm insists he used his position to protect Elisabeth and others, only for Hans to admonish him: 'That is supposed to be your justification, that you helped two or three people for a while? Herr Doctor Blohm, one day hundreds of artists who have been robbed of everything because of you and your racist politics will accuse you'. Hans' attack exposes a common defence at denazification trials at the time, namely that individuals who had defended a small number of Jews during the war should be spared prosecution for any other crimes. Here, it seems that Maetzig is seeking to place blame onto political functionaries. However, at the very point when it seems that the film is seeking to displace responsibility vertically, there is a self-correction. Hans continues to admonish Blohm, but he also broadens the scope of this attack: 'But it's our own fault. We never bothered with politics. We always thought things would not be so bad and believed as individuals, as artists, we could avoid responsibility. We are just as guilty as you!' Despite the clear attack on Blohm, the dialogue also highlights how the 'we' in Maetzig's film is imbued with a deeply critical tone that condemns both those who acted falsely and those who did not act at all.

The scene exemplifies the film's emphasis on the role of everyday acts by 'ordinary Germans' in upholding antisemitic prejudices and practices. A similar critique can be found in an episode shortly before the Reichstag fire when the characters travel to Hiddensee for the weekend. As the friends return from the holiday house, Bernstein suddenly stops and ominously states, 'I think I'll never see Hiddensee again'. When the others ask why, he looks straight forward and points directly at the camera and at the audience. The scene then cuts to reveal a man erecting a sign that reads 'Jews not wanted' (Figure 1.3). Earlier drafts of the screenplay indicate that the scene originally included a member of the SA who was overseeing the action, that is to say, the action was led by a readily identifiable National Socialist party supporter.[41] In the final film, however, the action is carried out by an 'ordinary German'. This recalibrates the relationship between action and agent by casting a local farmer rather than an ardent party member as the perpetrator.

The decision to cast a German civilian as the agent of an antisemitic act allows Maetzig to highlight the duplicity of the characters' actions and show that no one character is entirely villainous or without responsibility. Of course, such an approach is not without its own limitations. By placing all the characters on a spectrum of guilt and attributing individual responsibility for the failure to act sooner to *all* the characters, Maetzig arguably holds no *one* person to account. In so doing, he risks implying that Germans, motivated by little more than careerism and opportunism, inadvertently stumbled upon the 'twisted road to Auschwitz'.[42] Nonetheless, by challenging every character's conduct, Maetzig does not show his characters as 'helpless cogs in the wheels of the times', but rather demonstrates how Germans' individual failure to act created a climate for the societal propagation of persecutory actions by presenting the characters as cognisant, albeit naïve cogs in a wider socio-political system.[43]

Picking up the Pieces 39

Figure 1.3. *Ehe im Schatten* points the finger of responsibility at 'ordinary Germans' – and even the film's audience – for the persecution of Jews. © DEFA-Stiftung/Kurt Wunsch.

Finally, when discussing the film's negotiation of questions of responsibility, it is important to reflect on the fact that the first German feature film dedicated to Jewish persecution does so within the professional milieu of the acting community. *Ehe im Schatten* was a deeply personal project for Maetzig and several members of the cast and crew. Clear parallels existed between the experiences of Maetzig's family during the war and those of the Wielands in the film. Maetzig's Jewish mother (who was divorced from the director's father) died by suicide after the Gestapo arrived at the family house with the intention of deporting her to a concentration camp.[44] The actors Willy Prager (Silbermann) and Alfred Balthoff (Bernstein) played roles that drew heavily on their own experiences as Jews in the Third Reich, while Hans Schweikart, whose novella *Es wird nicht so schlimm* (*It Won't Be So Bad*) formed the basis for the film's screenplay, had directed Joachim Gottschalk in the actor's penultimate performance, *Das Mädchen von Fanö* (*The Girl from Fanö*, 1941).[45] But Schweikart was not simply active as a director during the Third Reich; he had considerable influence as the head of production at Bavaria Film. The participation of Wolfgang Zeller and Hilde von Stolz in *Ehe im Schatten* seems entirely incongruous with their roles in *Jud Süss*. Indeed, it is hard not to respond with a certain degree of cynicism to a letter forwarded from Veit Harlan to DEFA in which he repeats the (valid) claim that he used his position to help a number of Jews and adds that not only did he attempt to assist the Gottschalks, but that Gottschalk's suicide note had been addressed to him and Kristina Söderbaum – and was still in his possession.[46] At a time when actors, directors, cameramen and producers were still undergoing denazification trials in the German courts, we must ask whether *Ehe im Schatten* offered many of those involved in the film industry in the Third Reich an opportunity to distance themselves from the National Socialist regime. This is not to imply that the motivations of figures such as Hans Schweikart were insincere. But as a statement of political and moral attitude, participation in a film depicting National Socialist persecution was certainly an excellent opportunity for all involved to (re)position themselves on the right side of history.

Ehe im Schatten at Home and Abroad

The film's murder-suicide scene is frequently cited as a key example of Maetzig's use of dominant filmmaking tropes from Third Reich melodramas. A number of critics have rightly highlighted the similarities between Elisabeth's death in *Ehe im Schatten* and the death of the female protagonist in Wolfgang Liebeneiner's 1941 film, *Ich klage an*.[47] *Ich klage an* was envisaged as a pro-euthanasia film in which the protagonist, Thomas, administers a fatal overdose to his wife, Hanna, who suffers from multiple sclerosis. In contrast to antisemitic legislation, National Socialist euthanasia policies never found widespread acquiescence among the German population and it has long been argued that the employment of melodramatic tropes in *Ich klage an* was designed to encourage audiences to view Thomas' act of murder as one of compassion. The comparisons between the deaths of Hanna and Elisabeth imply that Maetzig, like Liebeneiner, drew on melodramatic tropes for the death scene in order to frame Elisabeth's murder as an act of compassion and, crucially, to indulge in an 'excess of effect over cause' that would allow audiences to overcome any apathy to the Jewish protagonist.[48]

Both sequences were shot by the same cinematographer and attributing the similarities between the two films to Friedl Behn-Grund can be seen to imply a direct interfilmic link between *Ich klage an* and *Ehe im Schatten*. This is, however, somewhat misleading. It is important to remember that the staging of Hanna's death in *Ich klage an* was itself far from unique. The death of a couple in love has long served as the apex of a frustrated love story in film, theatre and literature. The ending of *Ehe im Schatten* may resemble that of the 1941 film, but the Ufa production was already in dialogue with numerous other works taken from the stage and screen. It is no coincidence that we first encounter Elisabeth and Hans performing Schiller's *Kabale und Liebe*. The play is an archetypal example of a *Sturm und Drang* work, a movement that was pivotal in shaping the melodrama. Moreover, the protagonists' deaths draw heavily on the Wagnerian *Liebestod*, a recurring motif of nineteenth-century opera which was later adopted by filmmakers in Germany and beyond throughout the 1930s and 1940s. *Ehe im Schatten* was by no means unique in the employment of the *Liebestod* motif and numerous contemporaneous German, European and Hollywood films also used the same dramatic trope. There is, therefore, little reason to believe that spectators at the time would have perceived a specific reference to *Ich klage an* in Maetzig's suicide scene.

The argument that the film employs melodramatic tropes to appease domestic audiences also leaves an important question unanswered: if the use of melodramatic tropes in *Ehe im Schatten* was first and foremost a concession to German audiences, why did the film enjoy such widespread success abroad? By the end of the decade, *Ehe im Schatten* had been screened in seventeen countries,[49] had been named as one of the best foreign films of 1948 by *The New York Times*[50] and appeared on the 1949 Academy Award Reminder List.[51] To understand the success of the film abroad, it is important to return to the film's style. Although Ufa productions have become largely synonymous with melodramas, the style of the films produced during the Third Reich should not be conflated with an 'Ufa aesthetic'. National Socialist cinema never had a style to call its own. As Karsten Witte has discussed, it was deliberately shaped to imitate classic Hollywood cinema through a reliance on genre cinema, highly structured narratives and the fostering of a star system in which German film stars were positioned to emulate the on-screen image of American actors such as Katherine Hepburn (Marianne Hoppe) and Joan Crawford (Brigitte Homey).[52] Thus, when critics allude to the 'Ufa aesthetic' of *Ehe im Schatten*, they are, in fact, overwhelmingly referring to the dominant style of filmmaking of the period and, more specifically, to classic Hollywood models of filmmaking.

The stylistic continuities between German and American cinema help to explain the film's success abroad. The export of German films to America during the Third Reich fell dramatically after the outbreak of the Second World War, dropping from eight-five in 1939 to twenty-three in 1941 and just one in 1942.[53] However, German newsreel footage continued to be shown in a propaganda effort designed to demonstrate the brutality of the German enemy. Consequently, the image of German national cinema differed significantly between occupied and non-occupied countries. Audiences in France and the Netherlands, for instance, were exposed to Ufa films throughout the war and would have been fully accustomed to the style of *Ehe im Schatten* from earlier such productions from the Third Reich. Conversely the melodramatic style of *Ehe im Schatten* clearly came as a surprise to reviewers in the United States. In stark contrast to one French critic who reflected that, 'if, for extra-filmic reasons, one can only applaud this film produced on the other side of the Rhine, one nevertheless laments its artistic shortcomings',[54] a reviewer for *The New Yorker* proclaimed, 'it is a big relief to see a film about Germany in which everybody isn't clicking his heels and hollering 'Heil Hitler'!'[55] Indeed, the film's American distributors even saw fit to boast that *Ehe im Schatten* was 'the most important contribution for reparation on the part of the German film industry, thus making up in part for the immense calamity caused by the Nazis, in which the German film played an important part'.[56] The surprise revealed in such reviews is not that *Ehe im Schatten* is aesthetically innovative, but that it is reassuringly familiar. It is this point that, albeit for markedly different reasons, unites domestic and international receptions of the film.

Ehe im Schatten exemplifies the recurring discord between the content and the presentation of DEFA's Holocaust films. Throughout the course of the GDR, *Ehe im Schatten* was framed as evidence of the nascent socialist state's willingness to engage with legacies of Jewish persecution in the immediate postwar years. On the surface, *Ehe im Schatten* offered little political potential for the SED. In private correspondence, Maetzig stressed that he had 'made every effort to write this film as simply and as humanly as possible, to keep it free from any perceptible and heavy propaganda'[57] and that it was 'superfluous to say that we do not bring any party or day-to-day politics to our films'.[58] However, this deliberately depoliticized approach disappeared within a matter of months as East German officials became less concerned with 'coming to terms' with the past, so much as distancing the GDR from it.

Ehe im Schatten was strategically re-released during periods of German tension with the Federal Republic. In November 1958, East German newspapers reported that a screening of *Ehe im Schatten* had been disrupted by 'fascist bully boys' from the CDU's youth organization. Citing the incident as 'further evidence for the path of the Federal Republic towards fascism', the East German press reported that 'fascist hooligans' disrupted the screening through such loud 'jeering and whistling' that 'hardly one word of the action could be understood'.[59] With the arrest of Adolf Eichmann in 1960, the SED once again seized upon the opportunity to draw such associations. The arts newspaper *Sonntag* reported that *Ehe im Schatten* would be screened in Berlin in January 1960 'in order to support the protest against the antisemitic and fascist excesses in the Federal Republic',[60] while *Neues Deutschland* claimed that the re-release of the film in Sweden in the same year was a direct response to 'the fascist and antisemitic wave in the Federal Republic'.[61] The film was released again in 1980 as a direct response to the West German screening of *Holocaust* and once more in 1988 as part of the commemorations for the fiftieth anniversary of 1938 November Pogroms as evidence of the GDR's long-standing commitment to 'coming to terms' with the past.[62] Herein lies a certain irony in the state's position towards DEFA films depicting Jewish persecution. The SED's repeated attempts to utilize Maetzig's film in order to demonstrate its early dedication to the commemoration of the Holocaust resulted in the presentation of *Ehe im Schatten* as evidence of the 'coming to terms' with a past for which it took no responsibility.

Notes

1. An OMGUS report reads: 'In spite of the prohibition of non-licensed films in the American Sector, the Soviet-sponsored DEFA film *Ehe im Schatten*, a film dealing with the mixed marriage problem under the Nazis, was given a release because of its great educational value'. Cited in Gallwitz, '"Unterhaltung – Erziehung – Mahnung"', 283 note 15.
2. Joachim Gottschalk (1904–41) was a German stage and film actor best known for playing romantic leads. In 1930, he married the Jewish actress Meta Wolff. With the outbreak of war, Hans Hinkel, a member of the Propaganda Ministry who had been tasked with the 'dejudification' of German culture, demanded Gottschalk divorce his wife. Gottschalk refused and as a result was effectively barred from acting. In November 1941, Gottschalk committed suicide with his wife and son through gas poisoning. Newspapers at the time were banned from reporting his death.
3. Allan, 'DEFA's Antifascist Myths and the Construction of National Identity in East German Cinema', 53.
4. Maetzig, '*Aber eines Tages*. Screenplay'. BArch DR 117/2634.
5. The concept of the *Kulturnation* draws on the cultural bonds that united the Germanic lands before the creation of the German nation state in 1871. Here, Stephen Brockmann's definition is particularly helpful: 'The *Kulturnation* is the nation as it imagines itself to be, tied together by bonds of language, culture, religion, history and desire'. Brockmann, *Nuremberg: The Imaginary Capital*, 9.
6. Hake, *Popular Cinema of the Third Reich*, 214.
7. Altman, 'A Semantic/Syntactic Approach to Film Genre', 10.
8. Ibid.
9. Ibid.
10. Neale, 'Melodrama and Tears', 6.
11. Hake, *Popular Cinema of the Third Reich*, 113.
12. Neale, 'Melodrama and Tears', 21.
13. Landy, *Imitations of Life*, 14.
14. Allan, 'Sagt, wie soll man Stalin danken?', 257.
15. Musial and Knospe, *Kurt Maetzig*, 11.
16. Hilde von Stolz played the role of Greta Koch, a non-Jewish woman who Hans kisses just before the November Pogrom riots.
17. *Ehe im Schatten* was Kurt Maetzig's first feature film.
18. Rentschler, 'Germany: The Past That Would Not Go Away', 212.
19. Shandley, *Rubble Films*, 86–7.
20. Ibid.
21. Ibid., 84.
22. Bongartz, *Von Caligari zu Hitler, von Hitler zu Dr. Mabuse?*, 121.
23. Smith, *Melodrama*, 9.
24. The encounter between Elisabeth and the Secretary of State was one of several fictional additions to the real-life persecution experienced by Joachim Gottschalk and Meta Wolff. Gottschalk and Wolff committed suicide by gas poisoning, not by taking Verenol. The depiction of a Jewish character committing suicide with gas may have been considered too sensational so soon after the war, although it is worth noting that Käutner's *In jenen Tagen*, released just a few weeks before *Ehe im Schatten*, does just this, albeit off screen.

25. Of course, the term 'Holocaust' was not widely used in public or academic discourse in 1947 to describe the crimes committed against the Jews.
26. For more on how women who challenged the prescribed roles of the sexes under National Socialism were 'contained and eliminated' in National Socialist melodramas, see O'Brien, *Nazi Cinema as Enchantment*, 161.
27. *Razzia* (*Raid*, 1947); *1–2–3 Corona* (1948); *Straßenbekanntschaft* (*Street Acquaintances*, 1948). The figures are rounded up. For the exact figures, see DEFA, *Auf neuen Wegen*, 217.
28. *Frankfurter Rundschau*, 'Unsere tägliche Frage: *Ehe im Schatten*'; Geßner, 'Nachbetrachtung zu einem Film'; Leibelt, '*Ehe im Schatten*'. It should be noted that Hans Leibelt was an actor who appeared in *Ehe im Schatten*.
29. *Der Sozialdemokrat*, '*Ehe im Schatten*'.
30. Klaren, 'Zeitgemäße Filmstoffe: Filme, die wir drehen möchten'. See also Shandley, *Rubble Films*, 88.
31. Maetzig, 'Letter from Kurt Maetzig to Axel Eggebrecht', 2 October 1946.
32. A modified version of this image appeared on the film's poster.
33. Maetzig, 'Memorandum. Kurt Maetzig to Dr Klaren'.
34. Maetzig, 'Letter from Kurt Maetzig to Prof. Dr W. Liebbrandt'.
35. Maetzig, '*Verfolgte Seelen*. Draft Screenplay'.
36. Maetzig, 'Letter from Kurt Maetzig to Axel Eggebrecht', 17 January 1947.
37. The two screenplays are located in different archives. It is unclear which represents the earlier screenplay.
38. Maetzig, '*Aber eines Tages*. Screenplay'. BArch DR 117/2634.
39. Maetzig, '*Aber eines Tages*. Screenplay'. AdK, Berlin, Kurt-Maetzig-Archiv, Nr. 5.
40. Chamberlain, '*Todesmühlen*: Ein früher Versuch zur Massen-"Umerziehung" im besetzten Deutschland 1945–1946', 434.
41. Maetzig, '*Aber eines Tages*. Screenplay'. AdK, Berlin, Kurt-Maetzig-Archiv, Nr. 5.
42. Schleunes, *The Twisted Road to Auschwitz: Nazi Policy Toward German Jews, 1933–1939*.
43. Rentschler, 'Germany: The Past That Would Not Go Away', 212.
44. See also Brockmann, *A Critical History of German Film*, 189–90.
45. Schweikart, *Es wird schon nicht so schlimm! oder, Nichts geht vorüber!: ein Filmvorschlag*.
46. Filmbüro Shellhaus, 'Letter to DEFA'.
47. For example, Byg, 'DEFA and the Traditions of International Cinema', 30; Feinstein, *The Triumph of the Ordinary*, 26.
48. Neale, 'Melodrama and Tears', 7.
49. The film was screened in China, Albania, Bulgaria, Hungary, Romania, France, Belgium, Czechoslovakia, the Netherlands, Switzerland, the United Kingdom, Austria, Sweden, Norway, Finland, Denmark and the USA. Ackermann, 'Zum 5-jährigen Bestehen der DEFA', 211.
50. *The New York Times*, 'The Ten Best Films'.
51. The Reminder List is circulated to all Academy members who are invited to select individuals or films for consideration for an Oscar. Ilse Steppat, Paul Klinger and the film appeared on the list. There was no category for Best Foreign Language Film in 1947. Academy of Motion Picture Arts and Sciences, '1949 (22nd) Academy Awards, Reminder List of Eligible Releases'.
52. Witte, 'The Indivisible Legacy of Nazi Cinema', 24.
53. Spieker, *Hollywood unterm Hakenkreuz*, 338.
54. *Aux Écoutes de la Finance*, 'Aux Écoutes du Cinéma'.

55. *The New Yorker*. Reprinted in *The New York Times*, 'Display Ad 31: *Marriage in the Shadows*'.
56. Gramercy Publicity, 'American Film Programme for *Marriage in the Shadows*'.
57. Maetzig, 'Letter from Kurt Maetzig to Ilse Meyer and Lie Friedländer'.
58. Maetzig, 'Letter from Kurt Maetzig to Prof. Dr W. Liebbrandt'.
59. *Thüringer Tageblatt*, 'Antisemitische Krawalle in Bad Nauheim'.
60. *Sonntag*, 'Ehe im Schatten'.
61. *Neues Deutschland*, '*Ehe im Schatten* in Schweden aufgeführt'.
62. ZK der SED, 'Maßnahmen zum 50. Jahrestag der faschistischen Pogromnacht'.

PART II

1949–61

Just days after the founding of the GDR in October 1949, the new president Wilhelm Pieck declared that the 'economic, political and cultural advancement' of Germany lay in the new socialist East German state.[1] The sealing of the German–German border in 1961 following the emigration of more than three million East Germans to the West signalled the failure to convince many compatriots of this vision. The construction of the Berlin Wall came after a decade-long attempt to foster an intrinsic East German identity among the GDR's citizens through the *Aufbau des Sozialismus* ('building up of socialism').[2] The programme was designed to establish the political and economic structures of the new socialist state, as well as promoting the figurative 'Aufbau' of East German identity. Film played a vital role in the advancement of this new, socialist identity. Although *Aufbaufilme* ('building up films') were primarily concerned with stories of socialist heroes in contemporary society, films set during the National Socialist period continued to play an important role, not least through their celebration of the antifascist resistance fighter as an emblematic orientation figure for audiences. It is hardly surprising, therefore, that this period saw a rapid increase in the number of antifascist films with a total of twenty-five released between 1949 and 1961.[3]

The extent to which film was successful in contributing to the promotion of an East German identity is difficult to gauge, but it is clear that the SED's concurrent attempts to exert greater control over the studio served to stifle rather than stimulate the East German film industry. In 1950, eight films were completed. By 1952 this had dropped to just five.[4] The immediate postwar years may have been remembered by DEFA filmmakers as a 'wonderful period' in which 'we were very free and could make the films we wanted to make', but the period from 1949 to 1961 saw a rapid increase in the level of political influence over East German filmmaking.[5] In the months running up to the official founding of the GDR in October 1949, the SED quickly sought to tighten its grip on DEFA by replacing the studio's board members with trusted party officials. This culminated in the appointment of Sepp Schwab as DEFA's studio director in 1950. Schwab, who had no filmmaking experience whatsoever, was a hard-line party official who, according to former DEFA studio director Albert Wilkening, operated according to the principle of 'better too much suspicion than gullibility'.[6] His credo would set the tone for filmmaking in the GDR for years to come.

The early 1950s saw the rapid alignment of the East German film industry with state structures of operation and control. The 1952 resolution by the Politbüro, 'For the Upturn of Progressive German Film Art', marked a key milestone in the history of the East German film industry. The resolution led to the creation of Progress Film, the GDR's domestic film distribution company, and heralded the fundamental restructuring of filmmaking through the reclassification of DEFA as a 'Volkseigener Betrieb' (People's Own Industry, VEB) in 1953, a publicly-owned, vertically integrated company.[7] The 1952 resolution also paved the way for the creation of the Ministry for Culture and Hauptverwaltung Film (Central Administration Film or HV Film) in 1954, a department within the Ministry headed by the Deputy Minister of Culture, which served to tighten the SED's influence over the studio further.

Although film output increased in the mid-1950s, the underlying causes for the upturn actually owed far more to political events than to internal restructurings at DEFA. The workers' uprising of June 1953 led the state to make a number of concessions and to undertake a series of social reforms. This in turn heralded a more liberal climate in the GDR, as did the political and cultural thaw which unfolded across the Eastern Bloc after Stalin's death. The period of liberalization was used by DEFA's new studio director, Hans Rodenberg, as an opportunity to negotiate greater freedoms for filmmakers. Initially, DEFA's output did increase from fifteen films in 1954 to seventeen films the following year.[8] However, these freedoms proved short-lived. In May 1957, the Minister of Culture Johannes Becher, his deputy Anton Ackermann and the DEFA management were summoned to the office of the Culture Secretary for the Central Committee, Paul Wandel, who attacked the studio's production plan and criticized the absence of films dealing with workers' everyday lives.⁹ Speeches delivered by cultural functionaries at the 1958 Film Conference in Berlin also indicated that filmmaking was to return to the ideological dogmatism of 1952. By 1958, all leadership positions at the studio were occupied by party members. Similarly, seventy per cent of DEFA's directors and fifty per cent of its dramaturges were party members.¹⁰ As a point of contrast, party membership among the general population stood at just five per cent.

Victims and Heroes during the 'Aufbau' Period

At the same time as the so-called 'freezes' and 'thaws' were shaping the conditions in which DEFA's films were produced and released, parallel developments were also shaping Holocaust commemoration in the GDR. In 1953, the Association of Persecutees of the National Socialist Regime (Vereinigung der Verfolgten des Naziregimes or VVN) was replaced by the Committee of Antifascist Resistance Fighters (Komitee der Antifaschistischen Widerstandskämpfer or KdAW). Whereas the VVN represented all victims of National Socialist persecution, the KdAW was an organization concerned with ensuring a lasting legacy for political resisters. This not only resulted in the exclusion of Jewish victims, but it also led to their redesignation as 'Victims of Fascism' rather than the KdAW members' title as 'Fighters against Fascism'. From the outset, the KdAW was less a veterans' group as much as a lobbying organization that actively sought to shape memories of National Socialist persecution in the GDR. The influence of the KdAW was evident at the former concentration camps of Sachsenhausen, Buchenwald and Ravensbrück which at the end of the 1950s were designated National Sites of Admonition and Remembrance (*Nationale Mahn- und Gedenkstätten*). The KdAW was actively involved in designing the exhibition boards at the sites. Although Politbüro member Albert Norden intervened to warn the KdAW that they should be mindful of how they presented information at the former concentration camps to avoid accusations that 'the suffering of Jews under Hitler's fascism is not sufficiently observed in the GDR', the three sites were shaped by a clear desire to legitimize the GDR as an antifascist state in the present, rather than by a desire to remember the German crimes of the past.¹¹

The Holocaust was a present subject in East German film during the 'Aufbau' period, albeit a minor one. Mirroring broader commemorative trends in the GDR, the already diminished space afforded to Jewish persecution in DEFA's output was compounded by the dominance of the figure of the antifascist resistance fighter. The celebration of the antifascist resistance fighter not only threatened to push Jewish victims to the margins, it also risked instrumentalizing their victimhood. While idealized socialist heroes functioned as either exemplary father figures (as in Kurt Maetzig's Ernst Thälmann films) or offered an antifascist conversion by proxy for East German audiences (*Lissy* and *Sie nannten ihn Amigo*), Jewish characters were overwhelmingly reduced to peripheral figures (*Rotation*) or served as vehicles for the condemnation of resurgent antisemitism in the Federal Republic (*Zwischenfall in Benderath, Der Prozeß wird vertagt*).[12]

No other two films during this period focus on Jewish persecution to the same extent as Konrad Wolf's *Sterne* (1959) and *Professor Mamlock* (1961). Wolf is widely considered to be one of the GDR's leading filmmakers and he enjoyed high esteem among party officials and his peers. The son of playwright Friedrich Wolf, Konrad Wolf emigrated with his family in 1933 to the Soviet Union where, as committed socialists, they remained exiled throughout the Third Reich. In 1942, Wolf enlisted in the Red Army and was later part of a unit that was involved in the liberation of Sachsenhausen concentration camp.[13] After the war, he worked in a range of cultural roles in the SMAD before attending film school in Moscow in 1949. Wolf served as assistant director to Kurt Maetzig on *Ernst Thälmann – Sohn seiner Klasse* and two years later released his own debut feature film, *Genesung* (*Recovery*, 1956). Given Wolf's 'exemplary record as a soldier and socialist', it is perhaps of little surprise that antifascism should inform so much of his work.[14] However, the extent to which this inevitably led to the marginalization of Jewish persecution in the following two case studies requires closer examination.

Sterne and *Professor Mamlock* are two quite different films, but together they provide ideal case studies for exploring the representation of Jewish persecution during the 'Aufbau' period. In both films, we find a Jewish victim at the heart of a storyline that interweaves an antifascist narrative with Jewish persecution. It is certainly true that the Jewish characters risk becoming passive figures whose primary function is to facilitate the protagonists' antifascist conversion. However, the cinematographic means by which Jewish victimhood is conveyed complicates this reading. The strategic use of camera angles and montage compels the spectator to acknowledge the emotional cost of persecution. Moreover, although the films feature the antifascist conversion of two non-Jewish protagonists, both films underline the fact that this conversion occurs too late in the narrative to save the Jewish character whose death lingers over the final scenes.

One striking absence in both films is the figure of the perpetrator. In sharp contrast to *Ehe im Schatten*, there is no attempt to examine societal prejudices or to address the audience through a culpatory 'we'. Although senior Wehrmacht figures and Gestapo officers are shown to be agents of violence, both films reveal a notable disinterest in exploring questions of individual or collective culpability. As we shall see, *Sterne* and *Professor Mamlock* are far more concerned with the redemptive potential of antifascist conversions than they are with the relationship between victim and perpetrator. The two chapters in this section conclude by exploring the extent to which *Sterne* and *Professor Mamlock* became conduits for debates about East German identity in the past and present. By examining the marketing of the films at home and abroad, it becomes clear that the domestic and foreign distributors sought to shape the presentation of each film in order to foreground different elements depending on where and for whom the film was being distributed. While this is perhaps not remarkable in itself, what emerges from this comparative analysis is the ways in which DEFA films were strategically promoted domestically and internationally; DEFA omitted reference to antifascism for the sake of international success in the West at the very point this same narrative underpinned the 'Aufbau' of a new East German antifascist identity at home.

Notes

1. Pieck, 'An der Wende der deutschen Geschichte', 22.
2. The concept of the 'Aufbau des Sozialismus' dates back to a speech by Walter Ulbricht at the Second Party Conference of the SED in July 1952.
3. According to a publication by the Verband der Film- und Fernsehschaffenden der DDR (Film and Television Association of the GDR), DEFA produced four antifascist films (as feature films) prior to 1949. Twenty-five antifascist films were made between 1949 and 1961, compared to seventeen in the period from 1962 to 1972 and nineteen between 1973 and 1984. Verband der Film- und Fernsehschaffenden der DDR, *Das Thema 'Antifaschismus' in Filmen der DDR für Kino und Fernsehen*.
4. Feinstein, *The Triumph of the Ordinary*, 30.
5. Brady, 'Discussion with Kurt Maetzig', 83.
6. Mückenberger, 'Zeit der Hoffnungen', 26.
7. Foreign distribution came under the remit of DEFA-Außenhandel which was founded three years later in 1955.
8. Feinstein, *The Triumph of the Ordinary*, 38.
9. Ibid., 67–9.
10. Heimann, *DEFA, Künstler und SED-Kulturpolitik*, 271.
11. zur Nieden, '... stärker als der Tod: Bruno Apitz' Roman *Nackt unter Wölfen* und die Holocaust-Rezeption in der DDR', 97.

12. *Ernst Thälmann – Sohn seiner Klasse* (1954), *Ernst Thälmann – Führer seiner Klasse* (*Ernst Thälmann – Leader of his Class*, 1955), *Lissy* (1957), *Sie nannten ihn Amigo* (1958), *Rotation* (1949), *Zwischenfall in Benderath* (*Incident in Benderath*, 1956), *Der Prozess wird vertagt* (*The Trial is Postponed*, 1958).
13. Walk, 'Wolf, Konrad'.
14. Coulson, 'Paths of Discovery', 164.

Chapter 2

THE GERMAN DEMOCRATIC REPUBLIC'S AMBASSADOR OF GOOD WILL

Konrad Wolf's *Sterne*

Film officials and critics were divided over Konrad Wolf's *Sterne* (1959) from the outset. The point of contention was not the artistic quality of the film. Here critics at home and abroad were united in their praise of *Sterne*, a production which one East German reviewer described as 'one of the most moving films of recent times',[1] a West German critic considered 'one of the best DEFA films ever'[2] and which a British journalist termed an 'extraordinarily good film'.[3] Rather, the issue at stake was whether Wolf's film was underpinned by a celebratory antifascist narrative or if, against all expectations to the contrary, *Sterne* was a film that avoided rehearsing the familiar narratives of the past and instead was able to transcend the political and ideological parameters of its land of production.

If we look to domestic reviews of the film, it is clear that East German journalists frequently used the release of *Sterne* as an opportunity to attack the Federal Republic. Somewhat unsurprisingly, the SED's organ *Neues Deutschland* led the way in the East German press' overt attacks against the Federal Republic, describing the film as 'a wake-up call to all those who believe again today, they can stand by passively as the militarists in West Germany [*Westdeutschland*] prepare another horrific war'.[4] In a similar vein, the East German film magazine *Filmspiegel* used its review of the film as an opportunity to claim that in the Federal Republic 'one Jewish cemetery in every ten [is] desecrated, German citizens of Jewish origin are harassed and insulted, and it very rarely happens that even a blatant antisemite is held to account'.[5] West German cultural and political functionaries shared the East German press' reading of the film as being imbued with an overt political and ideological message, although obviously to markedly different ends. The West German Filmbewertungsstelle Wiesbaden (FBW), a film evaluation board made up of the federal states' ministers of education, concluded that the film ultimately served as a pretext for the celebration of communism and stipulated that its final sequences be removed or, as one West German critic termed it, 'amputated'.[6] When the film was released in the Federal Republic, it was screened without the film's concluding exchanges between the German corporal Walter and the Bulgarian partisan Petko.[7]

A basic synopsis of the film certainly does little to counter readings of *Sterne* as a film with an explicit antifascist narrative. The East German–Bulgarian co-production is set in a Jewish transit camp in the fictional Bulgarian town of Bankso and depicts the journey of Walter from a position of ideological indifference to the resolution to act for the sake of his love interest, the young Jewish woman Ruth. As his love for Ruth grows, so does his resolve to help her escape the fate of the other Jewish prisoners. His first act is to establish contact with the local Bulgarian partisans and to arrange for the delivery of much needed medical supplies to the camp. When he learns of the imminent deportation of the prisoners to Auschwitz, he meets the partisans again to try to arrange for Ruth's escape. But, as the film's framing device reveals, the actions come too late and Walter's penultimate act in the film is to watch the train carrying Ruth and the other prisoners disappear into a tunnel filled with smoke. The film ends with Walter walking away into the distance with a local partisan.

Despite what appears to be a clear narrative arc whereby a politically and ideologically indifferent young man comes into contact with communist partisans who open his eyes to the right course of action, reading the film as a straightforward antifascist conversion narrative is immediately complicated by two points. Firstly, East German journalists may have praised *Sterne* as a film that venerated 'the memory of the antifascist resistance fighter',[8] but this view was not actually shared by DEFA. In a document written just two months before the release of the film, officials reported that 'the film is hard for us' precisely because 'when you look at the Germans . . . an antifascist is not present'.[9] This view was echoed by DEFA studio director Albert Wilkening who conceded that, 'we are aware that this film is a very hard film for the

German spectator because it unrelentingly shows German guilt'.[10] Both statements are a far remove from the victim–victor presentation of the collective East German experience that underpinned official narratives of the National Socialist past and were certainly not views openly expressed in public. Secondly, in contrast to the conclusions of the FBW, reviews by West German critics expressed surprise at the lack of any obvious antifascist narrative. As one journalist for the *Hamburger Abendblatt* reflected, 'we have long known that over there they speak with a forked tongue', but in *Sterne* 'it is the gentle voice that speaks and we have no objections that it sounds good, as we know that falsehood can sometimes use truth'.[11]

Since it is unclear from the reviews whether West German critics were watching the re-cut version of the film, their surprise at the apparent lack of political and ideological undertones in *Sterne* is perhaps not entirely unexpected. Nevertheless, journalists outside of the Federal Republic – where the film did show in its uncut form – also expressed surprise at the apparent absence of didactic messages in the film. Writing in the French newspaper *Dimanche*, François Maurin described the film as 'without doubt one of the most beautiful films one has seen for many years among those which have tried to confront the most important subjects of our age',[12] while a journalist for the British newspaper *The Sunday Times* concluded that in spite of 'a few moments of political propaganda', *Sterne* was 'basically a non-political appeal against inhumanity'.[13] There was a certain irony to DEFA's response to such reviews. In September 1960, the studio's foreign distribution department, DEFA-Außenhandel, sent Konrad Wolf a series of articles published in the West German and international press praising the film.[14] However, in a crude attempt to conceal West German criticisms of the SED and its legitimacy, some reviews were redacted by officials to remove words and phrases considered derogatory to the GDR. Expressions such as 'east zonal' were crossed out, as were any references to the lack of democratic freedoms in the GDR.[15] The claim by the newspaper *Die Welt* that the film was able to 'transcend [the] party line and party jargon' was similarly removed.[16]

The different interpretations of the film raise an important question. How can *Sterne* be viewed as both a celebration of the antifascist legacy and as a production shaped by overt East German antifascist narratives to the point that the film's ending had to be removed as a precondition for its West German release, while also being praised for its ability to transcend national politics and, according to one DEFA report, being a challenging film precisely because of the absence of antifascist characters? Of course, audiences approach films with a complex matrix of expectations, models of reference and preconceptions, and to a certain extent the surprise of the Western reviewers was informed as much by the perceived absence of any overt ideological framework as by what was actually present in the film itself. But we must nevertheless ask how *Sterne* was able to appeal to both domestic and international tastes by simultaneously appearing to be a standard East German narrative of antifascist heroism while also being 'free of the trite rhetoric of Eastern propaganda'.[17] This chapter examines the implications of focusing on the personal and ideological development of Walter for the film's exploration of Jewish victimhood. The chapter concludes with an examination of the different marketing strategies adopted by the domestic distributor Progress Film and the international distributor, DEFA-Außenhandel, and what these in turn reveal about the malleability of the role of East German Holocaust films as an alternative space for the discussion of Jewish persecution at home and abroad.

Sterne's Reluctant Hero

Walter is far from the typical 1950s DEFA hero. Described in *Der Morgen* as having a 'sensitive nature',[18] he is a passive and ideologically indifferent character who is motivated by his love for an individual rather than by any political or ideological commitment to the collective. As Thomas Elsaesser observes, Walter never 'truly feel[s] at home' in the film and at no point does he ever speak in the first person plural with Kurt or any other member of the Wehrmacht.[19] But nor does Walter ever see himself as part of the antifascist resistance and he finds no more affinity with the antifascist resistance than with other members of the Wehrmacht. Only in the final moments of the film does Walter ask whether there is 'a force to oppose it [fascism]' and offer to provide the partisans with weapons. But even then, his motivation remains unclear: it appears that Walter is ultimately motivated to help Ruth *even though she* is Jewish rather than by a desire to save the prisoners *because they* are Jewish. As Walter himself says to Ruth, 'I never had the ability to think about all people. But I must help you, that is most important for me. . . . One must sometimes do something in order to prove to oneself that he or she is no pig'.[20]

Walter's listless identity as an outsider is established from the very start of the film. We first encounter Walter in movement as he runs towards a deportation train and in the opposite direction from the other marching Wehrmacht soldiers (Figure 2.1). This symbolic act of separation from the other German soldiers is reinforced in the opening lines of the film. Walter is formally introduced through an anonymous voiceover that explicitly announces, 'we could not even discover his real name. Therefore, we simply call him Walter in our story'. It seems no coincidence that the etymological meaning of Walter lies in the Old High German *Waltari* or 'ruler of the army'. The film encourages the audience to position Walter as an alternative point of orientation for the German soldier, the 'good German' as a counterweight to the active complicity of his peers in persecutory crimes. In this way, Walter's decision to act against the orders of his superiors is framed not only as an act of resistance within the context of the film's Second World War narrative, but also as an exemplary act for the postwar audience. As one reviewer for *Neues Deutschland* concluded, 'Walter stands for so many Germans who for a long time, too long, participated [*mitgemacht*], but also for the many who have finally found the courage to turn away from fascism'.[21]

In keeping with dominant trends of 1950s East German cinema, responsibility for Jewish persecution is displaced vertically onto higher-

Figure 2.1. Walter is repeatedly positioned as an outsider in *Sterne*. © DEFA-Stiftung/Lotte Michailowa.

ranking officers. Wolf presents three quite different images of the Wehrmacht through Walter, Kurt and the Hauptmann (Captain). The Hauptmann is presented with a particular lack of nuance as a brute who revels in the verbal and physical abuse of others. In his only extended scene in the film, the Hauptmann berates Walter for drawing when he should be monitoring the Bulgarian workers. As the Hauptmann leaves, Kurt enters, and he and Walter turn to see their superior reprimand the Bulgarian workers outside. Witnessing this, Kurt carefully closes the window, thereby creating a physical and symbolic barrier between the irascible Hauptmann and the far more genial lower-ranking pair inside.

Kurt is the most important point of contrast for Walter. Initially Kurt appears to be an affable character. In the film's opening scene, we witness him carefully lifting up a young child into a waggon in a manner that would ordinarily be considered an act of kindness and chivalry, were it not for the fact that the vehicle into which Kurt is placing the child is a deportation train. These subtle revelations establish the moral hypocrisy behind Kurt's charming personality. To position Walter as a sympathetic character capable of questioning the very actions Kurt carries out with no reflection, Wolf juxtaposes the responses of the two men in two similar sequences in order to demonstrate the characters' different behaviour towards the Jewish prisoners. In the first sequence, Walter walks along the perimeter fence of the transit camp and drops a half-smoked cigarette on the ground. A series of cuts establishes an exchange of looks between a Jewish prisoner and Walter, and the dropped cigarette on the ground. Walter sees the man's judgemental look and instead of stamping out the cigarette as he had instinctively planned, he lifts his foot at the last minute and instead offers the man the box of cigarettes. The Jewish prisoner declines, answering 'thank you, I don't smoke'. Walter, at this point still oblivious to the subtle act of defiance underpinning the man's refusal, shrugs and walks on (Figure 2.2).

This exchange anticipates a later sequence at the *Appellplatz* with Kurt and the Jewish prisoners. The scene begins with Kurt facing the Jewish prisoners, behind whom is a sign which reads 'Smoking Forbidden'. Kurt reprimands the collected Jewish prisoners for betraying the 'good faith' placed in them and for smuggling medication into the camp. After he approaches the prisoners and orders them to surrender the medication, the camera pans along the rows of prisoners and registers the individual, but nameless, faces through a point-of-view shot from Kurt's perspective. In contrast to the exchange of looks between Walter and Ruth, Kurt is confronted with hostility. The camera stops

Figure 2.2. The similarities and differences between Walter (left) and Kurt's (right) interactions with the Jewish prisoners reflect subtle variations in each character's values. © DEFA-Stiftung/Lotte Michailowa.

at the point at which Kurt selects a prisoner and draws back. Two soldiers throw the unnamed man's belongings on the floor including two rolls of medication. The rolls of medication resemble cigarettes and, as Kurt stamps on them, we are reminded of the earlier exchange between Walter and the Jewish prisoner. To reinforce the two men's instinctively different responses, Kurt is then shown smoking a cigarette in front of a Jewish woman as he continues to destroy the medication by stamping on the white tubes. Whereas the corrective look of the Jewish prisoner towards Walter caused an act of – albeit indifferent – generosity, an elderly woman's look to Kurt provokes nothing other than sarcastic pleasure as he mockingly thanks the prisoners for relinquishing their much-needed medication (Figure 2.3).

The displacement of responsibility onto higher-ranking elites in order to unburden the (implicitly working-class) corporal from the responsibility of National Socialist crimes seems entirely fitting with dominant East German narratives of the National Socialist past. However, if *Sterne* is so closely aligned to domestic trends in the discussion of the National Socialist past, how do we account for the international success of the film? The answer lies in Wolf's use of tropes that allow Walter's conversion to transcend its domestic production context and instead be reincorporated into other national and international frames of reference.

Attempts to unburden East Germans from the persecutory legacy of National Socialism were a core feature of DEFA's Second World War films of the 1950s, but the vertical displacement of responsibility also aligned the film with dominant filmmaking trends in the Federal Republic. Against the backdrop of escalating Cold War tensions, the Federal Republic's Western allies began to place increasing pressure on the West German Chancellor, Konrad Adenauer, to reconstitute a West German army. Such a prospect was met with deep ambivalence by the West German public and opposition to rearmament fluctuated between twenty-five and thirty-three per cent.[22]

It is no coincidence that during this same period there was a marked increase in the number of films depicting honourable German soldiers on screen:[23] approximately ten per cent of West German cinematic output between 1955 and 1960 was dedicated to the war film genre, as opposed to just three per cent in the first half of the decade.[24] As Robert Moeller has discussed, these films 'invariably told a story of noble German men who had been sent to fight battles they could not win' and, 'although doctrinaire Nazis were certainly present', they were customarily depicted as 'a mix of corruption, comic blundering and blind fanaticism'. As a point of clear contrast, 'the true German man wore a uniform because he had to' in order to defend the German nation rather than the National Socialist state. The message of such films was that while it was acceptable for (West) Germans 'once again to put on uniforms', soldiers and officers should be 'profoundly aware that not all orders should be followed unquestioningly'.[25] Read against this background, we can see the ways in which Walter also embodied the key ethos of the new Bundeswehr, namely the importance of 'innere Führung' ('inner

Figure 2.3. Sketches and photographs reveal Wolf's careful use of montage to contrast Walter (right) and Kurt's (bottom right) behaviour in two key sequences. © DEFA-Stiftung/Lotte Michailowa. Source: Akademie der Künste.

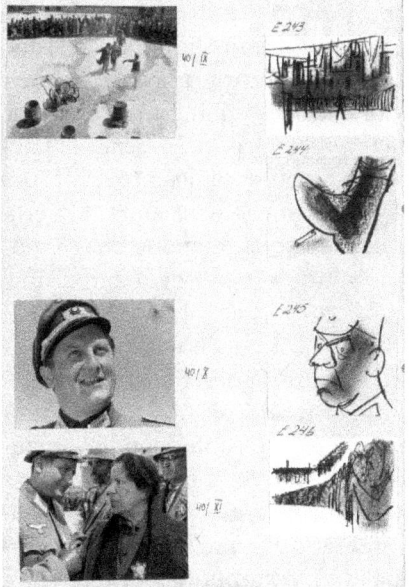

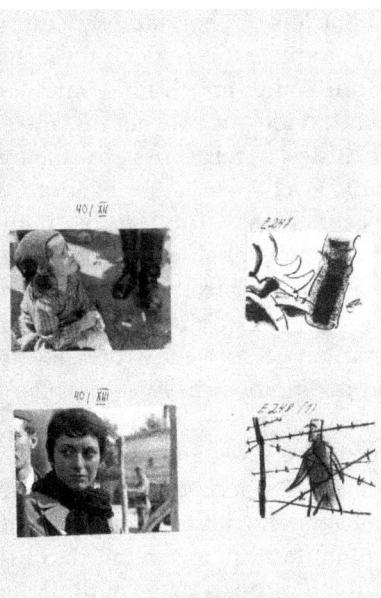

leadership') or the need to exercise personal and moral integrity, and the importance of questioning Prussian codes of obedience to one's superior. The release of *Sterne* in the Federal Republic thus came at a point at which West German audiences were highly conversant with the war film genre and when images of German soldiers acting against a superior's orders were an increasingly familiar presence on screen.

The visual and narrative presentation of Walter's developmental arc also allows for a third reading which lifts the film out of the specific East and West German context of the rehabilitation of the German soldier. Walter's decision to act against orders is repeatedly conveyed through a Judeo-Christian iconography. Churches, donkeys and crosses appear throughout the film and Walter's realization that he must act against orders in which he does not believe and follow a new path takes place as he walks hand-in-hand with Ruth to a church. Interestingly, one of the three cuts requested by the film's Bulgarian co-producers was the removal of a cross in this sequence. The request was discussed in detail at the film's pre-approval meeting between DEFA, the filmmakers and the Deputy Minister of Culture. DEFA's chief dramaturge, Konrad Schwalbe, acknowledged that while the sentiments expressed by the characters did not 'represent our world view', the calls of the Bulgarian co-producers to remove these sections of the film should be resisted since Walter and Ruth's 'rare poetic dialogue' corresponded to 'their world view'. It was not just the studio that was willing to tolerate the inclusion of religious conversion imagery: the Deputy Minister of Culture, Erich Wendt, also believed the scene would not lead to any 'false associations'.[26] The fact that both DEFA's management and a government minister should be so tolerant of the use of religious imagery as a visual backdrop to Walter's shift in attitude may seem surprising. However, while religious over political conviction was certainly not a favoured form of expression in the GDR, it was a familiar literary trope employed in 1950s East German literature to describe the 'pseudo-religious conversion in Soviet captivity' of former Wehrmacht soldiers into committed antifascists through a process of 'confession to conversion and redemption'.[27] The visual and narrative framing of Walter's conversion within a Judeo-Christian framework thus functions as both an antifascist conversion narrative and as a Pauline conversion narrative. Through these multiple textual and visual points of reference, Wolf is able to instil the film with a level of international mobility that allows audiences viewing it within the context of different frames of reference to engage with the narrative in spite of the overtly political and ideological framework of its country of origin.

The promotional materials developed for *Sterne* also reveal the extent to which the distributors were able to draw on different frames of reference when marketing the film at home and abroad in order to accentuate or elide references to antifascism. When we compare the opening paragraphs of the synopses published in the domestic, West German and international programme notes, it is clear that the film was marketed in significantly different ways depending on the country of release. The text prepared by Progress Film for East German audiences begins by proclaiming, 'On how many paths have people in Germany, under the impression of Hitler's insane war, come to new thought and action!' before introducing the film's 'hero', Walter, who is described as embodying a call for 'active action for humanity and international friendship'.[28] By contrast, the West German programme notes emphasize Jewish victimhood in the very first line: 'A goods train slowly sets off. On the doors, the words "Jews to Poland" have been written in chalk with a Star of David underneath'. Instead of framing Walter as an active hero, we are told that he 'can no more delay the waggons than he can delay the fate of the people inside who are being transported away'.[29] Whereas the synopsis for East German audiences presents Walter as the victim of an externally imposed political and ideological system, in the West German promotional materials he is instead rendered a helpless victim of fate who, in keeping with the protagonists of West German war films in the 1950s, is 'borne along by history rather than actively shaping it'.[30]

Beyond the German context of the rehabilitation of the German soldier, we find a very different presentation of the film. In the programme notes prepared for non-German audiences by DEFA-Außenhandel, the synopsis removes all mention of politics and instead appeals to audiences' own national traumas through the evocation of three bombed cities: 'A little town in a small country in an out-of-the-way corner of Europe: it seems very far away from the war in those years which we remember by the names of Stalingrad, Warsaw, Coventry'. Walter is recast as 'a clever, ironic German, weary of war, who ceased to believe in anything long ago' and who 'must break off a friendship to find love; and he must lose his love to discover the truth'. Although the 'greatest of all crimes' is cited as 'the crime of fascism', the synopsis concludes, somewhat oddly, with the statement, 'the earth must be a place for flowers, children, laughter'.[31] Of course, targeted marketing techniques are a common tactic used by film distributors. What is striking in the case of *Sterne*, however, is that a historical film made in the GDR – a country in which tightly prescribed readings of the past not only underpinned how the Third Reich was interpreted at home, but also how it was represented to the outside world – was deliberately presented in such a manner as to downplay, or even remove, the markers which would announce the film as an East German production. In the film and its marketing, Wolf and DEFA drew upon multiple textual and visual points of reference which instil the film with a level of international mobility that allows audiences to engage with the narrative in spite of preconceptions about the film's country of origin.

Defining the Jewish Victims

Despite the titular allusion to the 'Judenstern', the film's setting in a transit camp and the role of the Jewish protagonist Ruth in allowing Walter to realize that Auschwitz is not a 'vegetable garden' but rather a 'mill for human flesh', *Sterne* is primarily focused on the figure of Walter. To a certain extent, as the film's central interest lies in the personal and ideological development of Walter, it need not be entirely unexpected that the other characters serve as foils for his inner transformation. Nevertheless, the failure to accord the victims a comparable degree of development within the film to that of the Wehrmacht soldier certainly raises questions as to whether *Sterne* exploits Jewish persecution for the sake of ideological expediency. By reducing Jewish persecution to a vehicle for the assertion of the primacy of communist resistance, Wolf arguably presents Walter's transformation as a socialist conversion by proxy for East German audiences and allows them to circumvent questions about the legacy of the National Socialist past in the East German present. Otherwise incidental plot details also reflect the growing instrumentalization of Jewish persecution as a weapon with which to attack the Federal Republic. In an early sequence, Ruth's father reveals that he has a doctorate in German literature. Originally, the character stated that he had studied in Dresden,[32] but this was quickly changed to Munich, presumably in order to avoid any insinuation that the father could have been deported from a city now in the GDR.[33]

The film is heavily reliant on the codification of Jewishness according to reductive stereotypes. Ruth's (unnamed) father reprises the symbolic role of Dr Bernstein in *Ehe im Schatten* by embodying the stereotypical role of Jews as the guardians of German cultural heritage. During one scene, Ruth's father attempts to present Walter with an old copy of a Heine text. This could be read as an attempt to break down German–Jewish binaries: a non-German Jew hands a non-Jewish German the work of a seminal German author of Jewish heritage. However, the film does not consider these complexities and instead of serving as an example of the polysemic and composite identities of the Jewish characters, the film conversely further simplifies the two men's exchange through recourse to the nineteenth-century stereotype of Jews as the defenders of German culture.

It is important to stress that the film's problematic depictions of the Jewish victims did not go unnoticed by DEFA. At a meeting between the studio and the film's production team in February 1958, the film's screenwriter Angel Wagenstein was asked to develop the screenplay in order to present the Jewish prisoners in a 'more differentiated' manner.[34] Interestingly, the solution that was found was not a textual, but rather a cinematographic reworking of the screenplay. One of the key differences between the screenplay of February 1958 and that of June 1958 is the addition of extreme close-ups of the Jewish prisoners' faces in the Appellplatz sequence.[35] The decision to privilege shots of the Jewish prisoners' faces is key to Wolf's attempts to re-enfranchise his Jewish victims. When Kurt walks down the line of men, women and children, the camera slowly pans along the rows of prisoners and we are reminded of the freedom of movement afforded to the camera – and by extension, to the spectator – that is denied to the Jewish prisoners. At the same time, the look-to-camera of the Jewish characters silently acknowledges the gaze of the spectator. In so doing, the audience becomes both the subject and object of the look in a way that calls upon spectators to acknowledge their own failure to act and their passive presence during the act of persecution.

Even with the addition of the new sequences, however, it is questionable whether the film does in fact offer a 'more differentiated' presentation of the Jewish characters. Ruth is the only named Jewish figure in the film – other characters are listed as 'old Jewish woman' and 'nervous Jew' – and even Ruth remains underdeveloped.[36] Walter may achieve his moral awakening through Ruth, but she never emerges as a fully developed character in her own right. Rather, she serves as a counterpoint to the German soldier and poses moral questions to which Walter responds with actions. For instance, Walter responds to her accusation that 'You lot aren't people. Wild animals. All Germans are the same!', by arranging for the illicit delivery of medicine to the camp for a woman in childbirth. However, in keeping with her description as the film's 'moral conscience', there is a clear tendency to return Ruth to the camp once she has delivered her moral lesson to the German soldier.[37] In this regard, Ruth can be seen as analogous to the rag doll which Walter holds at the beginning and end of the film. As Walter walks nonchalantly through the market square at the start of the film, he stops to look at a stall with rag dolls wearing 'Judensterne'. The shot of dolls hanging from the wooden posts and Walter's casual tossing aside of the doll appears to anticipate the fate of the Jewish prisoners at the end of the film. After Walter contacts the Bulgarian partisans to arrange for Ruth's rescue, Wolf revisits the rag doll sequence. This time, Walter carefully picks up the doll before gently placing it back down again. The screenplay may describe how 'absent-mindedly, his hands play with her', but crucially Walter chooses to return the doll to the pile rather than keeping it.[38] Ruth may have changed Walter's perceptions of her, but ultimately her fate remains the same.

Recalibrating Resistance

The presentation of the Jewish characters is certainly problematic. Narratively, the Jewish characters remain undeveloped and their primary role in the plot appears to be to serve as a backdrop for Walter's moral awakening. What is particularly fascinating about *Sterne*, however, is that Wolf also offers a critique of the characters' failure to challenge the persecution of the Jews in the film. Visually, Jewish persecution haunts the film throughout and repeatedly serves to undercut episodes of happiness and celebration through visual reminders of Jewish victimhood. Immediately after the scene during which the Hauptmann berates Walter for neglecting his duties, Kurt and Walter retreat to the picturesque hills outside the town. The anonymous voiceover at the start of the film announces that Walter walks 'with a slight limp' and, as the two men relax in the sunshine, Kurt reveals that he and Walter had been posted in Leningrad where Walter sustained his injury. As Kurt's contrasts their experiences in 'Leningrad . . . [with] this quiet little island' where there is 'no war, only tranquillity', the stage is set for a conventional war film in which Walter, who is clearly the least enthusiastic of the pair, questions his fate and challenges his orders. Here the film appears to signal a desire to position Walter as a victim of circumstance. However, the film subtly undercuts this initial impression. The two men's seclusion in the 'peaceful valley' is first interrupted by Allied aeroplanes flying overhead and then, crucially, by the sight and sound of Jews being marched around the corner on their way to the deportation trains to Auschwitz. Even during the film's lighter moments, the fate of the Jewish prisoners haunts the characters. At the local funfair, the young Bulgarian partisan,

Figure 2.4. Subtle, but significant, reminders of Jewish persecution haunt the film throughout. © DEFA-Stiftung/Lotte Michailowa.

Blashe, enjoys a date with a young woman. As the couple walks off into the crowd, the camera lingers on a Ferris wheel in the background whose spokes form a Star of David (Figure 2.4). Through these subtle visual reminders, Wolf draws the spectator's attention back to the fate of the Jews in the film; their narrative voice may be pushed to the margins, but visually their absence punctuates the film throughout.

Nowhere is this more powerfully conveyed than in the film's closing scenes. The ending, and specifically the fate of Walter, was the only part of the film that underwent a substantial rewrite. The scenes were heavily discussed in a meeting in March 1957 between the filmmakers, DEFA officials and representatives from HV Film and the Ministry for Culture. In the original ending, Walter delivers weapons from the Wehrmacht armoury to the partisans. However, this ending came under criticism when the head of HV Film, Anton Ackermann, pointed to the fact that after handing over the weapons, Walter surrenders 'without a fight' which, argued the film official, allowed the film to 'end pessimistically'. During the meeting, Wagenstein then proposed a new ending in which Kurt realizes the key to the armoury is missing and raises the alarm. But this time it is Kurt who is too late and he arrives to discover that Walter has already distributed the weapons. A shootout takes place between the two men during which Kurt kills Walter.[39] This new ending was agreed upon by all present, however four months later Wolf wrote to Erich Wendt, the Deputy Minister of Culture, to discuss the ending again. In the letter, Wolf expresses satisfaction at a new 'simpler' and 'politically clearer' [eindeutiger] ending. This new ending, according to the director, offered 'a convincing unfinished conclusion with all the tragedy of the story of Walter and Ruth', while also sparing Walter from a 'tragic fated death'. Instead he 'remains alive and begins to tread a new path, a path that will inevitably lead him' to the partisan Petko.[40]

This is the ending used in the final film. It is unclear what provoked Wolf to rewrite the ending, but the new scenes are in keeping with the director and screenwriter's strategy of foregrounding Jewish persecution visually rather than narratively. After Walter fails to save Ruth, he returns to the officers' quarters. As he stands outside the building, we hear Kurt drunkenly socialising. Walter decides not to enter the building and instead leaves the physical and symbolic space of the German soldiers' headquarters and goes to meet the Bulgarian partisans. He seeks out Petko and asks, 'Is there a force to oppose it [fascism]?' to which the Bulgarian replies, 'Yes there is, there is'. In a clear reference to Walter's earlier exchange with the Jewish prisoner, Petko and Walter light each other's cigarettes in a symbolic act of mutual trust. As the men walk off together, Walter asks, 'you said you needed weapons?'. At this point, the voiceover returns and once again reflects, 'To us he was simply Herr Corporal. No one knew his name. That's why we called him Walter' and music gently plays over the image of the two men walking off in conversation.

To a certain extent, the ending is 'politically clearer'. In keeping with the gradual ideological awakening of the German corporal, the film implies an act of future resistance which might even lead to the death of the protagonist.[41] But the extent to which we can conclude that the ending is 'simpler' is certainly questionable. At the point at which the film appears to reach its dramatic conclusion, Wolf suddenly cuts to the train carrying Ruth. The image of the two men calmly walking away in conversation is replaced through a sharp cut to the frantic sight of the deportation train intercut with Ruth's face looking out of the barred window of the waggon. The voiceover provocatively asks, 'of course, you still remember. . .' and calm music is replaced with the Yiddish song, 'Es brennt' ('It is Burning'). As the smoke blows over Ruth's face, the song's lyrics are projected over her face in the same chalk-like cursive font we have just seen used by the German guards to write the Jewish prisoners' destination of Auschwitz on the waggon doors. The lines, 'You alone can help! If the town is dear to you, grab your buckets, quench the flames! Quench them with your own blood! Prove that you can! Don't just stand there! Don't let it happen! Our town is burning! It's burning! It's burning! It's burning!' serve as a clear imperative to act. The smoke clears from Ruth's face and she looks directly into the camera before the screen fades to black.

The film concludes with a clear call to act and the scene immediately preceding with Walter and Petko makes it clear how the film envisages this action: Germans fighting side-by-side with the international antifascist resistance. However, the decision to superimpose images of Jewish victimhood over this call to action complicates the message. Antifascist resistance is not explicitly linked to heroism and victory. The partisans were no more successful in their efforts to save the Jewish prisoners than Walter. The film's closing statement serves not only as an assertion that had Walter embraced antifascism sooner, Ruth would have been saved, but it also acts as a reminder that any resistance narratives should and must place Jewish victims at the core of its action. The ending is not without its own problems. Jewish victims are rendered passive figures who, as Judith Doneson has argued, await rescue by the film's Christian male protagonist.[42] However, at the end of a decade in which the already marginal topic of Jewish persecution had become an increasingly peripheral concern in East and West German war films, the force of Wolf's approach should not be underestimated.

The GDR's Trojan Horse?

Sterne is a complex film. It was produced and released during a period when the National Socialist past was routinely instrumentalized for political and ideological purposes in the present. Although the film was subsequently discussed in the East German press as part of DEFA's antifascist canon and as an indictment of the purported renascent militarism of the Federal Republic, what emerges from the film itself is not an unproblematic reaffirmation of antifascist narratives, but rather an ambivalent presentation of a solider inculpated in the persecution of Jewish victims. Yet *Sterne* demonstrates that not only was Jewish persecution a permissible theme in the 1950s, but that such films could be championed abroad, even if they did not unequivocally unburden East German audiences from the legacies of the past.[43]

In his pre-release report from January 1959, studio director Albert Wilkening recommended that *Sterne* should be sent to 'an international festival – if possible in a Western country'.[44] This conclusion was supported by the Ministry for Culture and a print was prepared for the Cannes Film Festival along with three thousand press booklets, thirty posters and one thousand press photographs.[45] The GDR's presence at Cannes was highly controversial and provoked a government level response from the West German authorities. To understand why the GDR's presence was so contentious, it is first necessary to situate the incident within the political climate of the late 1950s. By 1957, the GDR was only recognized by twelve countries, with not a single Western state among them. In an attempt to deny the SED legitimacy, the Federal Republic pursued its claim to be the sole representative of the German people (the so-called 'Alleinvertretungsanspruch') through a series of political treaties and economic trade agreements designed to secure the simultaneous diplomatic recognition of the Federal Republic and the non-recognition of the GDR. This strategy became known as the Hallstein Doctrine. Named after the Secretary of State for Foreign Affairs, Walter Hallstein, the Doctrine sought to combine the economic 'carrot' of privileged political and economic relations with one of the world's strongest economies with a diplomatic 'stick': any country with which the Federal Republic maintained diplomatic relations was not to accord any form of diplomatic recognition to the GDR. According to the Doctrine, any attempt to establish or maintain diplomatic relations with the GDR would be viewed as an unfriendly act which could result in the Federal Republic breaking off relations with the violating state. The Hallstein Doctrine presented the GDR with considerable problems. With its politicians and diplomats unwelcome in most of the Western world, the state increasingly invested in what can best be termed cultural ambassadors – artists, sportsmen and sportswomen, intellectuals and filmmakers – who were able to travel to countries to which East German politicians were routinely refused entry.

This was not the first time a DEFA film had played at Cannes. In 1956, DEFA was invited to submit a film to play out of competition for the following year's festival.[46] When the West German Foreign Office learnt of the intention of the organizers of the Cannes Film Festival to invite DEFA to submit an entry for the 1957 festival, officials at the Foreign Office ordered that 'the participation of a "governmental delegation" of the Soviet Zone of Occupation [SBZ] on an equal footing at the film festival in Cannes must be prevented at all costs'. While officials emphasized that the participation of 'the "government" of the

SBZ' would not constitute an act of official recognition of the GDR by the French government, it would, they stressed, nonetheless give support to 'the efforts of the SBZ in the assertion of its recognition under international law, since the SBZ is keen to promote itself at all international events in order thus to advance step-by-step international recognition'.[47] To appreciate why the Foreign Office was so concerned about any possible East German participation in the Cannes Film Festival, we must look to the invitation process. There was certainly a symbolic element to the Foreign Office's concerns as a dual German presence at the festival would compromise its claim to be the sole representative of Germany on the international stage. But this alone does not account for both its initial reaction and subsequent campaign to marginalize the GDR at the festival. Rather, their concerns were also driven by the political consequences of any East German involvement. Invitations to the film festival were issued to the Foreign Office of the submitting country. Thus, an invitation for East German participation would be sent to the East German government, thereby representing a diplomatic link with the GDR.[48]

In November 1958, the West German Foreign Office learnt that the festival organizers intended to invite the GDR to submit a film for the official competition in 1959. Following consultation with its Embassy in Paris, a Foreign Office official reported that the head of the festival organizing committee had assured the West German cultural attaché, Bernhard von Tieschowitz, that the invitation would be issued to DEFA rather than the East German Foreign Office, that films would only be announced under the name DEFA rather than the German Democratic Republic and that DEFA would be barred from presenting 'a politically-coloured film'.[49] Although East German participation at Cannes in 1957 had been marginalized and contained as a result of West German intervention, there were clear signs that government officials were concerned about the situation in 1959. Even with the renewed assurances from the festival organizers, officials at the Foreign Office concluded that an invitation to DEFA would represent 'a great success' for the GDR since 'the fact that DEFA may only be named as a quasi-private production company and consequently that its films would not be advertised under the denotation "The German Democratic Republic presents" is only of theoretical significance' since 'from experience, the most effective publications like the press, radio and also the semi-official bulletins take little notice of this distinction'.[50]

In principle, the situation in 1959 should have been far more straightforward than in 1957. Since *Sterne* was an East German–Bulgarian co-production, the name 'German Democratic Republic' could simply be removed from the film's credits. However, while the Federal Republic did manage to marginalize the GDR at the festival in 1957, its attempts to do so in 1959 were almost entirely frustrated. The film once again played with the opening words 'The German Democratic Republic presents' and the East German submission was unanimously praised for its content and style in the press.[51] To compound the Foreign Office's frustration, the East German film went on to win the Prix du Jury and reports of the GDR's success featured in newspapers around the world.

Given the often well-founded expectations of East German cinema, how did Wolf's film manage to win one of the main prizes at Cannes? The answer is two-fold. Firstly, DEFA's hand was greatly strengthened by its ability to present a film as polyvalent in its narrative and visual structures as *Sterne*. Secondly, the Ministry for Culture appears to have deliberately approved the selection of a film which placed DEFA's commercial and cultural interests above the SED's short-term political ambitions. At first glance, the selection of *Sterne* does not appear to serve the SED's immediate interests insomuch as the extent to which the film promotes the antifascist credentials of its country of origin is certainly questionable. A film which international journalists interpreted as exhibiting an 'unusual and wholly non-Marxist flavour' certainly seemed unlikely to achieve this goal.[52] However, *Sterne* provided the East German authorities with a far more subtle means of achieving recognition on the world stage through an 'ambassador of good will'.[53] Not only did the film win a major prize at Cannes, but it was also awarded a Gold Medal at the Vienna Film Festival, received a commendation at the Edinburgh Film Festival and was the only German film to play at the London Film Festival, all in countries with which the GDR maintained no official diplomatic relations. In addition, the film played in Denmark, Australia, Finland, Italy, Sweden, Tunisia, Luxembourg, Switzerland, the Soviet Union, Poland, India, Cuba and the United States. Reports of the international success of the film featured extensively in domestic newspapers with one journalist concluding 'the film *Sterne* proves once more that the political reality of the GDR cannot be argued away'.[54] Not everyone was so enthusiastic about the experience of Cannes, however. Writing to his wife during the festival, Wolf reflected, 'up until now it has been rather boring here – mediocre films, not much atmosphere, the usual star hype and bleak weather. No question of bathing. That apart there is not a lot to do – it is just a little provincial town'.[55]

Notes

1. Eylau, *'Sterne'*.
2. Kersten, 'Gegenwart blieb unbewältigt'.
3. *Guardian*, 'Horror and Humanity'.
4. Einhorn, *'Sterne'*.
5. von Schnitzler, *'Sterne'*.
6. *Filmkritik*, *'Sterne'*.
7. It was not only West German officials who were suspicious about the film's ideological message. Even though *Sterne* was an East German–Bulgarian co-production, the Bulgarian production partners expressed dissatisfaction with the depiction of Bulgarians as collaborators. For more on Bulgarian responses to the film, see Nadège Ragaru's discussion of the film in Ragaru, 'The gendered dimensions of *Zvezdi/ Sterne* (1959)'.
8. Jahn, *'Sterne'*.
9. DEFA, 'Protokoll über die Diskussion bei der Abnahme des Films *Sterne* am 13.1.1959. Sektor Filmabnahme und -kontrolle'.
10. Wilkening, 'Einschätzung des Filmes *Sterne* durch die Direktion, Dr Wilkening'.
11. *Hamburger Abendblatt*, 'Film guter Gesinnung: *Sterne*'.
12. Maurin, *'Étoiles'*.
13. *The Sunday Times*, 'Stars'.
14. DEFA-Außenhandel, 'Letter from DEFA-Außenhandel to Konrad Wolf'.
15. By referring to the GDR through reference to its geographical location, the terms 'east zonal' and later 'East Germany' [Ostdeutschland] were used in the Federal Republic to deny the legitimacy of the GDR as an independent state. *Rhein-Neckar Zeitung*, *'Sterne'*.
16. Beheim-Schwarzbach, 'Sterne der Sehnsucht, Sterne der Vernichtung'.
17. Miska, 'Da fängt eben der Marxismus an'.
18. Funke, 'Sieg über den Stacheldraht'.
19. Elsaesser, *German Cinema: Terror and Trauma*, 157.
20. The German uses 'man' and 'er'.
21. Einhorn, *'Sterne'*.
22. Corum, *Rearming Germany*, 37.
23. For example: *Es geschah am 20. Juli* (*It Happened on July 20th*, 1955), *Der 20 Juli* (*The Plot to Assassinate Hitler*, 1955), *Des Teufels General* (*The Devil's General*, 1955), *Der Stern von Afrika* (*The Star of Afrika*, 1957), *Der Fuchs von Paris* (*The Fox of Paris*, 1957), *Der Arzt von Stalingrad* (*The Doctor of Stalingrad*, 1958) and *Hunde, wollt ihr ewig leben?* (*Stalingrad: Dogs, Do You Want to Live Forever?*, 1959).
24. Wulff, 'Bundesdeutsche Kriegs- und Militärfilme der 1950er Jahre', 1.
25. Moeller, *War Stories*, 148.
26. DEFA, 'Protokoll über die Diskussion bei der Abnahme des Films *Sterne*'.
27. Biess, *Homecomings*, 127–8.
28. Progress Film, *'Sterne. Werbehelfer'*.
29. It is important to recognize that it is likely that DEFA was not responsible for the wording of the West German programme notes; they were most probably written by the West German distributor Europa Filmverleih. However, the significance here lies not in who wrote the text, but rather in that Walter could be recast as both a heroic 'Fighter against Fascism' and as a victim of circumstance.
30. Kapczynski, 'Armchair Warriors: Heroic Postures in the West German War Film', 20.

31. DEFA-Außenhandel, 'Stars/Etoiles'.
32. Wagenstein, 'Sterne. Draft Screenplay'.
33. Wagenstein, 'Sterne. Screenplay'. AdK, Berlin, Konrad-Wolf-Archiv, Nr. 383.
34. Brückner, 'Aktennotiz der Diskussion des Rohdrehbuches Sterne'.
35. Wagenstein, 'Sterne. Draft Screenplay'; Wagenstein, 'Sterne. Screenplay'. AdK, Berlin, Konrad-Wolf-Archiv, Nr. 383.
36. Wagenstein, 'Sterne. Screenplay'. AdK, Berlin, Konrad-Wolf-Archiv, Nr. 383 and Nr. 384.
37. Ameer, Riebe and Steuber, 'Ausgeblendet?', 7.
38. Wagenstein, 'Sterne. Screenplay'. AdK, Berlin, Konrad-Wolf-Archiv, Nr. 384.
39. Brückner, 'Aktennotiz der Diskussion des Rohdrehbuches Sterne'.
40. Wolf, 'Letter from Konrad Wolf to Erich Wendt'.
41. It is worth noting that the voiceover strongly implies that Walter does not survive the war.
42. Doneson, 'The Jew as a Female Figure in Holocaust Film', 18.
43. Parts of this section have previously been published in Ward, 'Screening out the East: The Playing out of Inter-German Relations at the Cannes Film Festival' in *German Life and Letters* 68(1) (2015). Reprinted with the kind permission of John Wiley and Sons.
44. Wilkening, 'Einschätzung des Filmes Sterne'.
45. DEFA-Außenhandel, 'Memorandum'.
46. The GDR submitted *Betrogen bis zum jüngsten Tag* (*Duped Till Doomsday*, 1957).
47. Auswärtiges Amt, 'Betr. internationale Filmfestspiele in Cannes 1957'.
48. For more on the GDR's participation in the 1957 Cannes Film Festival, see Ward, 'Screening out the East'.
49. Auswärtiges Amt, 'Aufzeichnung betr.: Teilnahme der DEFA an den Filmfestspielen in Cannes 1959'.
50. Ibid.
51. Auswärtiges Amt, 'Aufzeichnung betr.: XII. internationale Filmfestspiele in Cannes 1959'.
52. Marcorelles, 'Winners at Cannes'.
53. *Neues Deutschland*, 'Botschafter des guten Willens'.
54. Funke, 'DEFA Sterne leuchten in Cannes'.
55. Musial and Rittmeyer, *Konrad Wolf*, 113.

Chapter 3

REFRAMING VICTIMHOOD

Konrad Wolf's *Professor Mamlock*

Released to coincide with the fifteenth anniversary of the founding of DEFA, Konrad Wolf's *Professor Mamlock* (1961) is one of a series of films made in the early 1960s that responded to two developments in the commemorative narrative practices of the National Socialist past in the GDR. Firstly, the rapid escalation in Cold War rivalries between the two German states saw the SED launch a sustained campaign against the Federal Republic in an attempt to present the West German state as a hotbed for expressions of unreformed National Socialist political and economic interests. Secondly, filmmakers increasingly turned to the task of conveying antifascist narratives to a younger audience who had only experienced the Third Reich as children. In this way, the emergence of young antifascist heroes in 1960s DEFA films should be understood as a response to the specific challenges of attracting younger audiences to the East German collective narratives of their parents' generation.

Based on the 1933 play of the same name, *Professor Mamlock* explores the failure of the Jewish surgeon, Hans Mamlock, to acknowledge the threat posed by National Socialism to himself, to his family and to Germany.[1] As a patriotic veteran of the First World War and a proud member of the bourgeoisie, Mamlock repeatedly affirms his loyalty to his country and his belief in Germany's democratic institutions. Although he witnesses a number of antisemitic incidents in his hospital clinic, Mamlock refuses to countenance any discussion of politics or of the underlying causes behind the rise in antisemitism in Germany. Even the antisemitic bullying of his daughter, Ruth, fails to bring about a decisive shift in his attitude. He only abandons his adage that in his clinic 'there are doctors and patients, patients and doctors' when his colleagues and friends sign a declaration demanding that he – a Jewish surgeon – be removed from his post. Finally realizing the price of his passivity, Mamlock commits suicide in the hospital clinic. The film closes with the camera focused on the Jewish surgeon's lifeless body, over which Wolf superimposes the film's core ideological principle: 'there is no greater crime than not fighting when one must!'. Mamlock's refusal to act against the rise of National Socialism is contrasted with the behaviour of his son, Rolf, who actively engages in the communist fight alongside his fellow comrade, Ernst. Together, the two young men not only epitomize an idealized model of antifascist resistance, but they also serve as emblematic figureheads of the founding spirit of the GDR by demonstrating to a new generation of East Germans the need for young, engaged citizens to continue the fight against fascist oppression.

By its own admission, DEFA acknowledged that although *Professor Mamlock* did draw international interest, it was 'no box office hit'.[2] Wolf's previous film, *Sterne*, was able to transcend the specificities of its land of production through the employment of polyvalent narrative and visual structures, but there was little attempt to pluralize the ideological message of *Professor Mamlock* or to facilitate alternative readings. Instead, Wolf and DEFA seized the opportunity to draw analogies between the film's National Socialist setting and contemporary West German politics at every stage of the film's production. Correspondence between the production company and studio emphasized the 'parallels to the development in the Federal Republic today'.[3] While filming, Wolf gave an on-set interview in which he described the film as 'a warning to citizens in the Federal Republic' and upon its release, numerous reviewers drew explicit comparisons between the Third Reich and the Federal Republic.[4] The film was awarded a Gold Medal at the Moscow International Film Festival but, underlining the different marketing approaches now employed by the filmmakers and DEFA, the East German delegation used the opportunity of the international press conference to attack West German politicians.

Although *Professor Mamlock* drew praise at the Moscow International Film Festival, its reception in Western countries – where East German officials hoped it would find a new audience for its thinly veiled political attack against its Western neighbour – was far more mixed. The film was screened at film festivals and dedicated East German film weeks in Australia, Italy and the United Kingdom, but *Professor Mamlock* failed to draw the widespread praise of *Sterne*. Although Western reviewers frequently praised the cinematographic and technical accomplishments of the film, the plot's celebration of communist resistance coupled with the distinctly anti-Western rhetoric surrounding the film's release ultimately restricted its ability to cross borders. In sharp contrast to the – albeit far from politically unbiased – surprise expressed by the West Berlin *Filmbegutachtungskommission* towards what it termed the positive 'ethical content' of *Sterne*,[5] Wolf's 1961 film was not approved by the board which deemed the film's 'emphatically positive depiction' of the communist characters to be 'too obvious'.[6] In this way, the shift from polyvalent narratives to decidedly inward-facing productions which sought to draw explicit lines of continuity between the Third Reich and the Federal Republic announced what would become a key characteristic of DEFA's 1960s Holocaust films: the confinement of East German Holocaust films to the domestic sphere.

Although we may be tempted to conclude that *Professor Mamlock* represents an aesthetically accomplished film embedded within an ideologically reductive plot, Wolf's 1961 film is a key case study for the negotiation of victimhood, politics and spectatorial engagement in East German Holocaust film in the early 1960s. Firstly, while Wolf may explore Jewish and communist identities in tandem, what emerges from this pairing is not a hierarchy of victimhood, but rather a hierarchy of responsibility. Secondly, although existing studies of the film have focused on the father–son binary of Hans and Rolf Mamlock, a closer examination of the figure of Inge reveals the ways in which Wolf orientates his film towards a female spectatorship. Finally, an exploration of the hitherto overlooked figure of Ruth Mamlock reveals the extent to which Wolf sought to engage younger audiences through recourse to contemporary cultural trends. Collectively, these points underscore the complex means by which two impulses – the celebration of the antifascist resistance and the recognition of Jewish victimhood – are interwoven visually and narratively in ways which cast new light on the engagement with the National Socialist past in *Professor Mamlock*.

Victimhood and Responsibility

The film's presentation of Mamlock's persecution and downfall has been described as 'highly questionable'.[7] Throughout the film, the surgeon refuses to countenance any discussion of politics in his home or at work and he dismisses Rolf's friends as mere 'ruffians'. At the same time, Mamlock remains loyal to the *Kulturnation* ('culture nation'), German patriotic values and the German *Rechtsstaat* ('rule of law'), even when those same values are used to ostracize him from his place of work and later from society. Mamlock's home bears multiple signs of his fluency with Enlightenment ideas and values as reflected in his love of Beethoven and the framed quotation by Danton which hangs on his wall ('To defeat the enemy we must have audacity, more audacity, always audacity'). However, if recourse to nineteenth-century stereotypes of German-Jewish assimilation was employed in *Ehe im Schatten* and *Sterne* as a shorthand for the enduring power of German cultural values, then in *Professor Mamlock* this *Vaterlandsliebe* ('love for the Fatherland') becomes a means of condemning the titular character. Mamlock may begin the film with the assertion that 'there is no need to despair', but it is his deathbed reflection that 'there is no greater crime than not wanting to fight where one must!' that becomes the maxim of the film. Conversely, Rolf Mamlock and his friend Ernst offer an exemplary model of action. In contrast to Hans Mamlock, they are shown in constant motion, are overwhelmingly depicted outdoors and they consistently place the collective identity of the communist resistance above individual statements of apolitical indifference. In a symbolic embodiment of this sacrificial comradeship, Rolf only escapes arrest, persecution and death when the SA mistakes Ernst for Mamlock's son after the two young men swap berets and their identities become merged in their fight for the common cause.

The different responses of Hans and Rolf Mamlock to Germany's unfolding political crisis are introduced in the very opening scenes. As Mamlock concludes his monologue with the words 'there is no need to despair' against the aural backdrop of Beethoven's Ninth Symphony, the film cuts to a smoke-filled railway station where Rolf leads his comrade Kurt to Berlin. The subsequent cross-cutting between father and son reinforces these two quite different models of behaviour.[8] While Mamlock's friend insists the coming year will bring 'economic boom, prosperity, security', a cut to the streets of Berlin shows Rolf's friend warn that 'trouble is afoot'. Rolf's offer of refuge to a communist on the run on the streets of Berlin is contrasted with Mamlock, his wife and their friends standing patiently and waiting to welcome in the New Year with champagne flutes in the seclusion of the family villa. A series of match shots then juxtaposes Mamlock's toasting of the New Year with the drawing of a knife, an aerial shot of five people celebrating New Year in the Mamlocks' bourgeois family home with Rolf fighting in the chaos of the streets, a spinning record with a spinning car wheel and the Mamlocks dancing with the young communists fighting. Having established these two different models of conduct, Wolf then stages an exchange between the father and son in which Hans Mamlock insists that the world cannot be changed 'with a clenched fist, but rather with knowledge and understanding', a position that the film then systematically undercuts. To reinforce their divide, Rolf reminds his father that the reason behind their differing stances is not 'ferment or a generation gap', but rather 'a question of class'.

From the outset, Wolf was keen to stress the different emphasis in his adaptation of *Professor Mamlock*. Unlike earlier versions of the play and film, the focus of his adaptation resided 'primarily in the politically and artistically unusually powerfully structured tragedy of a liberal bourgeois intellectual' who comes into conflict 'with his social order and class'. This conflict, argued Wolf, 'can only be resolved by joining the working class'.[9] However, the juxtaposition of two models of behaviour immediately creates a hierarchy of conduct whereby the passivity of Mamlock is contrasted with the active resistance of his son. This is all the more problematic given that Mamlock is explicitly introduced as Jewish before a word of dialogue is spoken: the rolling text *in lieu* of opening credits concludes with the words, 'the writer tells the fate of a German doctor, of the Jew ... Professor Mamlock'. Of course, under National Socialist policy, Rolf Mamlock would also be considered Jewish, but aside from one explicit statement by the son, little mention is made of Rolf's Jewish identity. Instead he is both defined by, and self-identifies according to, his class identity. Here the film encounters a problem: Wolf risks uncritically associating Jewishness with passivity and communism with active resistance, thereby reinforcing the designations and distinctions of passive 'Victims of Fascism' versus active 'Fighters against Fascism'. Mamlock is the film's most prominent Jewish character and it appears that his death becomes a representative means of condemning Jewish passivity. The film features two deaths: the suicide of Mamlock and the murder of Ernst, but whereas Mamlock dies *from* his failure to act, Rolf's friend Ernst dies *for* the communist cause. However, we must be careful not to equate hierarchies of victimhood with critiques of responsibility because, upon closer examination, the film's critique of passivity and action is more complex than it first appears.

The film is punctuated by multiple episodes of antisemitism: the public humiliation of Mamlock and Ruth who are forced to walk the streets with the word 'Jew' daubed on their clothing, the removal of Jewish characters' surnames from buildings and the uninhibited antisemitic discussions among the nurses in the clinic (Figure 3.1). There is little doubt – as a journalist for *Bauernecho* concluded – that Mamlock is 'driven to his death because he is Jewish'.[10] The murder of the communist resister Ernst is certainly a shocking act of physical brutality, but

Figure 3.1. Hans Mamlock's victimhood may be explicitly aligned to his Jewish background, but the reasons for his persecution are less clear. © DEFA-Stiftung/Walter Ruge.

it is the emotional turmoil of Ruth and Mamlock's public humiliation which delineates the emotional arc of the film. However, despite the sympathy Wolf elicits for his Jewish characters, the film also seems to condemn his protagonist for failing to resist. Here the importance of distinguishing between Wolf's attempts to separate Jewish victimhood and class-based responsibility come to the fore.

During a discussion about the screenplay by the production group, it was stressed that the 'actual conflict' of the film revolved around a 'citizen betrayed by his class' and 'not that of the persecuted Jew'.[11] While the film does not circumvent Mamlock's victimhood as a Jew, it does denounce his passivity as a member of the bourgeois-liberal intellectual elite. Visually, there are no markers of Mamlock's Jewish identity other than those imposed on him physically and verbally as part of his anti-semitic humiliation by other characters. By contrast, the surgeon is consistently framed within a middle-class setting designed to elicit a critical response from the audience. In this regard, Mamlock's own relationship to his Jewish identity is actually similar to that of his son: it is incidental and plays no active role in either man's life. The key difference, however, is that whereas Rolf aligns himself with a communist and antifascist identity, Mamlock embeds himself firmly within the bourgeoisie.

In the opening sequence, Mamlock remembers his time fighting for Germany in the First World War with the words 'anything for the Fatherland' before reflecting, 'Always the courage to die, but never the courage to live. And you need courage to live'. At this point, Wolf superimposes a shot of the pistol which will later become Mamlock's suicide weapon and which bears the inscription, 'The Fatherland thanks its brave. Verdun 1916'. The implication is that the courage to live cannot be separated from the responsibility to act. Such an emphasis is entirely in line with the negotiation of victimhood and responsibility in Konrad Wolf's films more broadly. In keeping with Konrad Wolf's protagonists such as Friedel (*Genesung*, 1956), Lissy (*Lissy*, 1957) and Gregor (*Ich war neunzehn*, 1968), Mamlock is called upon to undergo 'a process of searching and reflecting',[12] or as the film's initial treatment terms it, the 'principle of the Wolferian tragedy with [a] truly revolutionary optimistic outcome: the next time – better'.[13] It is not his Jewish identity which condemns Mamlock to death, as much as his failure to embark on a Wolferian awakening by rejecting passivity and turning towards ideological awareness through a process of self-repositioning. Antisemitic persecution is undoubtedly at the heart of the film's plot and there is no attempt to divert attention away from the fact that Mamlock and his daughter are persecuted by others because they are Jewish. However, this clarity of cause is immediately complicated by the film's parallel critique of class. Mamlock may be persecuted because he is Jewish, but it is his failure to question his bourgeois values which sees him condemned by the film.

Where this call to act breaks down, however, is in the film's historical setting. The scrolling text at the start of the film alerts us to the core event that separates Friedrich Wolf's 1933 source play and Konrad Wolf's 1961 film: 'At the time, the death camps had not yet been set up, the gas chambers not yet invented, six million Jews not yet murdered. The Second World War was still on the distant horizon. Back then none of this had happened'. *Professor Mamlock* may use source material from the start of the Third Reich that was intended to serve as a call to action, but in Wolf's film this circulates in a post-Holocaust context when victimhood was no longer something that could be countered by individual agency. Although the film does not deny the presence of Jewish victimhood and indeed highlights the genocidal outcome of National Socialist persecution, Wolf remains strangely myopic to the nuances of persecution, agency and victimhood.

The Hard Way to Enlightenment

In his analysis of Konrad Wolf's films, Anthony Coulson identifies the recurring trope of characters who 'reassess themselves and their place in society' through a 'process of searching and reflecting'.[14] This transformative process underpins several of Wolf's films, whether through the economically, politically and morally compromised titular heroine of *Lissy*, the Wehrmacht soldier who becomes cognisant of his criminal and moral complicity with the National Socialist regime in *Sterne* or the conflicted returning soldier of *Ich war neunzehn* (*I Was Nineteen*, 1968). On each occasion, Wolf returns to 'protagonists steeped in false values or misled by the force of circumstances' who to varying degrees of success, are able to realize the errors of their ways.[15] *Professor Mamlock* appears to be aligned with this central tenet whereby Mamlock's misplaced faith in liberal values and his refusal to heed the warnings of his son mark the tripartite process of 'error, confusion and conversion' that is the hallmark of the Wolferian awakening.[16] However, although Coulson is correct to place *Professor Mamlock* within this tradition and to highlight the role of editing in allowing the audience to see and hear what Mamlock cannot and will not acknowledge, this reading nonetheless overlooks a key figure in the film: Dr Inge Ruoff.

We are first introduced to Inge as she leaves a beer hall named 'Deutsches Haus' ('German House') that is frequented by SA members and inside is adorned with banners bearing swastikas. By her side is Dr Hellpach who, we subsequently learn, has swapped 'his surgeon's knife for a revolver' and has become an ardent National Socialist. Inge's own views are revealed when she asks Mamlock, 'Do you approve of this infamous terror by the Communists and their intellectual backers, the Jews?' before adding, 'I can't work under a Jew anymore'. However, her growing romantic feelings for Rolf force her to question this position. In so doing, she transforms from a character who appears to subscribe to nationalist eugenics by declaring 'blood is fate!', to a character who urges Rolf to fight against the National Socialists with the words, 'go where you must! Go where you are needed!'.

Here we find clear parallels to Walter in *Sterne*. As in the director's 1959 film, the only character to undergo an onscreen political and ideological transformation is one whose support for the regime appears to define his or her onscreen presence at the start of the film. By the end of the film, Inge has been forced to reconsider her actions and loyalties. If Wolf was careful to create a hierarchy of culpability in *Sterne* through the juxtaposition of Walter and Kurt, then in *Professor Mamlock* the director overwhelmingly contextualizes Inge's antisemitic or fascist proclamations by situating them alongside Hellpach's virulently nationalist and fascist statements. In *Sterne*, Wolf draws attention to the different behaviours of Walter and Kurt by contrasting Walter's attempted exchange of cigarettes with Kurt's wilful destruction of medication. In *Professor Mamlock*, the director visualizes hierarchies of culpability through repeated shots of the characters' hands (Figure 3.2). In the hospital clinic – the location of Mamlock's eventual suicide – Inge is shown with her white-gloved hands raised. This is repeatedly contrasted with Hellpach's black-gloved hands that loom menacingly over the camera as he utters increasingly nationalistic statements such as 'Germany is everywhere, everywhere where German blood runs through our veins'. Only after Mamlock's suicide does Inge figuratively and literally lower her hands as she comforts the doctor in his final moments. As much as the titular hero may follow the 'hard way to enlightenment', it is ultimately Inge who undertakes a path of 'exploration and discovery' and who affirms 'a commitment to open-mindedness and change'.[17]

The significance of Inge's role in the 1961 film becomes even clearer when we consider Wolf's presentation of the character alongside the 1933 source play and the television film of *Professor Mamlock* broadcast

Figure 3.2. The symbolic use of hands as the white-gloved Inge and the black-gloved Dr Hellpach loom over Professor Mamlock. © DEFA-Stiftung/Walter Ruge.

in September 1958. In contrast to both the 1933 play and the 1958 television film, Wolf not only positions Inge as the only character prepared to comfort the dying Mamlock, but he also foregrounds her antifascist conversion. As Mamlock dies in front of her, she declares in tears, 'what happened here, we will not forget. We certainly will not forget. Never forget'. Strikingly, in the 1933 and 1958 versions of *Professor Mamlock*, these lines were not spoken by Inge, but by Mamlock's colleague Simon (Figure 3.3).[18] By reallocating the lines to Inge, Wolf signals that she is to be viewed as the moral voice of the film and as the character whose transformational journey is key to its Wolferian theme.

As Anne Barnert observes, Wolf's reallocation of the film's closing lines from Simon to Inge modifies the group of reference from a 'we' spoken by a Jewish character to a communist 'we'.[19] At the same time, the change also reflects subtle shifts in the position of female voices in East German cinema. Anke Pinkert has pointed to a recurring trope in DEFA's 1950s and 1960s films that bound together the 'cinematic imagination of social stability and future progress' with 'women's successful integration into the public realm as active and responsible citizens'.[20] In *Professor Mamlock* there is a clear attempt to appeal to female spectators.

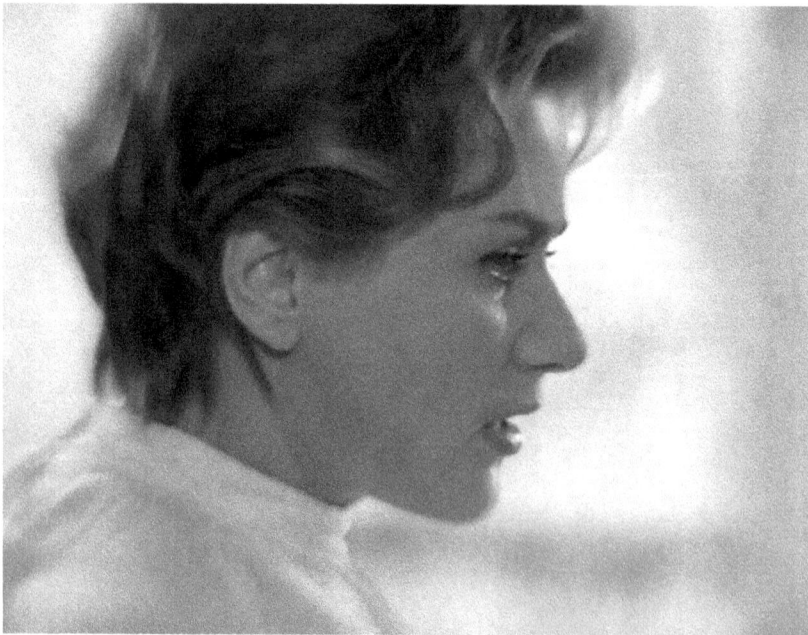

Figure 3.3. Inge's voice concludes the film and points to the antifascist future. © DEFA-Stiftung/Walter Ruge.

The film opens with a monologue delivered to camera by Mamlock which begins, 'You are full of worry. After the last genocide, will there be another war? You fear for your son, for your daughter, for your husband?', thereby signalling the imagined interlocutor is a mother and wife. It is important to stress that in spite of the increased prominence accorded to Inge and the film's privileging of female spectatorship, East German cinematic output during this decade remained dominated by the 'mature and resolute male comrade'.[21] Inge by no means challenges Rolf or Ernst as an idealized figure of the communist resistance. But to a certain extent, the failure to embody idealized models of behaviour renders her ideological trajectory all the more significant. In keeping with the precedent of Walter in *Sterne*, Inge demonstrates how flawed individuals can embark on the 'correct' path and, in so doing, the film once again offers audiences – this time male and female – a model of antifascist conversion by proxy.

The Girl with the Star

If the presentation of Inge was designed to appeal to a female audience, then the reworking of the character Ruth Mamlock can be seen as an attempt by Wolf to engage younger audiences in celebratory narratives of communist resistance. By examining a series of decisions made during pre-production, crucial changes made from the source text and the post-production marketing of the film by DEFA and in the press, it becomes clear that Wolf and DEFA sought to create synergies between Ruth Mamlock and the figure of Anne Frank. This strategy was particularly targeted at younger audiences and is symptomatic of an attempt by DEFA and East German filmmakers more generally to engage a younger generation in first-generation antifascist narratives.[22]

By the early 1960s, the figure of Anne Frank had become a global icon for both the six million victims of the Holocaust and for universalized victims of oppression and persecution more generally. Interest in Anne Frank in the GDR began in 1956 following the stage play adaptation of Frank's *The Diary of a Young Girl*. Just over a year after the play's Broadway debut, a production opened in Dresden's Theater der Jungen Generation (Theatre of the Young Generation).[23] This marked the start of a subsequent 'production wave' during which the play was staged in several small, medium and large theatres across the GDR, which culminated in a 1958 production of the play at the Deutsches Theater in East Berlin.[24] The theatrical adaptation was subsequently filmed and broadcast on East German television at peak time on 28 December 1958 and by 1961 it had been broadcast another three times.[25] Meanwhile, the first East German edition of *The Diary of Anne Frank* was published with Union Verlag in early 1957. Between the publication of the first edition in 1957 and 1990, a total of eight editions were issued with print runs of between 5,000 and 40,000 copies.[26]

The desire to harness the popular interest in Anne Frank for *Professor Mamlock* is clear from the behind-the-scenes casting decisions. When asked what drew her to the role of Ruth Mamlock in *Professor Mamlock*, Doris Abeßer replied, 'I am … so happy to be able to play Ruth because I have never played Anne Frank on stage'.[27] This reference to Anne Frank was far from coincidental; Abeßer's invocation of the fifteen-year-old victim of National Socialist persecution marks just one of several intertextual references in the film to the figure of Anne Frank. When the Deutsches Theater production of *The Diary of Anne Frank* was broadcast on East German television, Kati Székely made her acting debut as Anne Frank, Wolfgang Heinz played the role of Otto Frank and Ursula Burg appeared as Edith Frank. Székely played Frank again in the film *Ein Tagebuch für Anne Frank* (*A Diary for Anne Frank*, 1958) for which Heinz provided the narration.[28] Interestingly, DEFA sought to cast the same actors as the Mamlock family in *Professor Mamlock*: Heinz appears as Hans Mamlock and Burg as his wife, Ellen Mamlock. Arguably, the casting of Heinz and Burg in the film should not come as a complete surprise. After all, both had appeared in a stage version of *Professor Mamlock* at the Berliner Kammerspiel in December 1959. However, neither actor had been cast in the 1958 television film of *Professor Mamlock*. In fact, none of the actors from the television version appear in Wolf's film. Equally significantly, early casting lists compiled by DEFA reveal that the two actors considered for the part of Ruth Mamlock in the 1961 film were Doris Abeßer and Kati Székely.[29] No reason is given for the decision to cast Abeßer above Székely, but it is clear that DEFA still sought to present Abeßer as an Anne Frank figure to the public. DEFA's description of Abeßer in the film's publicity material refers to her 'childlike face which is framed by her short-cut, dark hair' in such a manner as to accentuate the parallels between the actress, her character and Anne Frank.[30] Such allusions were not lost on reviewers at the time who introduced their reviews with headlines such as 'The Girl with the Star'.[31]

Significant changes were also made to the source material. In contrast to the play, Wolf presents Ruth as politically naïve. The audience is introduced to Ruth as she is attempting to complete her homework while her older brother, Rolf, teases her. In the source text and the 1958 television adaptation, Ruth and Rolf quarrel and Ruth dismisses Rolf's political stance, claiming 'one day, the boys from the Deutscher Waffenring [German Arms Ring of Student Duelling Societies] will teach you intellectual hyenas some manners!'.[32] The film not only depicts the siblings' conversation as far more light-hearted and playful, but it also removes all of Ruth's politically-charged dialogue and instead presents her as a naïve young girl. Over the course of the film, Ruth becomes increasingly enlightened to the antifascist cause. In her encounters with Rolf and his friend, Ernst, both of whom play a significantly greater role in the film and serve as the production's ideological mouthpieces, Ruth displays a growing fascination with both their activities and their underlying motivation. Indeed, her question to Ernst, 'are you really doing all of this for communism?', appears less like a sceptical statement of incredulity at Ernst's 'wonderful idealism' as in the play and television film, but rather serves as an affirmation of her admiration for the antifascist resister.[33]

The most overt attempt to harness interest in the legacy of Anne Frank can be seen in the unusual decision by the studio to release a special edition programme aimed at young audiences to accompany the film. Entitled 'Our Family', the fifteen-page booklet takes the form of a diary combining text entries in a handwritten font with photographs bearing captions such as 'Mein Vati' ('my daddy') or 'Meine Mutti' ('my mummy'). The booklet begins with a forward from Ruth Mamlock: 'I started these notes a few days after the New Year's Eve celebration in 1932/33. I decided to create a small, extended family album that nobody would see. Maybe later, if I have children, but for now it is just the confidant of my thoughts, my moods. I think it's snazzy and it will take the place of a diary'.[34] Of course, one obvious difference between the fictional Ruth and the real Anne Frank is that the latter was murdered whereas Ruth is alive at the end of the film. Significantly, however, Ruth's diary continues after the film's narrative has ended. The final diary entry informs the reader that Mamlock has died and asks, 'It is inconceivable. What is to become of us?'. This appeal to the future has a double effect. The question appears to point to the Holocaust. However, interpreted within a postwar context, the question also anticipates a far more redemptive answer, namely the founding of 'the first socialist state on German soil'.[35] From the perspective of 1961, the answer to Ruth's question does not first and foremost invite any sense of national shame embodied in the Holocaust, but rather celebrates the redemptive and ideological victory represented by the foundation of the GDR.

Notes

1. *Professor Mamlock* is adapted from the 1933 play of the same name by the director's father, Friedrich Wolf.
2. DEFA, 'Thesen für die Aktivtagung'.
3. Wilkening, 'Letter from Prof Dr Wilkening to Ernst Hoffmann'.
4. *Zeit im Bild*, 'Väter und Söhne'.
5. Filmbegutachtungskommission für Jugend und Schule Berlin, 'Protokoll über die Begutachtung des Films *Sterne* am 21. Juni 1960'.
6. Filmbegutachtungskommission für Jugend und Schule Berlin, 'Protokoll über die Begutachtung des Films *Professor Mamlock* am 6.11.1966'.
7. Coulson, 'Paths of Discovery', 172.
8. See also ibid., 169.
9. Wolf and Egel, 'Handlungsaufriss (Fahrplan) für den Film'.
10. *Bauernecho*, '*Professor Mamlock*'.
11. Gruppe Heinrich Greif, 'Abnahmediskussion des Drehbuches *Professor Mamlock* am 27. September 1960'.
12. Coulson, 'Paths of Discovery', 165.
13. 'Wolferian' here refers to Friedrich Wolf, rather than Konrad Wolf. Wolf and Egel, 'Handlungsaufriss (Fahrplan) für den Film'.
14. Coulson, 'Paths of Discovery', 165.
15. Ibid.
16. Ibid., 166.
17. Ibid., 165.
18. See also Barnert, *Die Antifaschismus-Thematik der DEFA*, 239.
19. Ibid.
20. Pinkert, *Film and Memory in East Germany*, 131.
21. Feinstein, *The Triumph of the Ordinary*, 132
22. Parts of this section have previously been published in Ward, 'Zur strategischen Aneignung der Anne Frank-Figur in Konrad Wolfs Professor Mamlock (1961)' in Peter Seibert, Jana Piper and Alfonso Meoli (eds), *Anne Frank: Mediengeschichten*. Reprinted with the kind permission of Metropol Verlag.
23. Kirschnick, *Anne Frank und die DDR*, 37–9.
24. Ibid., 45–6.
25. Ibid., 46.
26. Ibid., 72.
27. Progress Film, '*Professor Mamlock*'.
28. Originally titled 'Anne Frank and her Murderers', the pseudo-documentary *Ein Tagebuch für Anne Frank* draws direct parallels between the murder of Anne Frank and the actions of West German politicians and businessmen. Although the title foregrounds the presence of the young Jewish girl, she is, in fact, a peripheral figure. The dominant figures in the film are not antifascist resistance heroes or working-class victims, but rather are Frank's perpetrators – perpetrators who were enjoying lucrative post-war careers in West German politics and business.
29. DEFA, 'Besetzungsvorschläge *Professor Mamlock*'.
30. Progress Film, '*Professor Mamlock*'.
31. *Neuer Tag*, 'Das Mädchen mit dem Stern'.
32. Wolf, *Professor Mamlock*, 21.
33. Ibid. 42.
34. Progress Film, 'Unsere Familie'.
35. Honecker, 'Rede Honeckers zum 40. Jahrestag der DDR'.

PART III

1961–71

East German filmmakers were quietly optimistic at the start of the 1960s. Although responses to the building of the Berlin Wall in August 1961 were mixed, most filmmakers and actors ultimately reconciled themselves to the hope that the sealing of the German–German border would stabilize internal political tensions, create a new sense of confidence in the GDR and consequently herald a new period of liberalization in East German filmmaking.[1] Their hopes were not entirely misplaced. Structural reforms within DEFA signalled that the studio was indeed committed to a new chapter in film production. The creation of seven Künstlerische Arbeitsgruppen (Artistic Working Groups, KAG) in 1959 partially devolved centralized filmmaking processes and gave filmmakers greater freedom within DEFA.[2] Although the studio and the Ministry for Culture maintained ultimate control, the creation of the KAGs was designed to increase both the quantity and quality of films produced. Each KAG comprised an artistic director, film directors, cinematographers, dramaturges, production leaders and production managers who were tasked with engaging in 'rigorous debate about fundamental questions of art and ideology' with the objective of promoting socialist cinematic art.[3] Changes were also made within the studio management and DEFA studio director Albert Wilkening was replaced by the young cultural official Jochen Mückenberger as part of a wider attempt by the Central Committee to recruit younger functionaries.[4]

These cultural reforms were accompanied by broader changes in East German society. If the 1950s were characterized by the 'Aufbau des

Sozialismus' ('building up of socialism'), then the 1960s were supposed to mark the 'Ankunft im Sozialismus' ('arrival in socialism'). The sealing of the border, or rather the erection of the 'antifascist protection wall' as it was described in the GDR, was followed by judicial, social and economic reforms in the GDR. The cumulative effect of these changes was to instil a new sense of confidence in filmmakers, the consequences of which played out in the films themselves. From the early 1960s, East German directors and screenwriters began to critique the social and political realities of 'everyday socialism' in the GDR. It was not just the content of the films that began to change. In keeping with parallel developments in Czechoslovakia, Poland and France, the GDR was on the cusp of its own 'new wave' in film as signalled by new levels of aesthetic experimentation.[5] However, the newfound freedoms proved to be short-lived.

The Eleventh Plenum of December 1965 was originally intended to be a platform to celebrate the economic achievements of the SED's New Economic System of Planning and Management (*Neues Ökonomisches System der Planung und Leitung*, NÖSPL).[6] The NÖSPL overhauled the centrally managed planned economy and introduced a series of market-based reforms such as greater autonomy for factories, increased emphasis on the importance of profit and the introduction of bonuses to incentivize worker productivity.[7] These restructurings would not have been possible without similar changes in the USSR where a process of economic decentralization was already underway.[8] However, the ousting of Nikita Khrushchev by Leonid Brezhnev signalled a return to political and economic orthodoxy in the USSR. The change in leadership had a ripple effect throughout the Soviet Bloc, but posed a particularly urgent problem for the SED. By this point, preparations for the Eleventh Plenum were well underway. The Plenum was intended to announce the successes of the second stage of the economic reforms, but by December 1965 the change in political mood was so pronounced that the Central Committee urgently sought to divert attention away from the now politically undesirable NÖSPL. Culture – and, in particular, film – provided the perfect scapegoat. The public criticism of DEFA was spearheaded by Erich Honecker who sought to refocus criticism on 'manifestations of immorality' and depictions of a 'lifestyle alien to socialism' which, he claimed, were propagated by artists in 'films, television programmes, plays, literary works and periodicals'.[9]

The films caught up in the wake of the Eleventh Plenum had no single unifying feature, but there were recurring characteristics. With the exception of *Der verlorene Engel* (*The Lost Angel*, 1966), all the banned films were *Gegenwartsfilme* ('films about everyday life').[10] The films frequently featured protagonists who were teenagers or young adults who found themselves in conflict with older East Germans. This generational tension was expressed through conflict with the state, whose representatives were often shown to be out-of-touch pedants who insisted on tedious processes and practices. It is important to stress that the aim of the filmmakers caught up in the wake of the Eleventh Plenum was never to challenge the authority of the SED, but rather to contribute to the development of the socialist state for the next generation, a process that they believed had been signalled by the reforms of the early 1960s. However, it was precisely the questioning of societal values through new, increasingly experimental aesthetic forms that made these films so vulnerable to attack.

The impact of the Eleventh Plenum cannot be overstated. It has been estimated that in the forty-six-year history of DEFA, a total of thirty East German films were banned, stopped mid-production or never released.[11] The fact that over a third of these were banned as a direct result of the Eleventh Plenum attests to the seismic impact of the events of late 1965.[12] The fallout from the Eleventh Plenum affected DEFA's output and blighted the careers of filmmakers and film officials. Nearly all of the 1965 production plan was shelved. Projects that were well into production were cancelled, while permission to start filming a number of new screenplays was revoked. The careers of several key figures within DEFA were either ended or severely impacted by this cultural-political *Kahlschlag* ('clearing of the ground'). Filmmakers were accused of 'sparking doubts about the policies of the GDR' by promoting certain views and 'tendencies' that were 'alien' and 'damaging to socialism', of showing the relationship between the individual and party leaders as 'cold and detached' and of propagating 'nihilistic, despondent and morally subversive philosophies'.[13]

A number of DEFA's leading directors who had hitherto been lauded for their exemplary filmographies suddenly found themselves subject to highly public criticism. DEFA founding member Kurt Maetzig, who had directed the unabashedly celebratory antifascist films *Rat der Götter*, *Ernst Thälmann – Sohn seiner Klasse* and *Ernst Thälmann – Führer seiner Klasse* found himself accused of contributing to 'an ideological pact with the enemies of socialism' which had 'sullied' the state with his film *Das Kaninchen bin ich*.[14] Maetzig was only permitted to continue his career after agreeing to pen a self-critical open letter in *Neues*

Deutschland in which he acknowledged his 'political [and] moral' responsibilities as a director.[15] Frank Beyer fell foul of the state following the release of his 1966 film, *Spur der Steine* (*Trace of Stones*) which was banned on account of its negative depiction of the party.[16] In contrast to Maetzig, Beyer – who had directed the antifascist action films *Fünf Patronenhülsen*, *Königskinder* (*Star-Crossed Lovers*, 1962) and *Nackt unter Wölfen* – was banned from directing at DEFA until 1972.[17] Studio and cultural officials were not spared from the fallout either and, over the following weeks and months, high-ranking cultural officials including Hans Bentzien (Minister of Culture), Günter Witt (Deputy Minister of Culture), Jochen Mückenberger (DEFA's studio director) and Klaus Wischnewski (chief dramaturge at DEFA) were all dismissed from office. The KAGs lost the autonomy granted to them at the start of the decade and became 'little more than vehicles for dividing responsibilities among dramaturges'.[18]

In the months after the Eleventh Plenum, there was a palpable nervousness among filmmakers and studio officials about the parameters of representation. To avoid any further transgressions, the studio opted for familiar and conventional projects. DEFA's output in the late 1960s came to be characterized by a return to the GDR's founding narratives, a heavy reliance on genre films and a steadfast desire to avoid controversial topics or, as the former chief dramaturge at DEFA Klaus Wischnewski termed it, 'information, affirmation and attempts with entertaining genres'.[19] The ways in which the two films in this section both uphold and challenge these dominant trends render them fascinating case studies for the exploration of East German Holocaust film in the aftermath of the Eleventh Plenum.

Instrumentalizing the Past

The 1960s was a period of transition in East German Holocaust film – although not necessarily in the direction of more inclusive understandings of victimhood and resistance. Two broader political and social developments played an important role in shaping East German Holocaust film during this decade: the GDR's explicit condemnation of Zionism and the coming of age of a new postwar generation. According to the 1963 edition of the East German *Meyers Taschenlexikon* (*Meyer's Pocket Encyclopaedia*), antisemitism was the 'hostile attitude towards Jews' which 'is manifest in racial aggression, restriction of rights [and] pogroms'.[20] The *Kleines Politisches Wörterbuch* (*Small Political Dictionary*) never carried a definition of antisemitism and instead referred readers to 'Racial Ideology'.[21] The 1988 edition did, however, contain an entry for 'Zionism', which it described as 'the chauvinistic ideology, the diverse organizational system and the racist, expansionist political practice of the Jewish bourgeoisie' and which, with the foundation of Israel, was raised to the level of 'state doctrine'.[22] Since Zionism, following a Marxist-Leninist reading, is an expression of bourgeois and imperialist powers exploiting the working classes, Jews could also be victims of Zionism. This framing of Jewish persecution underpins Wolfgang Luderer's *Lebende Ware*. As we shall see in the following chapter, the desire to condemn Zionism as 'upper-class nationalism and chauvinism' often risked inadvertently resurrecting antisemitic tropes – a point that became an increasing matter of concern for DEFA.[23]

The second key development that informed both the production and reception of DEFA's 1960s Holocaust films was the coming of age of the first generation of East Germans who did not experience the Second World War or who did so as children. Although the return to familiar genres resulted in an increase in the number of antifascist films produced, the ways in which the subject matter was approached began to shift significantly. One often overlooked aspect of this is the extent to which the figure of the antifascist hero changed after the Eleventh Plenum. The antifascist hero of the late 1960s was certainly less assured in his political convictions than his pre-Eleventh Plenum comrade. This contrast can be seen clearly between Frank Beyer's *Nackt unter Wölfen* and Konrad Wolf's *Ich war neunzehn* (*I Was Nineteen*, 1968). Based on Bruno Apitz's 1958 novel, *Nackt unter Wölfen* celebrates the resistance activities of the communist prisoners at Buchenwald concentration camp which included the hiding of a young Jewish boy and the liberation of the camp after an uprising by the prisoners.[24] Within a few years, the tone of the antifascist film had shifted significantly. The deeply ambivalent and subjective mode of Wolf's coming-of-age drama, *Ich war neunzehn*, lacks the celebratory tone of earlier antifascist films and instead affords the protagonist Gregor a space for reflection, circumspection and even doubt. *Ich war neunzehn* was loosely based on Wolf's own experience as a German who returns as part of the Red Army to liberate Germany, and Gregor's introspection and doubts render him a very different hero from DEFA's 1950s and early 1960s antifascist canon. In this way, Wolf's film has been described as an attempt to move away from the 'calcified ritualized antifascism that had functionalized art in the service of the party's heroic self-presentation'.[25] The changing mood that imbued the antifascist film in the 1960s alerts us to wider shifts in the depiction of the National Socialist past, and the clash between the lived experiences of audiences and the projected experiences of cinematic protagonists underscores much of the tension in *Das Tal der sieben Monde*.

It is the return to politically orthodox and culturally conservative material that makes the status of East German Holocaust films in the late 1960s so fascinating. Directors and officials may have been cautious about broaching any potentially controversial theme, but films discussing Jewish persecution continued to be made in the immediate aftermath of the Eleventh Plenum. In fact, the only non-children's film that survived the immediate fallout from the Eleventh Plenum was *Lebende Ware* (1966), a film set in German-occupied Hungary detailing the deportation of Jews. The first new film to be released after the Eleventh Plenum was *Das Tal der sieben Monde* (1967), a love story between a *Volksdeutscher* ('ethnic German') and a Jewish Pole set in German-occupied Poland.

Against the backdrop of the political and cultural orthodoxy of the late 1960s, the simple presence of the theme of Jewish persecution is significant, but this in itself reveals little about how the subject matter is treated or about the importance of this for East German filmic engagements with the Holocaust more broadly. When we look more closely at these two films, we find quite remarkable anomalies which, while not challenging the core tenets of antifascist memory, certainly fail to promote them. *Lebende Ware* may be an overt attack on the purported links between West German capitalism and National Socialist fascism, but it also omits any reference to antifascist resistance. In 1966, DEFA was under considerable scrutiny. At the start of the year, Franz Jahrow was tasked with reviewing the ideological suitability of DEFA's release schedules.[26] Had he so desired, *Lebende Ware* could have been modified or production could even have been stopped. But in spite of considerable pressure from DEFA's Hungarian co-producers to alter the screenplay, *Lebende Ware* presents Jews as the sole victim group of National Socialist persecution. A very different, but highly significant, point of tension also arises in *Das Tal der sieben Monde*. Kolditz's film does feature the antifascist resistance prominently, however it also includes two explicit references to civilian wartime rape. These two case studies examine how Jewish victimhood was presented during one of the most significant cultural 'freezes' to affect East German filmmaking and explore the debates embedded within – and provoked by – the films' storylines in relation to the prominence of Jewish victimhood and legacies of wartime rape.

Notes

1. For a range of reactions at the studio to news that the East–West border had been closed, see Feinstein, *Triumph of the Ordinary*, 122–4.
2. The seven KAGs were Roter Kreis, Heinrich Greif, Solidarität, Gruppe Berlin, Gruppe 60, Konkret and Stacheltier.
3. Georg Wege, 'Künstlerische Arbeitsgruppen im Spielfilmstudio', 336. Cited in Schittly, *Zwischen Regie und Regime*, 89.
4. Schittly, *Zwischen Regie und Regime*, 116.
5. Berghahn, *Hollywood Behind the Wall*, 141.
6. For an excellent overview of the Eleventh Plenum, see Morton, 'The Eleventh Plenum'.
7. Grieder, *The German Democratic Republic*, 58–60.
8. Feinstein, *Triumph of the Ordinary*, 154.
9. Honecker, 'Aus dem Bericht des Politbüros an die 11. Tagung des ZK'.
10. Richter, 'Zwischen Mauerbau und Kahlschlag', 207.
11. As Daniela Berghahn highlights, the decision to halt work on a film may not necessarily have been the result of censorship. Practical and pragmatic factors also led to the cancellation of projects. Berghahn, *Hollywood Behind the Wall*, 135.
12. The twelve banned films were *Denk bloß nicht, ich heule* (*Just Don't Think I'll Cry*, 1965), *Das Kaninchen bin ich* (*The Rabbit is Me*, 1965), *Fräulein Schmetterling* (*Miss Butterfly*, 1966), *Karla* (*Carla*, 1965), *Ritter des Regens* (*Knight of the Rain*, 1965), *Der Frühling braucht Zeit* (*Spring Takes Time*, 1965), *Berlin um die Ecke* (*Berlin Around the Corner*, 1965), *Wenn du groß bist, lieber Adam* (*When You're Older, Dear Adam*, 1965), *Jahrgang 45* (*Born in '45*, 1966), *Spur der Steine* (*Trace of Stones*, 1966), *Der verlorene Engel* (*The Lost Angel*, 1966) and *Hände hoch, oder ich schieße* (*Hands Up or I'll Shoot*, 1966).
13. Honecker, 'Aus dem Bericht des Politbüros an die 11. Tagung des ZK'.
14. Ulbricht, 'Brief des Genossen Walter Ulbricht an Genossen Prof. Kurt Maetzig', *Neues Deutschland*.
15. Maetzig, 'Der Künstler steht nicht außerhalb des Kampfes', *Neues Deutschland*.
16. Brockmann, *A Critical History of German Film*, 252–6.
17. According to Joshua Feinstein, Konrad Wolf was also considered by the SED to be one of the 'main representatives and intellectual authors of the fake ideological-aesthetic positions'. His prominence as a director and as head of the Academy of Arts protected him from undergoing a similar fate to Beyer. Feinstein, *Triumph of the Ordinary*, 191.
18. Ibid., 177.
19. Wischnewski, 'Träumer und gewöhnliche Leute', 216.
20. VEB Bibliographisches Institut, *Meyers Taschenlexikon*, 46–7.
21. Under 'Racial Ideology', the 1973 edition did contain the line, 'the key political-ideological feature of contemporary racial ideology is its close link to anti-Communism'. Dietz Verlag, *Kleines Politisches Wörterbuch* (1973), 698.

22. Dietz Verlag, *Kleines Politisches Wörterbuch* (1988), 1116.
23. Timm, 'Ideology and Realpolitik: East German Attitudes towards Zionism and Israel', 191.
24. For an excellent study of *Nackt unter Wölfen*, see Bill Niven's *The Buchenwald Child: Truth, Fiction and Propaganda*.
25. Pinkert, *Film and Memory in East Germany*, 151.
26. Feinstein, *Triumph of the Ordinary*, 177.

Chapter 4

CRIMES OF THE PAST AND POLITICS OF THE PRESENT

Wolfgang Luderer's *Lebende Ware*

Lebende Ware (1966) may have been one of the few films to have survived the *Kahlschlag* ('clearing of the ground') of films following the Eleventh Plenum, but it was never a popular film. It failed to find any widespread appeal among the general public and box office receipts reveal that just 267,423 tickets[1] were sold in the first three months of the film's release.[2] The film fared little better among critics. Although the acting performances were often praised in reviews, several journalists bemoaned the film's lack of 'artistic intensity'[3] and uncinematic aesthetic approach[4] that left 'many wishes unfulfilled'.[5] Nor did the various departments within DEFA greet the film with any great enthusiasm. Even before *Lebende Ware* entered pre-production, the film's own production team acknowledged that 'a first-class casting' of all key roles was necessary, not only in order to 'increase the export chances for this film', but also so that 'weaknesses in the composition and dialogue [could] still be overcome'.[6] DEFA approached Wolfgang Heinz – who had played the titular role in *Professor Mamlock* – for the role of Chorin. However, its efforts to cast the celebrated stage actor were ultimately unsuccessful[7] and the studio struggled to attract any prominent actors to the lead roles.[8] Scepticism about the quality of the film continued even after filming. Although the KAG Heinrich Greif and the DEFA studio management had underlined the international significance of the material,[9] DEFA-Außenhandel conceded that it would most probably only be of interest to audiences in other socialist countries.[10] In the event, the film only played in two other countries, Czechoslovakia and Hungary.[11] Even within the GDR, the film received a low-key release after DEFA took the decision to hold the film's premiere in Potsdam rather than at one of the usual high-profile locations at the International, Cosmos or Colosseum cinemas in East Berlin.[12]

Lebende Ware focuses on the real-life figure of the SS-Obersturmbannführer Kurt Andreas Becher and his financial exploitation of Jews in Hungary.[13] The film begins with Becher's arrival at the villa of the Jewish industrialist, Ferenc Chorin, in Budapest in March 1944. Enthralled by his affluent surroundings, Becher resolves to acquire not only Chorin's house, but also the source of the industrialist's wealth, the Manfréd Weiss Steel and Metal Works. Becher orders Chorin's notary, Wolfgang Mahlmann, to arrange for the transfer of Chorin's assets to him. In return for signing over the factory, Chorin and his family are granted exit visas to a neutral foreign country. News of Becher's actions quickly reaches the Zionist activist Rudolf Kastner, the Jewish Council of Budapest and Becher's colleagues in the SS.[14] With the assistance of Kastner, Becher agrees to provide wealthy Jews with exit visas in return for foreign currency, jewellery and works of art. These actions infuriate Adolf Eichmann who considers Becher's interference with transport lists an affront to his bureaucratic efficiency. Mahlmann becomes the victim of the two men's rivalry when, in an attempt to expose Becher's activities, Eichmann orders Mahlmann's arrest and interrogates him about Becher's financial scheme. Fearing further revelations, Becher orders Mahlmann's immediate deportation to Auschwitz. Meanwhile, it is revealed that Kastner has been manipulating transport lists to ensure his own friends and family are saved, while poorer Jews who are unable to buy their freedom are deported to Auschwitz. The film ends with Becher and Kastner fleeing Hungary to escape the advancing Red Army and, as the screen fades to black, three title cards announce the fates of Eichmann, Kastner and Becher.

Lebende Ware is a complex film. Its instrumentalization of the National Socialist past and the overt attempts to cast the Federal Republic as heir to the Third Reich situate the film firmly within the political climate of the 1960s. Furthermore, it struggles to offer nuance and depth in its engagement with the fate of the Jewish characters and Luderer's attempts to instil an anti-Zionist critique within the context of a Holocaust film repeatedly lead to simplistic characterization and reductive tropes to the point that the film errs worryingly close to replicating antisemitic tropes. However, the cultural-political significance of the film demands that we look more closely at Lebende Ware. Lebende Ware may boast the dubious accolade of being DEFA's only non-children's film to survive the fallout from the Eleventh Plenum, but it is also a film that places Jewish victimhood at its core and does not feature a single antifascist character or act of resistance. This chapter examines the implications of this for our understanding of the parameters of representation during one of the most contentious cultural-political periods in the GDR's history.

Setting the Scene

Lebende Ware may have failed to win critical or popular praise, but the film certainly had the potential to be a commercial success. It drew upon a familiar and tried-and-tested format that had proved popular on East German television: the Fernsehpitaval ('television pitaval' or 'television true crimes') series.[15] The director, Wolfgang Luderer, screenwriters Friedrich Karl Kaul and Walter Jupé, and the dramaturge Änne Keller had all already worked together on the Fernsehpitaval.[16] The Fernsehpitaval, which was described by one East German critic as one of 'the greatest political and artistic achievement of our television',[17] restaged historic events as political crime stories and focussed on real-life crimes in Wilhelmine Germany, the Weimar Republic and the Federal Republic. Lebende Ware shares the television series' overtly political agenda which, in the case of the Bonn Pitaval episodes, focussed on medium- or high-ranking National Socialists who subsequently occupied positions of power in the Federal Republic. Given the positive popular and critical responses to the television series, DEFA could well have expected Lebende Ware to replicate its success.

Lebende Ware is one of DEFA's most ideologically explicit Holocaust films. The transformation of Becher from a former 'fascist criminal'[18] to a 'respected citizen of the Federal Republic and multi-millionaire'[19] provided DEFA with an ideal case study for the indictment of the Federal Republic as a haven for former National Socialists who allegedly continued to abuse workers through financial exploitation. Lebende Ware was certainly not an isolated example of the instrumentalization of the National Socialist past for the politics of the present. Throughout the late 1950s and 1960s, the past was co-opted in films,[20] television series[21] and radio plays[22] to show the Federal Republic as a dangerous political enemy. These works ultimately served to uphold the claim made in the

GDR's controversial *Braunbuch* ('Brown Book') that 'in the West German Federal Republic thousands of people responsible for Nazi and war crimes not only remain unpunished, but also occupy leading positions in the economy, state, military and police, in education establishments, publishing houses and the mass media'.[23]

In early drafts of the screenplay of *Lebende Ware*, the relationship between the National Socialist past and the West German present was even more explicit. The film's treatment opens in 'a West German city' in 1964.[24] Mahlmann walks through the streets of the Federal Republic and he is almost run over by a black Mercedes, the occupant of which is revealed to be Becher. Having searched for him for years, Mahlmann confronts the West German businessman with the truth about the former SS-Obersturmbannführer's past, at which point the film cuts to an extended flashback of Becher in Budapest in 1944. The film closes by returning to the present with Mahlmann threatening to expose Becher no matter what threats are made against him. The 1964 storyline was subsequently removed, but the instrumentalization of Jewish persecution as a means of attacking the Federal Republic remained an important aspect of the film's marketing through the repeated (and dubious) assertions of historical accuracy.

At every stage of the film's production, the filmmakers were resolute that *Lebende Ware* was a factually accurate film. A synopsis of the film opens with the claim that, 'for the first time, this film reveals with detailed exactitude the process of a commercial murder', through the use of 'documents, international eyewitness accounts and authentic reports' which were intended to bring 'a criminal act to people's consciousness, frighteningly and explicitly, with objective exactitude regarding facts and persons'.[25] The filmmakers even seek to convey the historical accuracy of the material within the film itself through the use of title cards at the end. The three title cards that announce the fates of Eichmann, Kastner and Becher are designed to reinforce the film's political and ideological message. The first title card informs the spectator that Eichmann was executed. This is followed by a second card revealing that Kastner was assassinated. It is the final title card that delivers the film's key attack: 'Kurt Andreas Becher, SS Standartenführer, lives today in Bremen, Heerstraße 180. Personal wealth: 150 million DM!'. With this revelation, Luderer seeks to collapse the boundaries between the fictionalized Becher on screen and the real-life Becher in the Federal Republic. An earlier version of the screenplay even opened with the claim that, 'Insofar as the names of the main characters are the same as those of living people, and if the events reported here reveal similarities with actual occurrences, it is not a matter of chance!'.²⁶ This was removed from the final film, although a modified version of this statement did appear in the film's programme notes.²⁷

The pre- and post-production insistence on the historical accuracy of the film was evidently designed to create the impression that *Lebende Ware* was a truthful portrayal of Kurt Becher's activities in Budapest. In reality, Luderer's film is a highly selective retelling of the past. While it is important to remain sensitive to the specificities of the filmic medium, it is clear that the film does not indulge in dramatic licence so much as ideological reframing. What is particularly interesting in the case of *Lebende Ware*, however, is less the fact that changes were made – which, after all, is hardly indicative of a specifically East German malaise – but rather what those changes were and what these in turn reveal about East German presentations of Jewish persecution in the 1960s. It would be easy to dismiss *Lebende Ware* as little more than an East German exercise in Cold War propaganda, but production files cast an alternative light on the treatment of Jewish persecution which renders the film far more complex than it first appears.

(Re)Defining Jewish Victimhood

The first ninety seconds of *Lebende Ware* set the stage for the presentation of the Jewish characters throughout the film. The film opens with shots of a menorah, the Bimah and the Torah. The camera then slowly pans to reveal rows of men, women and boys attending a service in a synagogue as religious music plays in the background. This opening visual introduction to the Jewish characters bears no relation to the film's plot. No subsequent reference is made to the service, nor is the scene used as an opportunity to foreground individual characters who later appear more prominently in the film. Rather, the Jewish characters are presented as a homogenous group, undifferentiated and defined purely by religious affiliation. In so doing, the scene announces the film's overwhelming drive towards visual simplification and narrative reductivism.

Initially, Luderer does successfully convey the precarious position of the central Jewish character, Ferenc Chorin. At the start of the film, Becher summons Chorin to the villa to present him with an ultimatum: either Chorin signs an agreement which transfers the rights of his factory to Becher (who claims to be representing the SS, but is actually seeking to increase his own personal wealth) and in return he will receive exit visas for his family, or Becher will arrange for the immediate deportation of Chorin and his family to Auschwitz. From the moment he appears on screen, Luderer emphasizes Chorin's vulnerability by demonstrating the reconfigured power relationship between Chorin and Becher. While Becher's behaviour towards Chorin may appear cordial – he allows him to remove his coat which bears the 'Judenstern', he permits the visibly nervous man to sit down and he offers Chorin a cigarette and alcohol – his actions merely serve to accentuate the unequal power relations between the two men. When Chorin takes off his overcoat, he reveals another 'Judenstern' which is sewn onto his jacket. He may be offered a seat, but this allows Becher to circle around him which in turn emphasizes his vulnerability. Finally, Chorin may be offered cigarettes, coffee and cognac, but Becher's seeming largesse conversely serves to reinforce the SS-Obersturmbannführer's position as host towards the actual owner of the villa. As Chorin considers Becher's ultimatum, he is placed in a room with boarded-up windows, creating a clear sense of the walls closing in on the Jewish factory owner (Figure 4.1).

Although the film may convincingly convey the ways in which Chorin considers himself trapped by the ultimatum of the SS-Obersturmbannführer visually, Luderer nonetheless fails to replicate this subtlety in the narrative presentation of the Jewish characters. When Becher first proposes the transfer of the Manfréd Weiss Steel and Metal Works from Chorin's family to himself and the SS, Chorin refuses and states that Jews are not allowed to sell property in Hungary. Becher then suggests adopting a *Treuhand* agreement, whereby control (rather than ownership) of the factory would be transferred to him. Chorin refuses again,

Figure 4.1. Images of entrapment convey how Chorin becomes a prisoner in his own home. © DEFA-Stiftung/Dieter Jaeger, Hans-Joachim Zillmer.

this time arguing that he needs more time to make such a momentous decision. Even when explicitly threatened with death, Chorin hesitates and repeatedly refuses to sign the agreement. This reticence is never explained in the film. When Chorin insists the deal is 'impossible! That is out of the question', the audience may be tempted to concur with Becher who reminds the Jewish factory owner, 'you do not seem to be fully clear about your situation'. Despite this, Chorin continues to hesitate, pleading, 'the decision which you are demanding of me is so serious ... so serious, that one cannot immediately, so quickly, well, say yes or no!'. With no context provided to explain why Chorin may be so reluctant to sign over the factory when exit visas for his entire family are at stake, the audience is led to the conclusion that Chorin's unwillingness to comply is motivated by his desire to keep hold of his wealth and his industrial empire at the expense of his family's safety. This reading was not entirely undesired.

Chorin continues to be associated with visual markers of high levels of personal wealth even after he has signed over the ownership of the factory to Becher. He is driven to an airfield where he and his family are to be flown to Switzerland. As the chauffeur-driven car makes its way to the airfield, Chorin and his wife are driven past hundreds of Jews who are walking on foot as part of a mass deportation. As they speed past the blurred faces of Jewish deportees, Chorin lowers his eyes and tightens his grip on his suitcase. The scene illustrates the inequity of the Jewish characters' fates. Whereas Chorin's suitcase is packed for a flight to a neutral foreign country and safety, the nameless characters outside carry their suitcases to a concentration camp. The only factor that alters the characters' fates is Chorin's greater personal wealth.

The association of Jewish characters with excess wealth haunts the film throughout. After Chorin reluctantly signs over the rights to the factory, the Zionist leader Rudolf Kastner is inspired by the precedent set by the factory owner and encourages members of the Jewish Community to exchange money and jewels for exit visas. Kastner negotiates a deal with Becher and thereafter the Jewish characters are almost exclusively seen within the context of exchanging jewels and money (Figure 4.2). Within the space of just a few days, they are able to access suitcases full of foreign currency from relatives abroad and hand over jewellery valued at over seven million Swiss Francs. This visual codification of Jewish characters trading in wealth, increasingly surrounded by jewels and able to access foreign capital without difficulty errs uncomfortably close to rehearsing the antisemitic rhetoric of the very period the filmmakers sought to critique.

Figure 4.2. The filmmakers' desire to present the events of Budapest in 1944 as a critique of the inequalities of capitalism leads to a visual and narrative overemphasis on the Jewish characters' wealth. © DEFA-Stiftung/Dieter Jaeger, Hans-Joachim Zillmer.

The emphasis on the Jewish characters' wealth was not unintentional and is indicative of the ideological lens through which the film frames Jewish persecution. Although unquestionably clumsy in its execution, it is clear that the filmmakers tried to instil their examination of Jewish persecution with a critique of capitalism. The film shows how the perpetrators are motivated by the desire to increase their wealth and the victims are the product of wealth inequalities. These inequalities are crystallized in the character of Mahlmann. Mahlmann may play an instrumental role in facilitating the agreement between Chorin and Becher, but he becomes a victim of both the National Socialist regime and of economic inequalities. Ultimately, Mahlmann's fate is sealed when Becher fears the notary has revealed his money-making scheme to his rival, Eichmann, and orders his deportation to Auschwitz. However, Mahlmann's safety could have been secured by this point had Kastner or Chorin added his name to the list of Jews to receive a visa to leave Hungary for a neutral foreign country. In this way, the film presents Mahlmann's fate as the direct consequence of his inability to buy his freedom. The impact of antisemitism as a primary or even a secondary factor in understanding the perpetrators' actions remains entirely unexplored.

'Are We Morally Qualified to Do This?'

DEFA and the filmmakers were aware of the risks of incorporating Jewish victims within a Marxist-Leninist interpretation of National Socialist persecution and there were ongoing concerns about the presentation of the Jewish characters throughout the film's production. In their initial presentation of the material, Kaul and Jupé described their desire to depict 'the tensions that exist within the Jewish population' whereby 'the bourgeois elements, in particular those who as Zionists, are intellectual slaves of Jewish imperialism'. In spite of this explicit political framework, Kaul nonetheless worried that a discriminatory depiction of the victims could 'shift the weight . . . too much to the anti-Jewish side'.[28] Kaul was not alone in his concerns. Handwritten notes on the back of the film's pre-release evaluation indicate that the head of HV Film appears to have anticipated the question, 'Attitude and differentiation of the Jews. Are we morally qualified to do this?'.[29] Concerns about the implications of differentiating between Jewish victims continued even after the film was approved. When discussing the GDR's submission for the Karlovy Vary Film Festival in 1966, *Lebende Ware* was rejected as a possible choice by the Ministry for Culture precisely because 'it would be politically erroneous if we were to choose a film as the German contribution for an international festival which deals with differentiations among the Hungarian Jewish population'.[30]

Behind-the-scenes discussions between the filmmakers should not detract from the reductive depiction of the Jewish characters and the instrumentalization of their persecution in the film. But what these comments do reveal is an ongoing concern about a tension running throughout the film, namely the difference between what is depicted (Jewish victimhood) and how it is depicted (capitalist exploitation). Concerns were raised about the implications of the explicit political-economic interpretative framework, but the centrality of Jewish persecution was not questioned. It could be argued that the impact of the film's interpretative framework shapes the presentation of Jewish victimhood to such an extent that, to all intents and purposes, *Lebende Ware* does not address the National Socialist persecution of Jews. To do so, however, would be to dismiss the significance of this dominant mode of engagement with the National Socialist past in the 1960s in East German film. Moreover, the clear shortcomings of the film should not negate what the film does reveal. Firstly, *Lebende Ware* demonstrates the ability of East German filmmakers to discuss Jewish persecution without recourse to an antifascist narrative, even in the aftermath of the Eleventh Plenum. Secondly, behind the scenes discussions reveal the extent to which DEFA was willing to defend the place of Jews as victims of National Socialism, even when this placed them in direct conflict with their production partners.

Lebende Ware was envisaged as an East German and Hungarian co-production.[31] In the early stages of the film's development, the head of the KAG Heinrich Greif, Klaus Wischnewski, sent a copy of the screenplay to his counterpart at Hungarofilm, István Dósai. Dósai then forwarded it to a Hungarian historian for his assessment.[32] In July 1965, Dósai informed the East German production company of their findings. Dósai reported that the historian had concluded that the screenplay contained numerous historical inaccuracies and deemed that 'the authors of the screenplay have relied not so much on sources furnished with academic, critical apparatus as on secondary sources and memoirs'.[33] The criticism that a DEFA film distorted fact was all the more damning given it was issued by an East German ally. However, as the letter continues, it becomes clear that the criticisms were also a pretext for other objections. The historian (and by implication, the Hungarian studio) objected to the suggestion that 'the 19 March 1944 signified a tragedy only for the Hungarian Jews', arguing that 'we do not even find a small reference to what this violent German step meant for the whole country'. The concerns of the Hungarian studio resided far less in the historical accuracy of the characters, but rather in the decision to depict Jews as the sole victims of National Socialist persecution.

Although we must again be wary not to adopt a relativist position and overlook fundamental shortcomings in the film by virtue of greater failings demonstrated elsewhere, contrasting the Hungarian response to the screenplay with that of DEFA does serve as a revealing point of comparison. In spite of the evaluation by the Hungarian studio, the East German production company continued to defend not only the credentials of the filmmakers, but also the centrality of the Jewish persecution to the film's plot. In the production leader's subsequent five-page defence of the film to Dósai, Wischnewski conceded that while certain facts had been 'contracted and simplified' for reasons of length, this never came 'at the price of truth'. He continued that while 'the events in Budapest after the 19 March 1944 can be viewed and organized from quite a number of different aspects', their interest ultimately resided in 'the character of Kurt A Becher and his connection with the fate of the Hungarian Jews'.[34] Here Wischnewski refuses to recast the roles of victim and perpetrator. Had the filmmakers, the production company or DEFA sought a reason to reduce or even remove the presence of Jewish victimhood in the film, the Hungarian letter would have provided an ideal pretext to do so. Yet no such changes were made.

It did not go unnoticed by the East German filmmakers that the actual source of the Hungarian dissatisfaction with the screenplay resided in the film's emphasis on Jewish persecution. Evidently angered by the criticism levelled against him, Kaul attacked the Hungarian letter by insisting that:

> the Hungarians clearly found any objection proper for preventing the production of the film. Comrade Wischnewski and Herr Luderer concurred that the Hungarians had openly said that if the film had only related to the theft perpetrated against the Weiss Concern and the fact that the Nazis plundered Hungary economically, the film would have been of interest to them. The . . . liquidation of the Hungarian Jews is manifestly an allegorical theme for them, especially since they also pointed out in the letter that the occupation of Hungary by the National Socialists was a national misfortune for the whole of Hungary, which was not made sufficiently apparent in the film.[35]

Kaul's response once again challenges any notion that the reductive depiction of Jews in *Lebende Ware* can be attributed to an unwillingness by the East German film studio to explore Jewish persecution. Jewish persecution may be instrumentalized by the East German filmmakers, but the implication of Kaul's letter is that this is not 'an allegorical theme', but rather a subject in its own right. Of course, the screenwriter's defence of the film is by no means a ringing endorsement of its attitude toward Jewish victimhood. After all, ascribing the persecution of the Jewish characters to political-economic factors perpetrated by military and political elites ensures little space is afforded to the exploration of wider societal antisemitism in Germany or Hungary.

A Miscast Villain

No character in any of DEFA's Holocaust films better exemplifies the instrumentalization of Jewish persecution than the figure of Kurt Andreas Becher. Illustrating how in the GDR 'the genocide of the Jews was interpreted as a by-product of rampant profiteering', Becher was an ideal target for East German political and ideological attacks given that during the war he undoubtedly sought to exploit his position as a senior member of the SS for personal financial gain.[36] Becher both epitomized the relationship between fascism and capitalism in the past and also served as an ideal case study for inculpating the Federal Republic in the present. At the time of the film's release, Becher was one of the Federal Republic's most successful and richest businessmen. In fact, Becher was such a perfect villain that, upon release, reviews of the film frequently failed to differentiate between the cinematic Becher and the real Becher, with some reviewers barely even mentioning the film at all.[37]

Becher may have been an ideal target, but he is also a perfect cinematic villain. From the moment he appears in the film, Becher dominates the screen. Our first introduction to Becher is a sixteen-second medium close-up of his face and the film revels in the uninterrupted image of Becher, the epitome of the National Socialist perpetrator. This sustained focus on Becher continues to the end of the film. The film's closing title cards announce the fates of Eichmann and Kastner for ten seconds each, while Becher's fate is presented on screen for eighteen seconds. Indeed, the film's fascination with Becher is so pronounced that the filmmakers actually risk glamorizing the SS-Obersturmbannführer. As much as the real-life Becher corresponds to an archetypal 'capitalist-fascist' villain, the filmic Becher also fulfils the genre conventions of an antihero: he is a charismatic character who drives the action, outwits his nemesis, seduces a beautiful woman and, at the end of the film, escapes from the advancing enemy.

The discord between how Becher was intended to be portrayed and how he is played by the actor Horst Schulze is particularly surprising given that Schulze was only cast in the role after the first-choice actor was replaced on account of his 'undesirable' presentation of the SS-Obersturmbannführer. The actor was informed that his contract was to be terminated with immediate effect because there were doubts as to whether 'placing you in the role of this character would be right, in regard to type and temperament, vibrancy and impact'. Expanding upon this casting decision, Klaus Wischnewski added:

> Becher was – and must be – the eternally supremely confident, resilient businessman who, responding to the opportunity of the moment, is for a time leader of the SS. Your Becher would invert that relationship; he would become the SS leader who, likewise responding to the opportunity of the moment, does business. The director knows following the work carried out so far that this fundamental relationship is non-reversible. The whole effect of the film – which is based on this character – would be inverted and channelled into a wrong direction.[38]

The need to reinforce the desired political reading of Becher may well explain the explicit positioning of him as a villain in the film's marketing and in the press. Reviews described him as a 'devil in human form',[39] a 'professional fascist'[40] and 'the economic miracle's most miraculous child'.[41] To dispel any lingering doubts, a widely circulated interview with Schulze saw the actor posit, 'when I reflected on how this man had well and truly done what I was acting here, then his present respectable existence appeared inconceivable to me'.[42]

Interestingly, the film offers a second villain alongside Becher (and Eichmann): Rudolf Kastner. We first encounter Kastner in a room with representatives from Budapest's Jewish community. In the subsequent meeting, Adolf Eichmann instructs the group to form a Jewish Council. After he learns of Becher's scheme, Kastner persuades the other members of the Jewish Council to agree to Becher's 'deal' and to exchange money and jewels for exit visas. Kastner abuses his position by ensuring places are reserved on the list for exit visas for his friends and family while refusing to assist poorer Jews such as Mahlmann who cannot afford to pay. At the end of the film, Kastner flees Budapest with Becher as the Red Army approaches. His fate is announced in the final scenes of the film alongside that of Becher and Eichmann.

Unsurprisingly, the actions of the real life Kastner were far more complicated than the film allows. Kastner is most frequently presented as a compromised figure credited with having saved the lives of hundreds, if not thousands, of Jews but who, in so doing, worked with Eichmann and Becher.[43] It is true that Becher conducted negotiations with Kastner to provide exit visas for Hungarian Jews in exchange for money and goods. It is also true that Kastner secured the safe transit of a number of his friends and family. However, the filmmakers of *Lebende Ware* do not simply depict Kastner as corrupt; they also suggest he is, at least in part, as morally culpable as Becher. As Soviet troops approach Budapest in the film's final scenes, Becher discusses his actions with Kastner, who justifies his complicity with the SS-Obersturmbannführer by arguing, 'What I did happened with the intention of rescuing the Jewish people, of helping them!'. However, in a surprising shift in moral tone, the filmmakers make Becher the voice of condemnation. He reminds Kastner and the audience that, 'you have abused your position and brought all your relatives over the border – and the others have paid for it!'. Becher then delivers his final blow by stating, 'Dear Kastner, we are now sitting in the same rowing boat and it is starting to rock'. Becher's subtle modulation of the collective 'we' suddenly comes to signify not the Germans nor the SS, but a Zionist leader and a 'capitalist fascist' businessman.

Kastner's compromised moral status is conveyed in the film's final scene. As the car carrying Kastner and Becher creeps across Budapest, Kastner is cocooned from the crowds of Jews around him who are also fleeing the city. The car may afford him protection from the crowd, but it also imprisons him with the National Socialist (Figure 4.3).

Figure 4.3. The final scene suggests Kastner will be judged for his actions with Becher. © DEFA-Stiftung/Dieter Jaeger, Hans-Joachim Zillmer.

All that is visible through the car's rear window are the eyes of the fleeing Jews who appear to be casting judgement on the man an Israeli judge would later describe as having 'sold his soul to the devil'. In fact, this final scene may well have been intended as a premonition of Kastner's postwar fate: in 1957 he was assassinated beside his car by the right-wing militia group Lehi. The inclusion of Kastner's fate in the final title card concludes the film's criticism of the Jewish leader: he is positioned between the 'million-fold Jewish murderer' Eichmann and the 'multi-millionaire' Becher.[44] Meanwhile, no mention is made of the lives he helped save. Nor, it must be stressed, is any reference made to the 440,000 Hungarian Jews who were deported to the camps. Instead, the condemnation of the film's perpetrators takes priority over any commemoration of the victims.

Lebende Ware is clearly a product of its time through the explicit instrumentalization of Jewish persecution in pursuit of attacks against the Federal Republic. However, dismissing the film as an unproblematic reflection of dominant narratives neglects the significance of its subject matter. In a period of heightened cultural-political tensions when filmmakers and DEFA were wary of transgressing any notions of thematic permissibility, it is clear that Jewish persecution remained an acceptable theme. *Lebende Ware* might not have been commercially or critically successful at home or abroad, but the centrality of the Jewish victims in the film reminds us that the parameters of representation in the GDR did not exclude Jewish persecution, even during the most heated political and cultural times of the Eleventh Plenum.

Lebende Ware demonstrates once again that films depicting Jewish persecution were permissible in the GDR, even during so-called cultural 'freezes'. However, such is the film's preoccupation with the figure of the perpetrator, Jewish victimhood fades into the background. In this way, the film arguably renders the Jewish characters double victims of both the National Socialist regime and of the politics of memory propagated in the film. Moreover, the frequent reduction of Jews to passive victims means that presentations of Jewish characters often verge worryingly close to resurrecting National Socialist tropes. We must, therefore, ask whether a film that actively seeks to attribute the persecution of Jews to capitalism rather than antisemitism actually addresses the persecution of Jews as such or whether it ultimately rejects the specificity of their victimhood to the point that the characters are stripped of their Jewish identity. This exemplifies a perennial problem for the film historian. To what extent should archival documents, a text-based source, inform or even modify our reading of an audio-visual medium? The depiction of the Jewish characters in *Lebende Ware* is unquestionably reductive and the imposition of an overt political framework ultimately subsumes religious persecution within a critique of capitalism. This must inform our final reading of the film, but it should not allow us to overlook the significance of the film's singular focus on Jewish victimhood. Even during a period of heightened cultural political tensions, DEFA was still able to release a film that was far from a straightforward endorsement of two decades of state-endorsed memory.

Notes

1. Attendance figures for *Lebende Ware* are cited in: DEFA, 'Besucher- und Einspielergebnisse: Stichtag 8.12.66 = 13. Wochen'.
2. Compare this to *Der Fall Gleiwitz* (786,205), *Professor Mamlock* (720,620), *Nackt unter Wölfen* (586,414), *Die Abenteuer des Werner Holt* (1,812,476) and *Ich war neunzehn* (1,688,094). Berghahn, 'Liars and Traitors', 28.
3. *Neue Zeit*, 'Geschäfte mit der Angst'.
4. Sobe, 'Premiere in Babelsberg'.
5. Rümmler, 'Ein neuer DEFA-Film: *Lebende Ware*'.
6. Gruppe Heinrich Greif, 'Einschätzung der Gruppe zu dem Drehbuch *Lebende Ware*'.
7. Acker-Thies, 'Letter from Acker-Thies to Wolfgang Heinz'.
8. Hannjo Hasse, Peter Herden, Heinz-Dieter Knaup, Jürgen Frohriep, Otto Mellies and Thomas Weisgerber were all considered for the role of Becher. DEFA also approached the West German actor Hannes Messemer who also refused the role. Hasse was subsequently cast as Eichmann. DEFA, 'Besetzungsliste *Lebende Ware*'.
9. DEFA, 'Einschätzung zu dem Film *Lebende Ware*'.
10. DEFA, 'Handwritten Notes. Department for Film Production/Außenhandel/Progress'.
11. DEFA, 'Besucher- und Einspielergebnisse: Stichtag 8.12.66 = 13. Wochen'.
12. The decision not to hold the film's premiere at one of the GDR's designated premiere cinemas is all the more striking given that *Lebende Ware* was filmed in Totalvision

which required specialized projectors available in the aforementioned cinemas. Totalvision was an East German anamorphic lens analogous to CinemaScope. By developing its own lens, DEFA avoided paying licencing fees to the American patent holders. Heiduschke, *East German Cinema*, 97.
13. For more on the real-life Kurt Becher see Braham, *The Politics of Genocide*, 107–10 and Löb, *Dealing with Satan*, 231–41.
14. Rudolf Kastner's name is frequently spelt Rudolf Kasztner or Rezső Kasztner. This book uses the spelling adopted by DEFA and the filmmakers of *Lebende Ware*, namely Rudolf Kastner.
15. For more on the *Fernsehpitaval*, see Fischer, 'Historische Justizdramen: Der Fernseh-Pitaval des DDR-Fernsehens'.
16. Friedrich Karl Kaul was recognisable to East German audiences for both his legal work and as a media figure. He was the co-plaintiff at the 1963 Auschwitz Trials in Frankfurt and at the Düsseldorf Treblinka Trials in 1970 where he represented East German victims. During the pre-production of *Lebende Ware*, Kaul was regularly commuting between Berlin and Frankfurt to appear in court. Kaul was also a well-known media figure in the GDR. From 1947 onwards, he appeared in the printed press, on the radio and on television where he provided answers to the public's legal questions. As a media figure, however, Kaul was perhaps best known for his role in the *Fernsehpitaval* series in which he delivered political monologues and epilogues which established both the historical context and factual authenticity of the story. For more on Kaul, see Fischer, 'Historische Justizdramen'.
17. *Neue Zeit*, 'Im Netz politischer Intrigen'.
18. *Leipziger Volkszeitung*, '*Lebende Ware*'.
19. Gustmann, '*Lebende Ware*. Aktuelle Vergangenheit'.
20. For example, the documentary films *Ein Tagebuch für Anne Frank* (1958), *Aktion J* (1961) and *Der lachende Mann – Bekenntnisse eines Mordes* (*The Laughing Man*, 1966) and the feature films *Zwischenfall in Benderath* (1956), *Der Prozess wird vertagt* (1958), *Jetzt und in der Stunde meines Todes* (*Now and in the Hour of my Death*, 1963) and *Chronik eines Mordes* (*Chronicle of a Murder*, 1965). See also Schieber, *Tangenten*, 41–65.
21. For example, the *Fernsehpitaval* (1958–78) and *Dr Schlüter* (1965). For more on the depiction of the Holocaust in East German television, see Schieber, *Tangenten*, 66–94.
22. For example, *Alles beim Alten* (1959), *Der Schoss ist fruchtbar noch* (1960) and *Aussage unter Eid* (1964). For an excellent study into the Holocaust in radio plays, see Gerlof, *Tonspuren*.
23. The *Braunbuch* listed West Germans who occupied key positions of political, social or economic power and who had previously occupied positions of influence in the Third Reich. Nationale Front des Demokratischen Deutschland, *Braunbuch. Kriegs- und Naziverbrecher in der Bundesrepublik: Staat, Wirtschaft, Armee, Verwaltung, Justiz, Wissenschaft*, 8.
24. Kaul and Jupé, '*Lebende Ware*. Scenario'.
25. No Author. '*Lebende Ware*'.
26. Kaul and Jupé, '*Lebende Ware*. Scenario'.
27. The programme notes read: 'The plot of this film is not invented. The similarity of the main characters with persons alive and dead is by no means a coincidence; the names are – with individual exceptions – authentic'. Progress Film, '*Lebende Ware*'.
28. Kaul, 'Stoffexposé für einen Film mit dem vorläufigen Arbeitstitel *Lebende Ware*'.
29. DEFA, 'Handwritten Notes: Department for Film Production/Außenhandel/Progress'.
30. The Ministry for Culture actually selected Frank Beyer's *Spur der Steine* as the GDR's entry. The film would be banned in the aftermath of the Eleventh Plenum. Maaß and

Brasch, 'Letter from Wilfried Maaß and Horst Brasch to Kurt Hager', reprinted in Schenk, *Regie: Frank Beyer*, 108–9.
31. In the event, the only contribution of the Hungarian production partners to the final film was the inclusion of outdoor sequences shot in Budapest.
32. Dósai, 'Letter from István Dósai, General Director of Hungarofilm, to the KAG Heinrich Greif'.
33. Ibid.
34. This line is underlined in the original. Wischnewski, 'Letter from Klaus Wischnewski to István Dósai, General Director of Hungarofilm'.
35. Kaul, 'Gedächtnis-Protokoll über die Besprechung betreffend den Film mit dem Arbeitstitel *Lebende Ware* am 22. August 1965'.
36. Niven, 'Remembering Nazi-Antisemitism in the GDR', 205.
37. *Lausitzer Rundschau*, 'Ein Verbrecher wird angeklagt'; *Die Union*, 'Ein erregendes Dokument'; Penser, '*Lebende Ware*'; *Sächsisches Tageblatt*, 'Ein Leben kostete 1000 Dollar'.
38. Wischnewski, 'Letter from Klaus Wischnewski'.
39. *Die Union*, 'Ein erregendes Dokument'.
40. *Märkische Volksstimme*, 'Die Millionen des Kurt Andreas Becher'.
41. *Sächsische Neueste Nachrichten*, 'Blick auf die Leinwand: *Lebende Ware*'.
42. Progress Film, 'Progress-Presse-Informationen: *Lebende Ware*. Ein DEFA-Totalvisionsfilm der Gruppe Heinrich Greif'.
43. A particular source of controversy was the affidavit Kastner provided for Becher in conjunction with this denazification trial in which he wrote, 'there can be no doubt that Becher was one of the very few SS-leaders who had the courage to take a stand against the programme of extermination of the Jews and who tried to save human lives'. Reprinted in Löb, *Dealing with Satan*, 230.
44. Keller, '*Lebende Ware*'.

Chapter 5

'IN BABELSBERG, NOTHING NEW'

Gottfried Kolditz's *Das Tal der sieben Monde*

If the adaptation of a popular television series into a feature-length film failed to draw popular appeal or critical praise for *Lebende Ware*, then the decision to employ tried and tested genre conventions fared little better for the director of *Das Tal der sieben Monde* (1967). Film critics looked to Gottfried Kolditz's film to relaunch East German cinema after the fallout from the Eleventh Plenum.[1] Yet far from offering a new direction, *Das Tal der sieben Monde* was criticized in the press for its 'profound artistic weaknesses',[2] 'unrealistic dialogue'[3] and unconvincing performances.[4] As one reviewer for *Der Neue Weg* concluded, 'in Babelsberg nothing (better: still nothing?) new'.[5] The film fared little better with audiences: internal studio documents reveal that Kolditz's film was seen by just 208,854 people in its first three months of release.[6] Not even DEFA greeted the film with any great degree of enthusiasm and chose to hold the film's premiere in the distinctly unglamorous location of Dresden's Friedrich Engels Military Academy.

Das Tal der sieben Monde is set in 1944 in an unnamed valley in Poland where the German occupiers are overseeing the construction of a railway line intended to facilitate the transport of lead ore from the valley for use in the German armament industry.[7] Polish partisans plot to sabotage the railway line and are assisted in their efforts by Ulrich Banz, a German antifascist who has been in exile in the Soviet Union. Banz befriends the young railway worker, Rudek, a *Volksdeutscher* (ethnic German) who lives in the local village. Rudek is in love with a villager, Martyna, a Jewish Pole whose father has been deported to Auschwitz.[8] Through his contact with Banz, Rudek becomes increasingly aware of the need to resist the German occupiers. Here we find one of several similarities with Konrad Wolf's *Sterne*, both in the depiction of a relationship between a Jewish and non-Jewish character and, crucially, in the underlying reason for the male protagonist's decision to resist. Like Wolf's protagonist Walter, Rudek's decision to act against the German occupiers is ultimately driven by a personal motivation rather than by ideological conviction. One night, Martyna reveals to Rudek that she was raped by the German foreman of the railway construction site, Sanitter, shortly after her father was deported to Auschwitz. Upon this revelation, Rudek resolves to avenge Martyna. Meanwhile, Martyna learns that her father has managed to escape from Auschwitz and is being hidden by the local partisans. One night, she attempts to visit him, but she is followed by Sanitter, who attempts to sexually assault her. She escapes and Rudek becomes resolute in his desire to seek justice for Martyna. Banz attempts to persuade Rudek to abandon his 'private war' and join the partisan resistance. Rudek agrees to help the partisans secure ammunition but refuses to abandon his determination to kill Sanitter. He confronts the foreman and a shootout ensues during which Sanitter is killed. This action inadvertently instigates the partisans' sabotage of the railway line. Banz is killed during the action and another partisan is gravely wounded. Rudek carries the wounded man to safety and, the following day, Rudek, Martyna and the injured partisan flee the valley. The film closes with Rudek and the others being welcomed by the waiting partisans and his act of heroism finally allows him to be inducted into the antifascist communion.

DEFA may have been seeking to win back audiences following the political and cultural turmoil of the Eleventh Plenum, but it is questionable whether *Das Tal der sieben Monde* ever had the potential to shift popular and critical perceptions about the steady decline in quality of DEFA films. At the time, Kolditz was best known for his adaptation of fairy tales, the two lead actors were still studying at film school and at just seventy-three minutes long and with a budget of 987,300 Marks, *Das Tal der sieben Monde* was certainly a production with modest ambitions. In spite of its poor commercial and critical reception, however, Kolditz's film remains a key case study for understanding the filmic engagements with the Holocaust in the GDR. *Das Tal der sieben Monde* reflects the impact of the Eleventh Plenum on East German filmmaking and the manifold challenges facing DEFA at the end of the 1960s. The rise in television ownership placed the studio and its filmmakers under considerable pressure to win back audiences to the cinema. This challenge was made all the more difficult by the ongoing impact of the Eleventh Plenum. While the New Wave movements in Czechoslovakia and France pioneered new narrative and aesthetic approaches to filmmaking, East German filmmakers were severely restricted by the recent events of the Eleventh Plenum. The state's public criticism of formalist influences in the arts in the 1950s had already signalled that any narrative or aesthetic experimentations would not be tolerated. Indeed, filmmakers' tentative steps towards greater experimentation had been explicitly criticized during the Plenum and had led to accusations of subversive intent.

With the scope for innovation severely restricted, DEFA turned to popular genres in an attempt to attract audiences. *Das Tal der sieben Monde* strongly reflects this trend, not least through its celebration of the socialist realist hero. In its criticisms of formalism, the SED argued that artists were placing more importance on the formal aspects of a work of art than the subject matter. By contrast, Socialist Realism was celebrated for its optimistic presentation of a society 'moving forward in a positive way toward[s] a just and prosperous society' which, as Stephen Brockmann has argued, was accompanied by a positive hero designed to be both familiar to audiences and a model character to be emulated by audiences.[9] The figure of Banz in *Das Tal der sieben Monde* who, as the accompanying publicity material was at pains to point out, was based on the real-life antifascist resister Rudolf Gyptner,[10] certainly exemplifies the socialist realist hero whose life is 'patterned to show the forward movement of history in an allegorical representation of one stage in history's dialectical progress'.[11] Alongside these celebrations of antifascist resistance, Kolditz – who has been described as 'ostensibly the master of the DEFA genre picture' – draws on two further genres: the romance of two star-crossed lovers and the *Indianerfilm* or 'red western'.[12]

The desire to position the film as a genre-driven popular antifascist conversion narrative has important ramifications for the treatment of Jewish persecution. On the one hand, Jewish persecution appears to be integral to the film. The plot revolves around the 'mixed relationship' between a Jewish and non-Jewish character, the central female protagonist is Jewish, the deportation of her father to Auschwitz – and his subsequent escape from the camp – are critical events in the plot and Martyna's revelation to Rudek that she was the victim of sexual assault committed by a National Socialist German is the decisive moment that ultimately compels Rudek to resist the German occupiers. However, despite the film's setting in German-occupied Poland and the apparent prominence afforded to Jewish characters in the plot, the film's engagement with Jewish persecution is repeatedly obscured through the use of genre conventions that subsume the distinctiveness of the Jewish characters' identity and, most troublingly, the specificities of their persecution.

It would be easy to conclude that this circumventive engagement with antisemitism was symptomatic of a reluctance to engage with Jewish persecution in East German film, especially in the aftermath of the Eleventh Plenum and during a cultural 'freeze' when cultural political tensions inhibited the choice of material and a palpable unease surrounded the inclusion of potentially contentious subject matter. However, closer examination reveals a far more complex picture that brings to the fore surprising findings about what studio and party officials did and did not consider to be controversial topics. In this way, *Das Tal der sieben Monde* demonstrates both the limitations of East German cinema in the 1960s and also the possibilities that remained in spite of the climate of cultural orthodoxy.

Circumnavigating Victimhood

There is no doubt that Martyna is a victim in *Das Tal der sieben Monde*. The reasons for her victimhood, however, are far less clear. Kolditz's film is underpinned by an unresolved tension that derives from the film's attempt to use Jewish persecution as a narrative device while failing to engage in any commensurate causal interrogation into National Socialist or societal antisemitism. Martyna's vulnerability and her father's deportation to Auschwitz may be central to the plot, but the film repeatedly struggles to elevate the status of Jewish characters beyond that of a dramatic device. *Das Tal der sieben Monde* is blighted by weak characterization throughout and this unquestionably contributes to the superficial depiction of the two Jewish characters as well. Nonetheless, the elliptical depiction of the father and Martyna is compounded by the simultaneous lack of interest in the specificities of Jewish persecution and the concurrent instrumentalization of their persecution for dramatic and political expediency.

There are no other Jewish figures in the film other than Martyna and her father, and we learn little about either character. The father is one of the least developed characters in the film. He plays little part in the plot beyond establishing the pretext for Martyna's own persecution and, such is his superficial presence, he is only ever named in the film and in the production files as 'Martyna's Father'. What is particularly striking about the film's marginal interest in him is the fact that his experience constitutes one of the most significant episodes in the plot. We learn at the start of the film that Martyna's father has been deported to Auschwitz after he was denounced. It is later revealed that he subsequently escaped from the concentration camp during a prisoner uprising. Neither the details of the events leading up to his deportation nor the escape itself are explored. Instead, the father's imprisonment and escape become a platform for the celebration of antifascist solidarity as the partisans keep him hidden in the village. While the film may utilize the effects of antisemitic persecution (namely the deportation of Martyna's father) as a dramatic device that leads to an act of sexual assault committed against Martyna, it seems reluctant to investigate the causes of this: the Polish population remains remarkably blind to the effects of antisemitism. Polish villagers are never shown as *Mitläufer* ('fellow travellers'), let alone as collaborators or perpetrators.

It could be argued that the clear references to the father's Jewish identity and his deportation to Auschwitz mean that his status as a victim of National Socialist persecution is perfectly evident, even if any wider discussion of these episodes is conspicuously absent in the film. This point notwithstanding, however, it is hard to account for the marked lack of engagement with Martyna's Jewish identity. The sole danger Martyna faces stems from her identity as a young woman and it is this gendered identity that defines her victimhood in the film. There is no attempt to link Martyna's vulnerability to her specific identity as a Jewish woman in German-occupied Poland. The consequence of the realignment of Martyna's victimhood whereby she is rendered a victim of a sexual attack and not of antisemitism is compounded by the failure to afford any space to acknowledge, and certainly not to expand upon, the impact of the attack on the young woman. Although the film implies an ongoing trauma, little effort is made to explore this beyond demonstrating its transformative effect on Rudek. After the second assault by Sanitter, no further reference is made to either Martyna's Jewish identity or to her father. Instead, the film's focus shifts to the impact of the revelation on Rudek, which in turn serves as an opportunity to discuss the international solidarity of the antifascist resistance.

It is right to criticize both the realignment of Martyna's victimhood from a victim of antisemitic prejudice to the victim of a sexual attack and the superficiality with which her assault is then discussed. At the same time, the inclusion of two sequences dealing with sexual assault in the aftermath of the Eleventh Plenum is certainly surprising. Depictions of sex and violence had been heavily criticized by officials at the Eleventh Plenum who insisted that such subjects ultimately served as a pretext for social conflict and demonstrated a 'disregard for dialectical development'.[13] The thematic context of Das Tal der sieben Monde is clearly different from the contemporary focus of the Eleventh Plenum films. Yet the fact remains that during one of the most politically and culturally conservative periods in East German film production, we find two clear references to the sexual assault of a Jewish Polish woman. As Bill Niven has discussed, depictions of wartime rape were not taboo in East German culture, but they certainly took place within tightly controlled parameters which often circumnavigated the subject through 'silence, rumour and uncertainty'.[14] This is not to say that rape was depicted as a crime without perpetrators, but depictions circulated within clear political and ideological parameters. The inherent decency of the 'ordinary soldier' was preserved, while acts of sexual violence were projected onto the political and military elites. Meanwhile, reflections on the trauma experienced by the woman were conspicuously absent.

In this point we find a clear application to Das Tal der sieben Monde. The figure of the perpetrator is quickly externalized. The two attacks – the off-screen rape and the on-screen assault – are committed by a readily identifiable figure who has already been marked as morally and ideologically distinct from all other characters (Figure 5.1). As soon as Martyna reveals the details of the attack to Rudek, her victimhood becomes little more than a plot device for the facilitation of a heroic antifascist conversion. Despite the cultural conservatism of the late 1960s and the connotative potential of the subject matter, there is no evidence that the scenes were considered controversial. There is no reference to either of the two sequences in the initial evaluation of the screenplay by the KAG Roter Kreis from April 1966 or in response to the film's treatment from February 1966, both of which include the attacks. Neither the production company nor the studio considered it necessary to single the scenes out for special comment. On the contrary, the rape is explicitly mentioned in the film's promotional materials and a still from the second attack even featured in the film's press book.[15]

It is not just the timing of the film's release which makes the inclusion of rape sequences so surprising. The consequences of depicting rape in a film set during the Second World War were potentially explosive. The GDR's founding myth of antifascist resistance and international solidarity may have been powerful enough to allow for the development of

Figure 5.1. Martyna's attack is all the more shocking given the political and cultural 'freeze' shaping East German filmmaking in the late 1960s. © DEFA-Stiftung/Herbert Kroiss, Erich Krüllke. Source: Filmmuseum Potsdam.

a widespread collective amnesia about East Germans' passive or active complicity with the National Socialist regime, but it certainly could not efface the trauma suffered by German women. It is highly likely that the rape sequences in *Das Tal der sieben Monde* point to a wider myopia among East German cultural officials who either did not – or chose not to – realize that recasting the perpetrator and victim of rape would not preclude domestic audiences associating the sequences with acts of trauma in recent German history. Just two decades after the end of the Second World War, it is inconceivable that audiences would not have individual or collective memories about the traumas of the rape of German women by the Red Army.

An Early Indianerfilm?

The most surprising use of genre in *Das Tal der sieben Monde* is the employment of tropes from the Indianerfilm, a specifically East German reimagining of the western. Between 1965 and 1983, DEFA produced seventeen such films. The Indianerfilm fused the visual conventions of the western with 'an enlightening and educative purpose' to create what Gerd Gemünden has termed 'politically correct entertainment'.[16] Interestingly, there are a number of parallels between the conventions of the Indianerfilm and *Das Tal der sieben Monde*. The ideological premise of the Indianerfilm was to 'articulate an outspoken critique of ... colonialism and racism' and one need not look far to see the parallels between the sympathetically portrayed Native Americans and their 'heroic chief' in their struggle against 'greedy white settlers, treaty-breaking Army colonels, corrupt sheriffs, imperialist oil magnates and despicable plantation owners' and the antifascist communists who resist the expansionist actions of the capitalist National Socialist oppressors in the valley.[17]

The KAG most closely involved in the production of the Indianerfilm was Roter Kreis, the same production company behind *Das Tal der sieben Monde*, and Gottfried Kolditz would subsequently become one of the key directors of the Indianerfilm. We must be mindful of categorising *Das Tal der sieben Monde* as an example of a red western: Kolditz and the KAG Roter Kreis only released their first East German Indianerfilm, *Spur des Falken* (*Trail of the Falcon*), in 1968 – one year after the release of *Das Tal der sieben Monde*. But this does not mean that we should dismiss the parallels as simply fortuitous. Although the red western only became an established genre after the release of *Das Tal der sieben Monde*, the western was already establishing itself as a popular genre on both sides of the Wall. Following the Eleventh Plenum, DEFA was faced with a challenge which the studio's former head dramaturge, Klaus Wischnewski, termed the 'squaring of the circle'.[18] Increased state scrutiny meant that films had to conform to the new strict parameters of representation. Such control and doubt fostered a climate of distinct orthodoxy which only served to distance audiences further. However, at the same time, DEFA was being called upon to produce films that appealed to audiences at home and abroad. The Indianerfilm offered a partial solution to this problem: while they had a limited appeal abroad, Indianerfilme were hugely successful domestically. They offered what Evan Torner has described as the intertwining of entertainment with ideological allegory: audiences could draw upon 'an assemblage of state-approved, moralistic and consumption-driven alibis' for viewing the film, while state officials could be assured of the underlying ideological messages at the heart of the plot.[19] Approaching *Das Tal der sieben Monde* through the lens of an Indianerfilm allows us to consider how the ideologically desirable critique of colonization and occupation serves as a metaphor for National Socialist persecution and as a means of broadening the film's popular appeal in the aftermath of the Eleventh Plenum.

While the infusion of a strong message of socialist internationalism and antifascist unity was certainly a new addition to the western, the Indianerfilm left 'the genre's semantics mostly intact'.[20] In keeping with the traditions of the Indianerfilm, the protagonists in *Das Tal der sieben Monde* are associated with symbolically charged spaces. The film's hero Rudek is introduced as being in harmony with nature. He easily traverses the rocky terrain and uneven ground of the valley and at the end of the film he is able to flee the National Socialist attack because of his superior ability to navigate his way through the valley. Rudek also embodies the core values of the western's principled hero: he is a good worker, always acts honourably and, perhaps most significantly, is 'free from racial and religious prejudice'.[21] The colonial powers in *Das Tal der sieben Monde* are represented by Sanitter who is played by Hannjo Hasse. Described by *Der Neue Film* as 'DEFA's number one villain', Hasse also played the Hauptmann in *Sterne* and, just five months earlier, had appeared as Adolf Eichmann in *Lebende Ware*.[22] Spatially, Sanitter is overwhelmingly associated with the railway construction site in a clearing in the forest. Whereas Rudek aspires to integrate into the community, Sanitter is a destructive presence who seeks to plunder it. This once natural space has been taken over by the colonial invader, who seeks to expand his (or rather, the National Socialists') geographical and economic influence over the natural landscape through the building of the railway line.

In the Indianerfilm, the Native Americans were designed to represent victims of 'capitalist expansion' through 'unequal trade, theft and deceit to wilful starvation, random murder and organized genocide' and parallels can be found between the cowboys of the Indianerfilm and the depiction of Sanitter who, as a 'capitalist fascist' oppressor, exploits his victims economically and sexually.[23] In this way, Sanitter's plundering of the valley's natural resources and his sexual attack against Martyna come to represent the trauma of invasion and occupation. In keeping with the tradition of the western, the violation of the female's body serves as the pretext for the western's shootout. When Rudek arrives at the railway construction site to avenge Martyna, he and Sanitter engage in hand-to-hand combat (Figure 5.2). When Sanitter seeks unfair advantage by throwing dirt in Rudek's eyes, the young hero reaches for his gun in self-defence and fatally wounds the foreman. The partisans arrive to help Rudek escape capture. Just as the Indianerfilm sought

Figure 5.2. The use of set pieces from the Indianerfilm underpins scenes of confrontation and revenge in *Das Tal der sieben Monde*. © DEFA-Stiftung/ Herbert Kroiss, Erich Krüllke. Source: Filmmuseum Potsdam.

to glorify the collective struggles of the Native Americans against the occupiers, the image of the Polish partisans rallying behind Rudek represents a coming together of the anti-imperialist forces as a celebration of antifascist solidarity.

Semantically, the Indianerfilm may have drawn heavily from the globally recognizable genre of the western, but its underlying ideological message often situated the films as distinctly domestic products. Underpinning the Indianerfilm was an attack against colonialism and the West, criticisms that implicitly transcended the eighteenth and nineteenth-century setting to encompass modern-day society. It is clear that DEFA also sought to position the film as a contemporaneous political attack on the Federal Republic and the significance of frontiers takes on an additional meaning in the highly politicized context of the mid-1960s. In the film's 'Ideological Statement', *Das Tal der sieben Monde* is framed as a 'compelling argument against the objections to the Oder-Neiße peace border' by the Federal Republic and as a means of arousing 'anger and indignation against the imperialist forces, which, in the pursuit of their anti-humanist aims, ruthlessly put the peace between the nations at risk'.[24] Although there is no explicit reference to the Federal Republic in the film, the filmmakers evidently envisaged audiences would associate the invasion and exploitation of Polish lands by German occupiers with the contemporary Federal Republic.

The incorporation of familiar and popular genre tropes from the western reveals how filmmakers sought to appeal to audiences at the end of the 1960s in the aftermath of the Eleventh Plenum. It could be argued that the recourse to genre allowed Kolditz to embed potentially more controversial aspects – above all, the Jewish identity of the film's principal victim – in the plot. But while the model of the Indianerfilm offered 'politically correct entertainment' through its ideological critique, it also served to efface the specificities of the film's setting. *Das Tal der sieben Monde* subsumes the specificities of antisemitism in favour of a universal story of good and evil in which the triumphalism of the ending is predicated on the male hero's antifascist victory. There is little space in this presentation for Martyna's victimhood and certainly not for her Jewish identity.

Revisiting DEFA's Star-Crossed Lovers

The final genre that informs *Das Tal der sieben Monde* is the romance of star-crossed lovers.[25] The villagers' prejudice towards the relationship between Martyna, a Jewish Pole, and Rudek, a Volksdeutscher, threatens the couple's happiness from the outset. Here, the filmmakers encounter a problem. *Das Tal der sieben Monde* was envisaged as a celebration of Polish–German solidarity. However, in order for the plot to revolve around the difficulties of Rudek and Martyna's relationship, the filmmakers need to account for the external forces driving the couple apart. The solution found has important consequences for the film's engagement with Jewish persecution. When accounting for the villagers' hostility towards the couple's relationship, Martyna's Jewish identity plays no role whatsoever in their prejudice. Instead, the source of the division is reconfigured along national lines whereby Rudek's German identity is rendered the more problematic of the two 'undesirable' identities: the villagers shun Martyna for having a German lover, not because she is Jewish.

This recalibration was far from straightforward. The danger of 'German' becoming synonymous with 'National Socialist' was clearly a concern from the outset for the production company. A pre-release report by the KAG Roter Kreis stressed the 'immeasurable relevance' of the film precisely because of its great contribution 'to the clarification of the political, moral and class content of the concept of "German" as we understand it'.[26] As Manuela Gerlof has argued, in East German official discourse, the Second World War was presented as a political and ideological rather than national conflict in which the 'capitalist fascists' oppressed the working classes as part of their expansionist war. This meant that in contrast to dominant modes of remembrance in the Federal Republic, the GDR did not foster a *'Tätergedächtnis'* ('perpetrator memory'), but rather memory discourse was shaped by a victor–victim framework according to which 'German National Socialism' was described as 'Hitler fascism' (*'Hitlerfaschismus'*).[27] In *Das Tal der sieben Monde*, the film's strong antifascist narrative emphasizes ideological rather than national affiliation and, in so doing, allows for a redemptive repositioning: only communism can allow Germans to transcend the nationally determined designation of persecutor and enter into an international fellowship as victor of fascism.

In *Das Tal der sieben Monde*, the filmmakers therefore needed to reposition Rudek so that he is not condemned alongside Sanitter on the basis of his national identity, but rather is saved through his collaboration with the communist partisans. The film frames this ideological awakening as a challenge for Rudek who must prove his loyalty to the partisans in order to transcend their preconceptions of Germans as National Socialists. The young antifascist Josef introduces the quest Rudek must undertake by reflecting, 'There are fascists and there are decent Germans. We do not know what he is yet'. This journey is not without its own challenges. The younger partisans may support Rudek in his journey to antifascism, but his transformation is only complete when the older partisan, Skutella, finally accepts him into the international antifascist community. In an early exchange between Rudek, Martyna and Skutella, the older partisan reacts with visible anger when he learns that Rudek is German. Although Rudek insists 'you don't have to lump me together with them!', Skutella admonishes Martyna for associating with the Volksdeutscher telling her, 'Your father is in Auschwitz. Babka is hanging in Wjatki. And you are looking for a German for yourself and you have no secrets from one another?'. At this point, Skutella drops the cigarette Rudek had just given him. The scene recalls Konrad Wolf's *Sterne*. Just as the Jewish man's silent refusal to accept a cigarette from Walter in *Sterne* marks the beginning of the German soldier's realization that he must act against his fellow Germans' murderous actions, Rudek's exchange with Skutella sets in motion the young man's realization that he should question his own passivity. Later in the film, Skutella again refuses a cigarette from Rudek. When Rudek challenges Skutella about his hostile behaviour, he replies, 'You are a German, aren't you?', to which Rudek indignantly replies 'I am not Hitler!'. Through the refusal of the cigarette, Skutella stresses the need for Rudek to define himself through actions rather than words: 'You lay rails so Hitler can continue to wage war and so he can kill even more Poles in Auschwitz. Does he need to kill Martyna too for you to understand what is going on?'. Only when the protagonist has proved he is a 'decent German' by avenging Martyna and killing Sanitter does Skutella accept Rudek's offer of a cigarette (Figure 5.3).

Whereas Rudek must prove his antifascist credentials over the course of the film, Ulrich Banz offers the audience an unproblematic presentation of the 'decent German'. Banz, a German who, we are told, emigrated to the Soviet Union to join the antifascist struggle in exile, enters the film by parachuting into occupied Poland to join the local communist resistance. Narratively, Banz is intended to be a character who would 'underlin[e] the necessity of the common fight against the common enemy' and thereby celebrate the need for 'proletarian internationalism'.[28] However, Banz's presence ultimately exercises a disruptive force over the film. The dynamic, physically imposing and exemplary

Figure 5.3. Rudek's attempts to prove he is a 'decent German' are contingent upon his acceptance into the antifascist communion. © DEFA-Stiftung/Herbert Kroiss, Erich Krüllke. Source: Filmmuseum Potsdam.

antifascist casts an overbearing shadow over Rudek. While Rudek appears to have a somewhat listless and purposeless existence in the village, save for his work on the railway, Banz enters with a clear mission and ideological purpose which culminates in his selfless sacrifice in death to protect his comrades during the uprising. The audience's emotional sympathies lie with the star-crossed lovers, yet in comparison to the conviction and actions of Banz, Rudek appears passive and even emasculated.

Banz may be the more compelling presence on screen, but within the context of 1960s DEFA films, he appears oddly out of step with contemporaneous antifascist heroes. Antifascist films in the 1950s were characterized by idealized socialist heroes who either functioned as exemplary father figures (such as Kurt Maetzig's *Ernst Thälmann* films) or who offered an antifascist conversion by proxy for audiences (for instance *Rotation*). Through this victim–victor binary, such productions established clear distance between the GDR and the National Socialist state. By the late 1960s, however, the image of the antifascist protagonist was changing. Symptomatic of wider international trends, the coming of age of a new generation of filmmakers and audiences ushered in a new, more critical stance towards the 'conventionalized heroism of the antifascist canon'.[29] This was most evident in the evolving image of the protagonists whereby physically, emotionally and increasingly ideologically broken males formed the narrative focus for the antifascist film. Banz is an anachronistic hero. He may embody a certainty of purpose reminiscent of first-generation antifascist screen heroes, but the actor Karlheinz Liefers was making his film debut and brings none of the professional or extra-filmic gravitas to the role audiences had come to expect from the seasoned antifascist hero. Nor does he reflect the vulnerability of the 1960s young hero of contemporaneous antifascist films such as *Ich war neunzehn*. If *Das Tal der sieben Monde* was conceived as an opportunity to showcase new talent following the Eleventh Plenum, Kolditz's film ultimately serves to expose the studio's ongoing dependency on tried and tested aesthetic models and rehearsed narratives – and the limited life expectancy of such an approach.

The poor popular and critical reception of *Das Tal der sieben Monde* should not divert our attention away from a very important and yet simple point: the film was deemed unremarkable by the state and studio. It is precisely because the film did not encounter any political difficulties that it makes such a fascinating case study. Firstly, the inclusion of two instances of sexual assault appear to have caused no controversy among studio or state officials. Secondly, despite the cultural and political freeze engulfing the GDR, it was still possible to include Jewish victims as principal targets of National Socialist persecution. Here, however, we reach the core conundrum raised by the film. Is *Das Tal der sieben Monde* significant for its incorporation of Jewish characters in spite of its use of genre conventions that unquestionably detract from the film's National Socialist context or does the reliance on genre tropes serve to subsume the themes of Jewish persecution to such an extent that *Das Tal der sieben Monde* cannot truly be considered a film that engages with the Holocaust? The answer lies in-between these two options. The use of genre conventions does impact the already reduced interest in Jewish persecution and, as a work of filmic art, we must conclude that the film offers little engagement with the fate of the Jewish characters. However, the film retains its importance because of the context of its production and release. It is true that Jewish persecution is subsumed within the film's heavy use of genre conventions, which in turn serve to foreground the heroism of the antifascist resistance. However, the film also appears to have been approved at every stage of production without any discussion of the inclusion of Jewish characters. *Das Tal der sieben Monde* may not be a memorable example of aesthetic innovation, but in its status as the first film to be completed after the fallout from the Eleventh Plenum, the film serves as an important reminder that even during the most politically and culturally fraught period in East German film history, Jewish persecution was both a permissible and present theme.

Notes

1. Schirrmeister, 'Wird besonders die Jugend fesseln'.
2. *Neue Zeit*, 'Bedrohte Liebe in schwerer Zeit'.
3. *Mitteldeutsche Neueste Nachrichten*, 'Der neue Film'.
4. Lücke, 'Konflikte ohne Tiefe'.
5. *Der Neue Weg*, 'Gültiges und Routiniertes'.
6. DEFA, 'Besucher- und Einspielergebnisse: Stichtag 11.05.66 = 13. Wochen'.
7. Kolditz's film is based on the 1963 novel of the same name by Harry Thürk.
8. Martyna tells Rudek that her father was deported from Pszczyna, a town just twenty kilometres from Auschwitz. However, the film does not appear to be set here.
9. Brockmann, *A Critical History of German Film*, 220.
10. Progress Film, '*Das Tal der sieben Monde*'.
11. Clark, *The Soviet Novel*, 46.
12. Torner, 'Gottfried Kolditz (1922–1982)', 18.
13. Honecker, 'Aus dem Bericht des Politbüros an die 11. Tagung des ZK'. See also Feinstein, *The Triumph of the Ordinary*, 173.
14. Niven, *Representations of Flight and Expulsion in East German Prose Works*, 41.

15. The synopsis in the press notes from DEFA-Außenhandel includes the lines: 'On her way, she is attacked by Sanitter, Rudek's foreman at the building site. He had caused the arrest of her father. She narrowly escapes from being raped'. DEFA-Außenhandel, *'Das Tal der sieben Monde'*.
16. Gemünden, 'Between Karl May and Karl Marx', 400.
17. Ibid., 399.
18. Wischnewski, 'Träumer und gewöhnliche Leute', 216.
19. Torner, 'The DEFA Indianerfilme', 228.
20. Fisher, 'A Late Genre Fade', 180.
21. Roman, *From Daytime to Primetime: The History of American Television Programs*, 25.
22. *Der Neue Weg*, 'Gültiges und Routiniertes'.
23. Gemünden, 'Between Karl May and Karl Marx', 400.
24. Hartwig, 'Ideologische Begründung. *Das Tal der sieben Monde'*.
25. This was reflected in taglines for the film that included, 'The story of a dangerous love' and 'The testing of lovers from Alwernia'. Progress Film, *'Das Tal der sieben Monde*: Film Werbung'.
26. Gruppe Roter Kreis, 'Einschätzung. *Das Tal der sieben Monde'*.
27. Gerlof, *Tonspuren*, 31–2.
28. Kolditz, 'Sonne und Schatten über den Beskiden', *Schweriner Volkszeitung*.
29. Silberman, *German Cinema: Texts in Context*, 158.

PART IV

1971–80

In the early 1970s, the GDR made a series of breakthroughs on the world stage. This progress arguably owed as much to the election of Willy Brandt as Chancellor of the Federal Republic in 1969 as it did the appointment of Erich Honecker as General Secretary of the SED in 1971. The election of Brandt, who had risen to political prominence as the mayor of West Berlin between 1957 and 1966, brought about a marked change in policy towards the GDR. Throughout the 1960s, Brandt and Egon Bahr – who had worked alongside Brandt as spokesperson for the Senate of Berlin – promoted a policy of 'Wandel durch Annäherung' ('change through rapprochement'). This policy of increased normalization between the Federal Republic and the GDR underpinned Brandt's attempt to improve formal relations with the GDR during his time in office and paved the way for the eventual mutual recognition of the two German states through the Basic Treaty of 1972. This, in turn, led to the international recognition of the GDR by the United Nations in 1973, by the Federal Republic's Western allies in 1973 and, perhaps most significantly for the SED, by the United States in 1974.

The external validation of the GDR ushered in a new sense of confidence at home. With the GDR now recognized as a country in its own right by the West, Honecker embarked on a period of demarcation from the Federal Republic. Instead of continuing to present the GDR as offering a political and economic model for all Germans, the state began to stress its own intrinsic East German identity. This policy of 'Abgrenzung' ('demarcation') was most visible in the symbolic renaming of several institutions from 'German' to 'of the GDR' in the early 1970s including the German Academy of Arts (to Academy of Arts of the GDR), the Association of German Journalists (to the Association of Journalists of the GDR), the German Writers' Association (to the Writers' Association of the GDR) and German Television which became Television of the GDR. This period of change also impacted domestic cultural politics. Many artists believed that the change of leadership from Ulbricht to Honecker would usher in a new level of cultural tolerance that many had been anticipating since the building of the Berlin Wall. Initially, their hopes appeared to be realized. Just two months after his appointment, Honecker announced that, as long as a strong socialist position was maintained, there could 'be no taboos in the field of arts and literature'.[1] This position was reiterated at the Sixth Plenum of the Central Committee of the SED in July 1972 by Central Committee member and cultural functionary Kurt Hager. Hager announced that 'no area of life, no sphere of human coexistence in our society, no stirring of life can be "unimportant" for art'. However, the notoriously hard-line functionary added a telling addendum: artists were expected to follow 'the rules of the game'.[2] This was to have important repercussions for artists in the second half of the decade.

Initially the SED's words appeared to be matched with actions. To all appearances, filmmakers were able to enjoy unprecedented levels of artistic freedom. Two previously banned films, Ralf Kirsten's *Der verlorene Engel* (banned 1966) and Konrad Wolf's *Sonnensucher* (banned 1958), received theatrical releases in 1971 and 1972 respectively. It is with considerable irony, therefore, that at the very point at which the state was loosening its grip on filmmakers, DEFA was facing a new crisis. Production output had dropped from between twenty and twenty-five feature films per year in the early 1960s to between fifteen and twenty films in the 1970s – a trend that both reflected, and was compounded by, the studio's ongoing financial problems.[3]

DEFA's already reduced output of films was further disadvantaged by their decidedly conservative nature following the Eleventh Plenum. This exacerbated the decline in ticket sales further as the public abandoned the cinema as its preferred source of entertainment in favour of television programming. It is no coincidence that the decrease in the average number of cinema visits between 1960 and 1970 from 13.8 to 5.4 visits per person[4] coincided with an increase in television ownership from roughly one million at the start of the 1960s to 4.8 million by 1972.[5] In the face of this new form of cultural and economic competition, the DEFA management opted to collaborate with the state-owned television studio, Deutscher Fernsehfunk (DFF). Not only did this lead to a wider dissemination of films for DEFA, but it also significantly reduced the studio's own production costs. As DEFA's most important client, DFF commissioned around thirty films each year which provided the film studio with an additional annual income of approximately 42 million Marks.[6] The relationship between DEFA and DFF has been described by Thomas Beutelschmidt as one of 'cooperation and competition'.[7] Although increasing levels of television ownership continued to impact DEFA's audience figures, the film studio was able to compensate for its loss of cinema revenues through a steady stream of income from television productions. In return, DFF was able to draw upon the highly trained personnel and technically superior resources of the film studio. This partnership of convenience produced some of the most celebrated East German productions of the 1970s including *Jakob der Lügner* (1974), *Die Leiden des jungen Werthers* (*The Sorrows of the Young Werther*, 1976) and *Die Verlobte* (*The Fiancée*, 1980).

Honecker's proclamation of a new era in East German cultural politics nonetheless proved to be short-lived. With hindsight, this should perhaps have come as little surprise since it was Honecker who had spearheaded the attack against filmmakers at the Eleventh Plenum. Fearing that artists had been given too much freedom, cultural officials quickly attempted to re-establish their control over the film industry. However, if the SED's aim was to reduce the purportedly 'subversive' impact of artists' critical voice in society, then the outcome was disastrous. In November 1976, the Biermann Affair irrevocably damaged the relationship between East German artists and the state. Wolf Biermann, who had moved to the GDR from the Federal Republic in May 1953, was a singer of *Lieder* (political songs and poems) and had long been an outspoken critic of the SED for its failure to uphold what he considered to be 'true' socialist ideals. As a result of his outspoken criticism of the party, Biermann was issued with a performance and publication ban. He nonetheless continued to perform for small, private gatherings and, much to the anger of the SED, his work was regularly smuggled out of the GDR and published in the Federal Republic. To the surprise of many, Biermann was granted permission to tour the Federal Republic in 1976. While performing on stage in Cologne in November 1976, Biermann once again criticized the SED leadership.[8] His comments were widely broadcast by the West German media which, it is important to remember, could also be received in much of the GDR. In response, the Central Committee announced that the singer was to be stripped of his East German citizenship with immediate effect on account of his 'gross violation of his civic duties'.[9]

The decision to strip Biermann of his citizenship provoked an unprecedented public outcry by East German artists. In an open letter of protest, twelve leading artists including Christa Wolf, Sarah Kirsch,

Jurek Becker and Volker Braun called upon the SED to revisit its decision. The following day, nearly one hundred artists added their names to the letter. Although the party leadership had anticipated moderate displeasure with its actions, the scale of the protest was entirely unexpected. In an attempt to quell the growing criticism, the SED cracked down on the dissenting artists, a number of whom were prohibited from working as a result. The artists' insurmountable disenchantment with the SED, coupled with the state's desire to rid the GDR of these prominent and vocal critics, resulted in several of DEFA's best-known figures both in front of and behind the camera emigrating on a semipermanent or permanent basis to the West.[10] In an attempt to regain control over the increasingly embarrassing mismanagement of the situation, Honecker appealed to artists as 'comrades in arms and allies in our collective work towards the advance of socialism and communism'.[11] Kurt Hager was less reconciliatory in his tone and accused the Federal Republic of seeking to 'unsettle the creative forces in the East German cultural sector' by creating 'a psychosis of fear and hopelessness', before proceeding to describe artists who had left the GDR as 'strangers to socialism' and individuals who had 'lost their way'.[12] If the Eleventh Plenum indelibly marked the future course of East German film production and direction behind the camera, then the Biermann Affair changed the face of the acting talent in front of it forever.

Symptoms of Change

Although the cultural thaw of the early 1970s was precipitated by the appointment of Honecker as First Secretary of the Central Committee, wider demographic shifts within and beyond the GDR's borders were also leading to a tentative redrawing of East German film's engagement with the Holocaust. As discussed in the previous chapter, the movement away from celebratory heroic narratives was already underway at the end of the 1960s. By the early 1970s, a new generation of filmmakers sought to engage with the legacies of fascism through different aesthetic and narrative forms. For the first time, East German filmmakers approached the National Socialist past through comedic modes in films such as *Meine Stunde Null* (*My Zero Hour*, 1970), *Am Ende der Welt* (*At the End of the World*, 1974) and *Jakob der Lügner* as well as through new themes and protagonists. *KLK an PTX – Die Rote Kapelle* (*KLK Calling PTZ – The Red Orchestra*, 1970), for example, explores resistance among the middle classes, a theme which had previously only been explored in the West. Meanwhile Ralf Kirsten's *Ich zwing dich zu leben* (*I'll Force*

You To Live, 1978) explores the appeal of the Hitler Youth and focuses on the attempts of a father to convince his son to leave the organization.

These generational shifts also impacted East German cinematic engagements with the Holocaust. This new generation of filmmakers understood that if films about the past were to appeal to younger postwar audiences, then the ways in which the past was presented also had to change. In a revealing interview with the East German weekly arts newspaper, *Sonntag*, the screenwriter of *Jakob der Lügner*, Jurek Becker, addressed questions of shifting generational engagements with the Holocaust. His reflection that, 'it is of little use making a film today that does not want to do anything other than tell people of 1975 how terrible life was then. The spectator can all too easily start to think, why are they telling me this, I already know it all' is indicative of Becker's belief in the need to engage audiences emotionally in victims' stories and fates. Becker elaborated, 'I have no emotional access to a mountain of corpses. Crimes which are committed against groups of people [*Völker*] must be broken down by art into crimes committed against individuals. My contemporaries need to be able to understand that this injustice was perpetrated not only on the insane number of six million, but on couples, on families, on individuals'.[13]

The importance of emotional above cerebral engagements with the National Socialist past underpins the most significant shift from the eyewitness generation to the postwar generation. This new generation of filmmakers and audiences had no direct experience of perpetration or victimhood in the Third Reich. This shift plays out in the films themselves and from the mid-1970s onwards we find that the call to resist is slowly replaced with the need to remember. These films are characterized by a move away from stable narratives of the past and exemplary heroes, a development that comes to the fore when we place *Die Bilder des Zeugen Schattmann* (1972) and *Jakob der Lügner* (1974) side-by-side. Visually and narratively, *Die Bilder des Zeugen Schattmann* offers a far more didactic presentation of the past that is underscored by a clear ideological message that frames the film. Whereas Jung-Alsen uses the framing device of a court trial at which the protagonist Frank Schattmann gives his testimony as a reliable and eloquent witness, Beyer's *Jakob der Lügner* is punctuated by dreams, memories and flights of fantasy during which memory is shown to be unreliable and pluralistic.

It would nonetheless be overly simplistic to view generational shifts as a caesura in East German filmic engagements with the Holocaust. Placing these two case studies side-by-side brings important shifts in the depiction of Jewish persecution to the fore, but it also reveals the complex ways the two films seek to negotiate dominant cinematic and commemorative modes of discussing Jewish victimhood beyond the established norms of the period. *Die Bilder des Zeugen Schattmann* may celebrate antifascist resistance, but it also offers one of the most visually shocking images of Jewish persecution in East German film. It was also the only German film ever to shoot on location at Auschwitz. On first viewing, *Jakob der Lügner* marks a clear break with the antifascist narratives of Jung-Alsen's film. As we shall see, the antifascist storyline was written out of *Jakob der Lügner* and the sole victims of National Socialist persecution are Jewish. However, the film's casting decisions complicate this reading. Furthermore, although Beyer's film does signal a move away from celebratory antifascist narratives, the marketing of the film domestically shows the limitations of the studio's and press' willingness and ability to accommodate such changes. The two case studies in this section thus demonstrate the ways in which East German Holocaust film not only reflect political and social developments in the GDR; they also exemplify how these films offer a unique space for the discussion of victims, National Socialist persecution and dominant frames of reference in the GDR both on- and off-screen.

Notes

1. Honecker, 'Zu aktuellen Fragen bei der Verwirklichung der Beschlüsse unseres VIII. Parteitages'.
2. Schittly, *Zwischen Regie und Regime*, 173.
3. Hake, *German National Cinema*, 141.
4. Feinstein, *The Triumph of the Ordinary*, 214.
5. Wischnewski, 'Träumer und gewöhnliche Leute', 223.
6. Berghahn, *Hollywood Behind the Wall*, 220.
7. Beutelschmidt, *Kooperation oder Konkurrenz?*.
8. The SED's decision to grant Biermann the opportunity to criticize the state by allowing him to tour in the West might appear odd. However, with the opening of the Stasi files in the early 1990s, it transpired that the party leadership had been discussing what measures to take should Biermann leave the GDR since 1973 and was awaiting an opportune moment to enact its plans. Biermann's concert tour in the Federal Republic provided such an opportunity.
9. *Neues Deutschland*, 'Biermann das Recht auf weiteren Aufenthalt in der DDR entzogen'.
10. For example, director Egon Günther, screenwriters Jurek Becker and Klaus Poche and actors Angelika Domröse, Jutta Hoffmann, Manfred Krug and Armin Mueller-Stahl. Allan and Sandford, *DEFA: East German Cinema, 1946–1992*, 15.
11. Cited in Rinke, *Images of Women in East German Cinema*, 47.
12. Cited in ibid., 46–7.
13. Voigt, 'Lust auf Leben'. In the interview, Becker largely discusses his novel rather than the film. However, given the interview was conducted in 1975, there is a clear overlap between the text and film.

Chapter 6

NEW ENCOUNTERS ON WELL-WORN PATHS

Kurt Jung-Alsen's *Die Bilder des Zeugen Schattmann*

The developments unfolding in East German society in the early 1970s were not only the result of the change of leadership in the GDR. The coming of age of the first postwar generation who had only experienced life in the Third Reich as children (if at all) brought questions of national identity to the fore. These questions were not only directed towards contemporary East German society and the extent to which the state could truly claim the 'Ankunft im Sozialismus' ('arrival in socialism'), they also anticipated an albeit tentative exploration of the hitherto unchallenged narratives and commemorative practices surrounding the National Socialist past. While there was no clear caesura separating first and second-generation narratives of the past, it is clear that in the early 1970s, the ways in which the National Socialist past was remembered and commemorated in the GDR were changing. The realignment of dominant frames of reference comes to the fore in Kurt Jung-Alsen's *Die Bilder des Zeugen Schattmann*. The film not only represents one of the final first-generation narratives of the National Socialist past, it also exemplifies the ensuing tension that resulted from first-generation narratives delivered to second-generation audiences.

Die Bilder des Zeugen Schattmann is based on the 1969 novel of the same name by Auschwitz survivor Peter Edel.[1] It is important to address from the outset that this case study is not a cinematic film, but rather a four-part television film that was first broadcast on East German television in May 1972. Although this point does differentiate *Die*

Bilder des Zeugen Schattmann from other films examined in this book, the inclusion of *Die Bilder des Zeugen Schattmann* in a study of East German Holocaust film is important for two key reasons. Firstly, the film embodies the generational shifts among filmmakers and audiences that shaped filmic engagements with the past in the 1970s. As this chapter demonstrates, *Die Bilder des Zeugen Schattmann* acknowledges the need to engage younger audiences who were not witnesses to the time period depicted, but in so doing, the film struggles to break free from the familiar narratives of resistance and engagement so frequently employed in films from 1950s and 1960s. Secondly, although *Die Bilder des Zeugen Schattmann* is a television film, it was almost entirely a DEFA production: Kurt Jung-Alsen was a prominent DEFA director, the actors were contracted to DEFA and the technical crew was employed by DEFA. This was by no means exceptional in the 1970s. According to Thomas Beutelschmidt, roughly fifty per cent of DEFA's output between 1959 and 1990 constituted co-productions with East German television, Deutscher Fernsehfunk (DFF).[2]

Die Bilder des Zeugen Schattmann uses the framing device of the 1964 trial of the West German civil servant Hans Globke who was convicted *in absentia* of crimes against humanity by the East German Supreme Court.[3] The film opens as the protagonist Frank Schattmann takes to the stand to testify. After his opening statement, the camera cuts to an extended flashback of Frank's life in Berlin in 1943. The main setting for Part One, 'Der Freitagabend' ('Friday Evening'), is the home of the former army doctor – and the uncle of Frank's wife, Esther – Dr Bernhard Marcus, who is celebrating Shabbat with his family and friends. At the start of the flashback, we discover more about the protagonist's background. Frank is 'half-Jewish' and as a young boy, he struggled to understand the ostracism faced by his father but not by his 'Aryan' mother. Over the course of the first part of the film, we learn about the persecution experienced by each of the Jewish characters through a series of flashbacks. As the members of the group reflect upon the discrimination they face in their daily lives, Frank becomes increasingly angry and berates them for their passivity. In contrast to the other members of the group, Frank resolves that he and Esther must act. Part Two, 'Der Entschluss' ('The Decision'), builds on Frank's will to action as he and his wife join the communist resistance. Their plans are interrupted when Frank is detained, initially not because of his communist affiliations, but rather on account of his Jewish identity. Here the film explores the Rosenstraße protest in which 'Aryan' wives publicly protested at the arrest of their Jewish husbands and children and demanded their release. Frank is subsequently released, only to be re-arrested upon his return home after he is denounced. Part Three, 'Die Wiederkehr' ('The Return'), draws on the familiar 1960s trope of the West German state as a hotbed for unreformed and unrepentant National Socialists. The film focuses on the fictional character of Herr Koberschulte, a West German civil servant, and his activities during the Third Reich when he was Frank's interrogator after his arrest. The final instalment, 'Die Vorladung' ('The Summons'), shows how Frank attempts to come to terms with the past by returning to Auschwitz years later to reflect on his experience and the fates of his friends and family.

On first viewing, *Die Bilder des Zeugen Schattmann* appears to rehearse familiar narratives from DEFA's 1960s Holocaust films. From the celebration of exemplary acts of communist solidarity and resistance to the explicit indictment of West German officials, *Die Bilder des Zeugen Schattmann* seems to break little new ground. However, in spite of these familiar narrative tropes, two points emerge which offer a new image of the Holocaust in East German film. Firstly, the film's protagonist Frank Schattmann is a Jewish character who joins communist comrades to engage in active resistance. He is not a passive victim whose primary (if not sole) purpose in the plot is to be saved; he is a figure who acts with conviction and agency. Secondly, *Die Bilder des Zeugen Schattmann* was the only East German production ever to receive permission to shoot on location in Auschwitz. While this in itself might appear an interesting, but ultimately minor production detail, it is highly significant for the film's treatment of its subject matter. The depiction of the former camp plays a key role in the film's call to remember and reflects the challenges of delivering this message to a new generation of East Germans. This chapter examines the ways in which *Die Bilder des Zeugen Schattmann* marks a key juncture in East German filmic engagements with the Holocaust through the gradual erosion of unambiguous heroic narratives in favour of a tentative questioning about how to remember a different generation's past.

Shaping Jewish Identities

Die Bilder des Zeugen Schattmann is shaped by a complex interweaving of Jewish and communist identities. Jewish persecution underpins the narrative. Production documents refer to the film's focus as the 'fate of Jews in Germany' and, although communist prisoners are subjected to torture under interrogation, far more screen time is dedicated to depictions of Jewish above communist persecution.[4] However, while the film does indeed portray Jewish victimhood visually, narratively it celebrates the antifascist resistance. As the example of *Professor Mamlock* highlights, bringing these two identities together was by no means unique within East German Holocaust film. In Wolf's 1961 film, this resulted in the separation of Communist and Jewish identities based on the active 'Fighter against Fascism' versus the passive 'Victim of Fascism'. The interaction of these two identities in *Die Bilder des Zeugen Schattmann* is more complex. Although Frank is persecuted on account of his Jewish identity and resists as a communist, this does not inevitably lead to the demotion of the former as a secondary identity. For the first time in an East German production, we are offered a Jewish protagonist whose victimhood *and* resistance drive the plot.

Our first introduction to Frank is in the film's framing device during the trial of Hans Globke in 1964. Frank is called to the stand to deliver his testimony and cites 'wearing the yellow star' as the event that had the greatest impact on his life. He then proceeds to detail the effects of antisemitic discrimination on his daily life, from being forced to leave school, to working in a forced labour factory and the impact of the ban against Jews using public transport. At this point, the film begins to introduce its antifascist resistance narrative. Frank obliquely asserts that he had no desire to continue to live in this way and consequently 'made a decision'. For the first time in his testimony, Frank becomes the active agent of the sentence. The screen fades to black and a flashback begins to reveal what this 'decision' was.

On first viewing, the extended flashback to 1943 appears to signal the divergence of Jewish and communist identities whereby Jewish identity is aligned with victimhood and passivity, and communist identity is aligned with resistance and action. From the outset, Frank is marked as a character who is ill at ease with the imposition of National Socialist constructions of Jewish identity. The flashback begins with a shot of Frank waiting outside a Siemens factory. His face is turned away from the camera, which has the effect of obscuring his identity while also foregrounding the 'Judenstern' pinned to his coat. We see the external marker of identity imposed on Frank before we see the individual who bears it. At the end of Part One, Frank tears off the 'Judensterne' from his and Esther's coats: Frank will wear the 'Judenstern' when he is forced to, but he will not internalize National Socialist projections of his identity. In Part Two, we discover that Frank has attached his 'Judenstern' to a pin which allows him to attach and detach it easily. What is particularly interesting about *Die Bilder des Zeugen Schattmann* is that the film does not adopt a similar symbolic attitude to its protagonist's Jewish identity for the rest of the film. It is clear that Frank does not identify religiously, culturally or politically with his Jewish friends and relatives, but this does not mean that Frank's Jewish identity becomes tangential to the plot. Rather, Jewish victimhood continues to play a crucial role, even after the introduction of the communist resistance storyline.

In Part One, Frank and Esther arrive at the house of Esther's uncle, Dr Bernhard Marcus, where they meet family and friends for the Shabbat meal. As the group is seated around the table, we discover the impact of National Socialist discrimination and societal antisemitism on each character. The extended sequence, which lasts over an hour and a half in total, provides a unique exploration of antisemitic persecution in East German film. No other film provides such an explicit picture of both the acts of antisemitism that punctuated the characters' daily lives nor demonstrates the impact of antisemitism on such a range of primary and secondary characters. The characters' experiences can be divided into two groups. The first group comprises characters who describe their loss of status or feelings of helplessness. Martha reveals that she carries a vial of Veronol and insists that Frank reveals to her 'when [she] must be ready' so she can take her life. Renate laments her loss of status from an opera singer to someone who packs rotting entrails in buckets for a living. Gerson reflects that he used to work as a general agent for leather goods and was an art collector, but now works at the municipal refuse services. The final and most shocking revelation of the evening comes from the former army medic Dr Marcus who announces he is to be deported the following day.

Whereas Martha, Renate and Dr Marcus all share what they have experienced with the assembled group, four characters – Dr Sonnenschein, Julius, Jakob Dankowitz and Dr Marcus' son Fritz – all relive their persecution through flashbacks that they do not discuss with the others. These traumas, which are shared with the audience but not with Frank, have an important modifying function in the film. To Frank, Sonnenschein appears to be unmoved by the discussions around him and is simply enjoying cake with friends against the backdrop of stories of ongoing persecution. As he eats, the film cuts to a flashback which begins with Sonnenschein resting in a scrap yard. We then see a man wearing a National Socialist pin towering above him. The man forces him to repeat his name not as Sonnenschein ('sunshine'), but as 'Schrottschwein' (literally 'scrap pig'). The action then cuts back to the present to show Sonnenschein finishing his cake. Similar strategies are used for

Julius, Jakob and Fritz. Fritz and Julius are harassed at their places of work and Jakob is forced to hide from the Gestapo who accuse him of spreading propaganda after his daughter writes to him from London.

These short flashbacks have two effects. Firstly, they serve to reveal the different and sustained ways in which both primary and secondary characters have experienced antisemitism in their everyday lives and the silent toll such experiences bear on them. Secondly, they complicate Frank's outbursts and accusations of passivity. Over the course of the dinner, Frank becomes visibly agitated. As the group members break off their discussion of life in the Third Reich, Frank interrupts and angrily asks, 'are we simply supposed to celebrate and eat cake? It's the same old long, trivial witness speeches and never once saying, "we must do this and that". We're just so small, aren't we? We can't do anything, just wait. What are you all waiting for then? For a miracle? For the Messiah?'. This is one of the few times in Part One when Frank uses the collective 'we'; overwhelmingly he criticizes the group through an externalizing 'you' (*ihr*). However, what Frank does not see – but what is visible to the audience – are the unspoken levels of discrimination and persecution experienced by all the characters. The other Jewish characters may appear passive and unwilling to act, but Frank's rush to judgement is revealed, at least in part, to be shortsighted as he remains ignorant of the true extent of the other characters' daily experiences.

This more sympathetic reading of the presentation of Jewish and communist identities nonetheless begins to break down when we consider how these episodes are framed within the film's broader class-based ideological framework. This is particularly apparent in an argument between Dr Marcus and Julius. In *Die Bilder des Zeugen Schattmann*, Dr Marcus assumes the mantle of DEFA's stereotype of the assimilated and culturally fluent Jewish German. As he prepares to present himself to the authorities for deportation, Dr Marcus reflects upon how, despite being a decorated veteran of the First World War, he has become an undesirable presence in Germany. At the same time, he continues to express hope in 'our fellow countrymen'. When Julius asks who these 'countrymen' are, Dr Marcus clarifies: 'the Germans. I haven't yet stopped counting myself among them. Despite everything'. He then urges Julius to understand their persecution as part of a wider 'misfortune' [*Unglück*], adding that they are not the only victims, but rather that 'millions of people are affected, and we are only a small part'. Julius responds by attacking Dr Marcus' 'Prussian' mentality and views that verge on those of 'an antisemite'. Frank's intervention at this point reveals the complexity of the film's intertwined presentation of victimhood, persecution and resistance. The film unquestionably reveals Julius' persecution to be driven by his Jewish identity, but Frank challenges the passivity of the former antique dealer and accuses Julius of choosing to bemoan the loss of antiques rather than deciding to act against the National Socialist forces responsible for his oppression.

As Dr Marcus and Julius reflect on Germany's shift of national, political and cultural values from those of Heinrich Heine to those of Heinrich Himmler, Frank's resolve to act becomes ever stronger. The arguments between the group members may reveal different attitudes towards Jewish persecution, but only Frank insists that they must engage in active resistance. By the end of Part One, he has fully distanced himself from the other Jewish characters. To reinforce this divide, Jung-Alsen distinguishes Frank visually from the group. After the Shabbat meal, the group prepares for prayer. As each character covers his or her head, Frank purposefully puts on his beret. This is the last shot of Frank as a constituent member of the group. As the collected friends and family members begin to pray, the camera pans around the room and Frank is deliberately positioned off-camera. By excluding Frank from demonstrative displays of Judaism, Jung-Alsen reinforces the effect of divorcing Frank from the other Jewish characters. From this point onwards, the film continually returns to shocking visual examples of Jewish persecution, including against Frank. Narratively, however, and as Frank's communist mentor Helmut Wall stresses in Part Two, Jewish persecution is framed as 'a class question and nothing else'.

Confronting Acts of Persecution

In *Die Bilder des Zeugen Schattmann*, there is a clear willingness to show the agents of the persecutory acts – who are exclusively German – and to acknowledge that antisemitic persecution was carried out not only by the Gestapo and the SS, but also by 'ordinary Germans' on the streets of Berlin. Two sequences in particular reveal the candour with which the film depicts acts of Jewish persecution on screen: the shooting of Dr Marcus and the arrival of Frank at Auschwitz. Visually, the two episodes are shocking for their willingness to confront the spectator with the actions and consequences of antisemitic persecution, but at the same time they also exemplify the film's inability to reconcile the causal reasons for the characters' persecution with how this is framed within the narrative more broadly.

In Part One, Jung-Alsen establishes Dr Marcus' pride as a patriotic German and his belief in the inherent decency of Germans and the country's institutions. The tragic consequences of these misplaced beliefs are exposed in the third instalment of the film. Dr Marcus and Dankowitz arrive at Theresienstadt in a deportation train. As Dankowitz helps Dr Marcus out of the waggon with his two bags, we see that the doctor has pinned an Iron Cross in First and Second Class to his coat above the 'Judenstern' he is forced to wear. An officer sees the medals and informs his superior who has been watching the new arrivals from a distance. The senior SS-Sturmführer, now holding a horsewhip, approaches the doctor in his car. He sarcastically greets the 'Herr General' and derisively enquires whether Dr Marcus stole the medals. Refusing to be mocked, Dr Marcus stands to attention and announces his military record to which the Sturmführer replies, 'and you wore them just for us? For your arrival in the Jewish paradise?'. In the background, increasingly unsettling music accentuates the overwhelming sense of unease. The officer sarcastically demands that the 'veteran of the Kaiser's army' be accorded the respect he deserves. He orders the gathered prisoners to cheer Dr Marcus and declares, 'I cannot expect the Herr General to march to the accommodation!'. He then walks down the line to look for a 'horse' and, upon seeing a woman dressed in an expensive fur coat, orders her to fall 'down on all fours, Rebekka!' Dr Marcus is dragged forward and ordered to sit on the woman who collapses under the weight of the doctor. As he tries to run away, Dr Marcus is shot down by a guard (Figure 6.1).

This four-and-a-half-minute sequence is possibly the most shocking example of Jewish persecution in East German film. From the moment Dr Marcus and Jakob arrive, the camera aligns the audience's view with that of the perpetrators. When the camera focuses on the face of the officer, the use of shot/reverse shot cuts back to the victims and acknowledges the direct effect of the officer's words and actions on Dr Marcus and the unnamed woman. Crucially, at the point at which Dr Marcus is shot, the camera adopts a point-of-view angle that shows the doctor's murder from the perspective of the guard who shoots him. There is no alternative heroic identificatory figure with whom the spectator can align him- or herself, nor is the spectator able to adopt the position of victim.

The murder of Dr Marcus is shocking for its direct brutality and striking for its unambiguous framing of the underpinning antisemitism behind the act. The depiction of Frank's persecution, however, is less clear cut and exposes the tension created by attempting to present Frank as a

Figure 6.1. The point-of-view shot forces the spectator to witness the murder of Dr Marcus from the perspective of the perpetrator. © Foundation Deutsches Rundfunkarchiv (DRA)/rbb media.

victim of antisemitism, while simultaneously reframing his persecution within a different ideological framework. Jung-Alsen repeatedly draws attention to the discrepancy between how Frank is viewed in the Third Reich and how he self-identifies. Frank is initially arrested on account of his actions with the communist resistance, but by this point he has already been detained because of his Jewish identity. Even when he is being interrogated by Koberschulte, it is clear that Frank is unable to escape how he is viewed by the National Socialist state – and thus the reasons for his persecution (Figure 6.2). The film continually reminds the audience that the reason the National Socialist state persecutes Frank is firstly because of his Jewish identity and secondly on account of his communist affiliations. When Frank arrives at Großbeeren, once again wearing the 'Judenstern', he is confronted by an officer. When asked 'What are you?', Frank flatly responds 'I am a Jew'. The officer repeats his question before striking Frank to the ground. As the officer kicks Frank, he shouts the question again and forces Frank to repeat a series of antisemitic labels. As Frank repeats the names '*Geltungsjude*' ('half-Jew'), 'criminal' and '*Saujude*' ('sow Jew'), he becomes increas-

Figure 6.2. A poster by the communist resistance is pinned to Frank's shirt, on top of which Koberschulte pins Frank's 'Judenstern'. © Foundation Deutsches Rundfunkarchiv (DRA)/rbb media.

ingly weak. Eventually, Frank lifts himself to his feet and shouts 'Communist. I am a Communist!'. Upon revealing his 'true' identity, Frank collapses and his body shuts down in an act of self-preservation. When he wakes up in the next scene, he is being tended to by a fellow communist prisoner who welcomes him as a member of the resistance.

The significance of the narrative insistence on communist resistance as a progressive identity that situates Frank within an international fellowship becomes clear in Part Four. A flashback to Frank's arrival at Auschwitz shows him and the other prisoners being herded through the camp gates and into a shower room. An SS officer orders all the Jewish prisoners to step forward. Frank is then summoned by the officer, who is holding a bar of soap. The camera zooms in to reveal the letters 'RIF' or as the officer remarks, 'Rein Judisches Fett' ('pure Jewish fat'), a reference to a rumour in the 1940s that bars of soap in camps were made from the fat from the corpses of Jewish prisoners.[5] The officer throws the bar of soap at Frank's head and orders the men to strip. The men are then forced to run outside into the snow where they are hosed down with cold water by a Kapo, which causes one prisoner to fall to the ground with exhaustion. In the scene, Frank's humiliation and suffering is associated solely with his Jewish identity, but when we next see Frank in the concentration camp, he is being tended to by a Polish communist in an act of international solidarity.

This sequence establishes the basis for a crucial exchange in the film's present-day storyline. Having returned to Auschwitz in 1964, Frank attempts to locate his former Polish comrade, Bolkowski. He visits Bolkowski's home where he meets a different prisoner with the same name. The man asks, 'Are you also former Auschwitzer? A German? Where from? The GDR?'. When Frank and his partner Andrea reveal their East German identity, they are welcomed wholeheartedly by the Polish man into his home. The three of them then visit Frédéric Chopin's house which, the film is at pains to show, is a site visited by nationalities from around the world. Frank and Andrea take their seat within this international community to listen to a piano recital. Having situated the two East Germans in the fellowship of the international community, the film cuts to the trial of Hans Globke, the National Socialist functionary and West German civil servant whose actions are condemned in front of the world's press. Only antifascism is shown to offer Germans an identity of international solidarity in the past and present. The film then returns to the courtroom setting and Frank concludes his testimony by affirming why he chose to speak: 'I have said all this . . . for the people who suffered with me, who helped me to battle through and to continue on my path in our country. I have testified for those who can no longer speak for themselves and for those who work for a world in which young people know no racial and national hatred'. In this way, Frank comes to personify the founding spirit of the GDR. This desired reading was not lost on reviewers at the time. Writing in *Der Morgen*, Christoph Funke concluded that Frank represented 'the millions of Jewish citizens who have been persecuted and murdered by fascism' and 'those amongst them who joined the communist-led antifascist resistance', as well as standing for 'the survivors who used the opportunity to build a socialist German state to ensure that a repeat of fascist crimes is impossible forever more'.[6]

Lines of Continuity

One of the strongest markers of the film's ties to first-generation engagements with the Holocaust on screen is the explicit instrumentalization of National Socialist persecution for political attacks against the

FRG in the present. Part Three juxtaposes the film's present-day setting of 1964 with the flashback sequences from 1943 depicting Dr Marcus' murder, Jakob Dankowitz's arrest and Frank's interrogation. The two sequences are brought together through the figure of Commissioner Koberschulte who, we discover, has subsequently forged a career as a successful civil servant in postwar Munich. Koberschulte is seated in a small Munich tavern at the same table as Dankowitz, who has travelled from England to visit Frank in East Berlin. After Koberschulte discovers that Dankowitz also lived in Berlin, he enquires why the man no longer plays the piano. Dankowitz shows Koberschulte his injured hand. 'An accident?', asks Koberschulte. 'That's what some people call it nowadays,' answers Dankowitz tersely.

This marks the start of a series of exchanges between the two men designed to expose how Koberschulte's euphemistic language is a means of avoiding more direct confrontations with Germany's past. When Koberschulte then asks how the injury happened, the film cuts to an extended flashback in which we witness Dr Marcus' murder at Theresienstadt. Koberschulte misinterprets Dankowitz's description of his experiences as a forced labourer and enquires how long he was held as a Soviet prisoner of war. When Dankowitz corrects him, Koberschulte appears unaffected by Dankowitz's announcement that he is Jewish. The former Gestapo officer claims that he had Jewish friends in school, but proudly proclaims that in the Federal Republic a person's background is of no consequence: 'a human being is a human being', he asserts. Koberschulte then boasts of the ways in which the Federal Republic both respects its Jewish citizens and allows them to 'forget' the past. When Koberschulte adds that he has hitherto had so few opportunities to speak to 'people of your type', Dankowitz curtly replies, 'that's what Hitler's Final Solution did'. Koberschulte then dismissively sighs, 'let's leave the past. No hard feelings'. The use of Koberschulte as a means of directly linking the crimes of the National Socialist past with the West German state of the present exemplifies the film's crude instrumentalization of the past as a means of attacking the Federal Republic in the present. Here the film breaks little new ground. What is surprising, however, is the two men's discussion of the GDR and specifically the Berlin Wall.

Die Bilder des Zeugen Schattmann is by no means a subversive film, but alongside the explicit condemnation of the Federal Republic, we find a surprising willingness to voice criticisms levelled against the GDR. Koberschulte and Dankowitz's conversation is intercut with flashbacks from 1943, the longest of which is the interrogation of Frank. It is clear that Frank's 'enhanced interrogation' is driven by his identity both as a Jew and as a Communist. Meanwhile, the audience is intended to view Koberschulte as a class enemy in the past and present, and he dismisses the Russians as a 'foreign, spiritually primitive mass' who must 'free the Zone'. Interestingly, when Dankowitz seeks clarification, it is he who refers to the GDR as 'East Germany', the geographical rather than political name that was acutely disliked by the SED. When Koberschulte asks Dankowitz whether he will visit his relative (Frank) in East Berlin and Dankowitz simply shrugs, Koberschulte interprets this as his reluctance to visit a city with 'a concentration camp wall around it'. Unmoved, Dankowitz calmly replies that 'inevitably, to a certain extent' he has 'a different concept of concentration camp walls' than Koberschulte. He continues, 'I often read about this "Wall", but I also always read about these comparisons with "concentration camp" and "ghetto"'. However, Dankowitz argues, these same people 'purport to have known nothing about ghettos and camps' during the Third Reich: 'As people were burnt to death in ghettos, as millions were driven into gas chambers – they didn't say a single word. They should have. But they took part in it themselves'. Yet now, he argues, these same people claim to be fully informed about what they are like. Here Dankowitz turns his attention to the present and tells Koberschulte that in the Federal Republic, 'a number of prominent people who remained silent in the past are only too willing to shout about this Wall', because on 'the other side of the Wall [the GDR], there are people in power who were brought to the scaffold when they didn't stay quiet about certain things'. At this point, the camera pans suddenly and the action cuts abruptly to a sequence in 1943 in which Frank is undergoing an interrogation by Koberschulte. The desired reading is evident: through the figure of Koberschulte, the film seeks to suture the Federal Republic in the present and the National Socialist state of the past. What is remarkable about the two characters' dialogue, however, is the willingness – and ability – to give voice to the highly sensitive issues of human rights and sovereignty in the GDR.

Returning to Auschwitz

Die Bilder des Zeugen Schattmann is the only East German film to be shot on location at Auschwitz (Figure 6.3). According to Elke Schieber, this was only possible thanks to the author of the film's source text, Peter Edel.[7] Edel's active engagement with the KdAW brought him into con-

Figure 6.3. Frank Schattmann and Andrea Wohlfahrt visit Auschwitz so that future generations can see the past through Frank's eyes. © Foundation Deutsches Rundfunkarchiv (DRA)/rbb media.

tact with the Polish Committee for Resistance Fighters and he was able to draw in these contacts to secure filming permission from officials at Auschwitz.[8]

In *Die Bilder des Zeugen Schattmann*, much of the present-day action in Part Four takes place in and around the Auschwitz memorial site. Frank returns with his girlfriend, Andrea Wohlfahrt, in preparation for delivering his witness statement at the Globke trial. As Frank takes Andrea through the camp complex, he recalls what he experienced during his imprisonment there and reflects on the fate of his family and friends. He guides her from the barbed wire fence, to the different buildings and barracks, and finally to the gas chambers. In the literary source material, Frank returns to Auschwitz with a former antifascist comrade, Ernst. The change is key to understanding not only Andrea's role in *Die Bilder des Zeugen Schattmann*, but also the film's aims more broadly. Frank returns with a character who has never been to Auschwitz and who has not heard his story before. As they walk through the grounds, Frank reflects, 'Make the incomprehensible comprehensible? The unfathomable fathomable? Who can do that? I have tried, time and again, to draw . . .

But what use are pictures?', to which Andrea replies, 'Letting others see with your eyes, I think'. Andrea's response announces her role as an indirect witness to the events. She becomes the dramatic device who gives occasion to Frank's narration and instigates the sharing of experiences between the witness generation and East German citizens.

In an interview included in the film's press notes, Jung-Alsen noted that *Die Bilder des Zeugen Schattmann* was aimed at 'the generation who no longer knows that period from their own experience. In the character of Andrea, th[e] young spectator is led through Auschwitz. [The spectator], like the young woman, learns to comprehend that there are two very different things: to know about Auschwitz and to experience Auschwitz'.[9] Here the film encounters a difficulty that is by no means unique to *Die Bilder des Zeugen Schattmann*. The absence of any wider framework means that the spectator becomes dependent on Frank's individual experience to instil the images with meaning. Jung-Alsen argued that the character of Andrea was designed to guide young spectators' engagement with the camp. How this deeper understanding is to be reached, however, remains unclear. Revisiting the concentration camp may be designed as a means of 'letting others see with [Frank's] eyes', but this is accompanied exclusively by the narrative of a first-generation victim. If Andrea is indeed designed to facilitate engagement with the past for new East German audiences, then the film seeks to achieve this by bequeathing rehearsed narratives to the next generation. *Die Bilder des Zeugen Schattmann* may break new ground visually, but it does so on a well-worn path.

The intertwining of Jewish and communist identities in *Die Bilder des Zeugen Schattmann* is complex. Jewish persecution is not relegated to a secondary concern in the film's celebration of active resistance. The film repeatedly returns to examples of the everyday persecution Jews experienced in Germany as well as in concentration camps. However, Jung-Alsen attempts to force a story of religious persecution within the interpretative parameters of class-based persecution. In order to transpose this interpretative framework onto a story which overwhelmingly features Jewish characters, *Die Bilder des Zeugen Schattmann* attempts to differentiate between working-class and bourgeois Jews. The film may repeatedly insist that 'the "racial question" can only be understood and solved as a "class question"', but the consequence of this is the erroneous condemnation of the majority of the Jewish characters on account of their (purported) passivity.[10]

Despite its reliance on class-based narratives, *Die Bilder des Zeugen Schattmann* nonetheless constitutes one of the most important East German Holocaust films. The ways in which the film forces the spectator to confront Jewish persecution visually are both surprising and shocking on account of their unflinching candour. *Die Bilder des Zeugen Schattmann* also once again demonstrates how East German film repeatedly created a space for alternative discussions about East German collective identity in the past and present. Although the film's explicit interpretative framework leaves little opportunity for alternative examinations of the causes of Jewish persecution, the narratively superfluous inclusion of the ways in which the Berlin Wall could be compared to the ghettoization of East Germans nonetheless remains remarkable. Ultimately, however, *Die Bilder des Zeugen Schattmann* is unable to overcome two core tensions. Firstly, the film gives unprecedented visibility to Jewish persecution, but it attempts to frame this within a class-based discourse. This results in a divergence between the visual and narrative presentations of Jewish persecution that the film is never able to reconcile. Secondly, the filmmakers demonstrate an acute awareness of the need to engage younger audiences, but they fail to acknowledge that it was not sufficient simply to cast younger actors in all too familiar roles: what was required was a new approach to different material.

Notes

1. For a detailed study on the production history of the film, see Schieber's *Die Bilder des Zeugen Schattmann: Recherche zu einem Fernsehfilm*.
2. Beutelschmidt, 'No TV without Film', 125.
3. Hans Globke had worked in the Office for Jewish Affairs during the Third Reich and co-authored several legal commentaries and regulations stripping Jews of civil liberties. In 1953, he was appointed Secretary of State of the West German Federal Chancellery where he served as a close aide to Chancellor Konrad Adenauer.
4. Teichmann, 'Letter from Production Leader Teichmann to Benz'.
5. RIF actually stood for *Reichsstelle für industrielle Fettversorgung* (Reich Centre for Industrial Fat Provisioning).
6. Funke, 'Frank und Esther – ein Menschenschicksal'.
7. Schieber, 'Spuren der Erinnerung', 72.
8. Correspondence between Peter Edel and the KdAW and the Working Group of Former Prisoners of Auschwitz Concentration Camp (Arbeitsgruppe der ehemaligen Häftlinge des Konzentrationslagers Auschwitz) shows that Edel regularly participated in commemorative events in the GDR and at Auschwitz. He was also invited to several events by the Jewish Community of Greater Berlin. See files 744 and 747 in Edel's papers at the Akademie der Künste.
9. Fernsehdienst der DDR, *'Die Bilder des Zeugen Schattmann'*.
10. Interestingly, this synopsis was translated into English, French and Spanish, indicating that the film was envisaged for a Western export market. Fernsehen der DDR, 'New Films of GDR Television Import–Export'.

Chapter 7

RETURNING TO THE PAST

Frank Beyer's *Jakob der Lügner*

In March 1977, *Jakob der Lügner* received the GDR's first and only Oscar nomination for Best Foreign Language Film. Unlike other Oscar categories, a country's designated national film board must first select the film it wishes to be considered by the Academy for the category of Best Foreign Language Film. In the case of the GDR, the recommendation was made by DEFA-Außenhandel and the final decision resided with the Ministry for Culture. As its submission, the Ministry for Culture approved the selection of *Jakob der Lügner*, a film set exclusively in a ghetto, in which the sole victims of National Socialist persecution are Jewish and in which not a single communist character features.

The nomination could not have come at a more politically sensitive time for the Ministry for Culture. On 9 November 1976, DEFA-Außenhandel informed HV Film that the GDR had been invited to submit a film for the 1977 awards ceremony.[1] HV Film then forwarded the letter to the Minister of Culture on 16 November – the eve of the Biermann Affair.[2] The following two weeks were among the most turbulent in the history of East German culture. On 17 November, the SED suddenly announced its decision to strip the musician Wolf Biermann of his East German citizenship as punishment for his repeated public criticism of the party. Over the following days, a number of artists signed an open letter of protest including the film's director Frank Beyer, the film's screenwriter Jurek Becker and one of the film's actors, Armin Mueller-Stahl.[3]

The nomination of *Jakob der Lügner* meant that Beyer was automatically invited by the Academy to attend the ceremony and a press conference in Los Angeles. This posed a potential problem for the state. Were he permitted to attend, the press conference could open the door to questions about the treatment of Biermann or even risk providing Beyer a platform to criticize the actions of the SED. Revoking the invitation, however, would risk drawing unwanted attention to the ongoing fallout from the Biermann Affair. It is telling that a memorandum dated 16 February recommends that Horst Pehnert, head of HV Film, should conduct a conversation with Beyer to establish 'clear guidelines for his appearance'.[4] Ultimately the long-term gains appear to have outweighed the short-term risks for the SED. The memorandum concludes that the opportunity 'for a DEFA film to reach a wide public in the USA for the first time' and thereby allow the GDR 'to become politically and commercially active' was of primary importance, even if that meant funding extra attendees in order to ensure 'the delegation's offensive and propagandistically effective appearance in terms of party politics'.[5]

The approval of a film that features no antifascist characters, that focuses solely on Jewish victimhood and that was made by a director and screenwriter who had publicly spoken out against the SED as the GDR's first entry for the most prominent film awards ceremony in the world is highly surprising. This is even more remarkable given that the film had been cancelled a decade earlier and the director had been banned from working for DEFA since 1966. By tracing the production history of *Jakob der Lügner* from its first treatment to the Oscar nomination and by analysing the themes of Jewish victimhood and National Socialist persecution in the film, this chapter examines the extent to which *Jakob der Lügner* was considered a controversial production by DEFA and the Ministry for Culture and the implications of this for our understanding of East German Holocaust film.

Set in a ghetto in Central Europe, *Jakob der Lügner* tells the story of a Jewish pancake shop owner, Jakob, who becomes entangled in a web of lies after claiming to possess an illegal radio.[6] One night, Jakob is sent to the police station for allegedly breaking the nighttime curfew but, to his consternation, he is allowed to leave when the officer concedes that he has committed no offence. While waiting to see the officer, Jakob overhears a radio broadcast announcing that the Russians are only twenty kilometres away from the neighbouring town of Bezanika. His attempts to tell his fellow ghetto prisoners the news about the advancing Red Army fall on deaf ears: they do not believe it is possible that he could have left the police station alive. In an attempt to make the others believe his news, Jakob lies and tells them that he heard the news on his secret radio. Soon he is inundated with requests for information from the other prisoners and, for the first time, hope prevails in the ghetto. Suicides stop and Jakob is forced to invent more good news to maintain the hopes of all those around him. Jakob struggles under the pressure of maintaining his lies and he reveals the truth to his best friend, Kowalski, who, bereft of hope, dies by suicide. Shortly thereafter, it is announced that the ghetto prisoners are to be deported. The film ends with a conversation in a train waggon between Jakob and the eight-year-old girl, Lina, during which she asks him whether clouds really are made out of cotton wool as he had claimed. Lina's puzzled expression closes the film as she begins to realize that Jakob might not have told her the truth.

The complex production history of *Jakob der Lügner* renders Beyer's film a fascinating case study into East German Holocaust film. It would, nonetheless, be a mistake to conclude that the importance of the film resides solely in its evolution from page to screen. *Jakob der Lügner* is a fascinating case study not only for what it presents, but also for how it presents its subject matter. Beyer's film marks a new chapter in East German Holocaust film. Discussing the 1974 film a number of years later, the director stated he was keen to distance *Jakob der Lügner* from 'the mass of mediocre and bad films in which the same types of resistance fighters always encounter the same type of evil Nazis and SS men' of which he believed 'the audience were sick and tired'.[7] As Beyer himself observed, *Jakob der Lügner* 'has nothing informational, nothing educational in meaning'.[8] Instead, it personalizes the story of fictional Jewish characters during the Third Reich as a means of exploring broader, universal themes. In so doing, the film offers a markedly depoliticized presentation of the past that appeals to audiences' own experiences beyond the Third Reich. This chapter places previously undiscussed archival material alongside an analysis of the ways in which the film engages with Jewish victimhood and persecution. Such an approach reveals the extent to which the state viewed *Jakob der Lügner* and its subject matter as controversial and exposes the ways in which the film's presentation of Jewish victimhood and persecution both mark a break with the past and yet also offer subtly familiar modes of depiction.

Establishing Contexts

To understand the extent to which *Jakob der Lügner* was – or was not – considered controversial at the time of its release, we need to unravel the film's complicated production history. In January 1963, screenwriter Jurek Becker submitted a treatment to DEFA,[9] which was followed by a draft screenplay in 1965.[10] By the autumn of the same year, Frank Beyer had joined the project as the film's director and, having revised the draft screenplay together, Becker and Beyer submitted a screenplay to DEFA on 15 December 1965, the eve of the Eleventh Plenum.[11] Just eight months later the project was cancelled. By the end of 1966, Becker had begun to revise his screenplay into a novel which became a rare example of a bestseller on both sides of the Berlin Wall. The international success of the novel led to the resurrection of plans for a film in 1972. These plans were finally realised in 1974 when *Jakob der Lügner* was filmed as a co-production between DEFA and Fernsehen der DDR (DDR-FS).[12] The film premiered on East German television in December 1974 and received a theatrical release in April 1975. A year later, it had been nominated for an Academy Award and by the end of the decade, *Jakob der Lügner* had been screened at the United Nations headquarters in New York and exported to twenty-four countries including eleven Western European countries, Japan, the USA, Canada and even Israel.[13]

In accounting for the cancellation of the project in 1966, several critics have pointed to the submission date of the screenplay and concluded that it was simply the wrong script at the wrong time. The restrictions placed on the studio and its filmmakers in the aftermath of the Eleventh Plenum, it has been argued, made it impossible to shoot a screenplay that solely focused on the persecution of Jews.[14] It is true that *Jakob der Lügner* entered pre-production during a period when the fallout from the Eleventh Plenum was still influencing film policy. This certainly had direct consequences for director Frank Beyer, whose contract with DEFA was terminated in July 1966 for the supposed ideological shortcomings of his 1966 film, *Spur der Steine*.[15] It has been argued that the resurrection of the film project was only possible thanks to the cultural and political thaw in 1972 that was precipitated by Erich Honecker's appointment as General Secretary of the SED. However, this reading is challenged by two hitherto overlooked points. Firstly, the studio actually approved the screenplay for *Jakob der Lügner* after the Eleventh Plenum when the political and cultural fallout was still unfolding. Secondly, the decision to remove the film's most explicit references to the Red Army was not made by Becker after the film was cancelled, but rather came at the behest of the film's production company (KAG) in a process that started in 1965. Furthermore, DEFA invested considerable resources into defending the project in the face of significant opposition, not from East German cultural officials, but from the film's erstwhile Polish production partners.

Jakob der Lügner did not just go through two production phases, it also underwent several draft screenplays during which the content – and above all, the ending – of the film changed in important ways. The first record of the film is a treatment from January 1963 which was followed by a scenario in February 1965. Both the 1963 treatment and the 1965 scenario contain the figure of a Red Army soldier who, in the final scene, leads Lina away by the hand and symbolically into a new (East) Germany.[16] This is not the ending used in the 1974 film. In the final version of the screenplay, the Red Army does not appear: the film finishes with the failure of the Red Army to arrive in time to liberate the Jewish prisoners. It has been argued that Becker's decision to omit the figure of the heroic Red Army soldier was the result of his sense of disillusionment following the Soviet invasion of Czechoslovakia in 1968 during the Prague Spring. However, different versions of the screenplay and correspondence from the film's production company reveal a far more complex course of events.

In actual fact, the figure of the Red Army soldier would not have featured in the film had the project been completed in 1966. When the screenplay was submitted in December 1965, it was unclear how the film would end. The final scenes of the submitted screenplay conclude with the Red Army implicitly liberating the ghetto: in the background of the shot, a Russian tank 'steamrolls over the post towers and barbed wire and drives into the ghetto'.[17] The film concludes with Jakob's suicide and no Red Army soldier appears. However, it is clear from correspondence in the film's production files that there was no certainty that this ending would, in fact, be used. Even before the screenplay had been submitted, Klaus Wischnewski, head of the KAG Heinrich Greif, contacted Professor Lothar Berthold at the SED's own Institute for Marxism-Leninism to establish whether the Red Army had ever liberated a ghetto.[18] This was followed by enquiries to other institutes in the GDR, Poland and the Soviet Union. The decisive response appears to have arrived in February 1966 from Professor Bernard Mark, the Director of the Jewish Historical Institute in Poland. In his reply, Mark unequivocally stated that 'no division of the Red Army and also no partisan group ever liberated a ghetto' and concluded, 'the conception of Herr Becker's screenplay, which in general we very much liked, nevertheless contains the risk of a happy ending. Unfortunately, there was in reality, nowhere, not in any ghetto, a happy solution of that kind'.[19] Following receipt of Mark's letter, a meeting was called by the KAG at which the production group members, Beyer and Becker were informed that the ending needed to be changed as 'the liberation of a ghetto by the Red Army is not historically provable'.[20] Becker's new ending was discussed on 10 June 1966. During the meeting, it was once again stressed that the change of ending was necessary because 'in regard to the actual fate of Jews in Eastern Europe, there must be no idealization of reality, especially by Germans'. The revised ending proposed by Becker in 1966 largely corresponds to the filmed ending of the 1974 film insofar as it ends with the deportation of the Jewish prisoners in a train waggon. The only notable difference between the final version of 1966 and the film ending of 1974 is the inclusion of the motif that the 'the Russians are already in Bezanika' in order to undercut the (on-screen) accusation that Jakob is a liar and to uphold the implicit (off-screen) presentation of the Red Army as a liberating force.[21]

Why might the KAG – and by extension DEFA – have been so concerned about the historical accuracy of the screenplay? After all, no such concerns had been raised three years earlier during the production of *Nackt unter Wölfen*, a film also directed by Frank Beyer. Here, history was freely rewritten so that Buchenwald concentration camp was not freed by American troops, but rather was an act of heroic self-liberation by the communist prisoners. It may very well have been the distortion of the historical record in Beyer's 1963 film which accounted for the sudden drive for historical accuracy in 1966. *Nackt unter Wölfen* was submitted to the Moscow International Film Festival in 1963 and was considered by the Ministry for Culture to be a strong contender for the main prize. However, after the film lost to Federico Fellini's *8 ½* (1963), the Deputy Minister of Culture, Hans Rodenberg, informed members of the Central Committee of the film's failure to secure the main prize. While Rodenberg offered several possible reasons for the film's disappointing performance, Bill Niven has argued that the most likely was the intervention of the Polish jury member, Jan Rybkowski, who complained that the film offered little more than a 'varnishing over reality' because it failed to show 'how the mountains of corpses at Buchenwald were moved with bulldozers'.[22] Extensive efforts were made to ensure the visual authenticity of the camp setting through the acquisition of original log books and passes from the Institute for Marxism-Leninism, original identity cards from the Museum for German History and woollen blankets from local prison authorities.[23] The historical accuracy of the plot, however, left much to be desired. Against this backdrop, the production company's wish that there was no embarrassing repetition of *Nackt unter Wölfen* when preparing *Jakob der Lügner* gains context.

Had the omission of an antifascist character and the film's sole focus on Jewish victimhood been considered too controversial, there were multiple opportunities prior to its cancellation in July 1966 when DEFA or the Ministry for Culture could have intervened. The first opportunity came in February 1966 when the new studio director, Franz Bruk, requested approval for the project from the head of HV Film. When permission was received later in the month, explicit reference was made in the accompanying evaluation to a meeting between DEFA and Franz Jahrow in HV Film's production department. Jahrow had been tasked with reviewing all potentially controversial projects. The report stated that further development of the screenplay was necessary 'to make the specifics of socialist realism visible', not least through the 'portrayal of socially progressive forces', but concluded that 'the material at hand concerns a story line which is, artistically, extraordinarily successful, [and] one that is filled with a quite profound humanistic spirit' and approved the film for release.[24] Had HV Film harboured any doubts about the suitability or desirability of the project, it could have delayed or even cancelled production, yet no such instruction was made.

At the start of July 1966, the screenplay for *Jakob der Lügner* had been approved and filming was due to begin that summer. The screenplay presented Jews as the sole victim of National Socialist persecution and contained no heroic antifascist figure. The picture of the past presented in *Jakob der Lügner* may have worked against dominant and conventional National Socialist persecution, but it was not deemed controversial by cultural officials in the GDR. This was not the case for Polish film officials. Beate Müller has carefully traced the influence of the film's Polish production partners on the fate of the film in 1966 and 1974.[25] As on-location shooting was due to take place in Poland, DEFA enlisted support from the Polish ZZRF production company. However, at the end of June 1966, the head of ZZRF contacted the KAG Heinrich Greif to announce that it was withdrawing support for the project citing lack of capacity. The head of production, Günter Althaus, consequently informed DEFA that under such circumstances there was 'absolutely no more possibility of realization for this year'.[26]

The timing of the Polish withdrawal occurred the very same day as Beyer's previous film, *Spur der Steine*, was abruptly withdrawn from cinemas for its perceived infringement of the SED's cultural and political values. It is true that DEFA made no attempt to find an alternative director and it would be easy to conclude that this was indicative of its desire to cancel a contentious project. However, the decision to cancel the project when Beyer was no longer available may well have been motivated by pragmatic rather than political concerns. As Beate Müller argues, financial pressures were more compelling for DEFA than political sensibilities. The withdrawal of nearly the entire year's production output meant that in 1966, DEFA was facing significant financial difficulties and was reluctant to pay for on-site technical support in Poland in East German Marks.[27] Beyer may have been considered an unreliable director, but the project itself was consistently approved during the far more turbulent months of early 1966. In short, suggestions that the East German authorities considered the script 'too focused on Jewish suffering and too flippant about the Soviet contribution to the liberation of Germany',[28] and indeed Beyer's own assertion that 'the DEFA management did not have the courage for such a film at this time', are not supported by the film's production history.[29]

We are nonetheless left with the question as to why the East German studio resurrected the project in 1972. Commercial considerations appear to have been the core motivation. When it became clear that the film would not be made in 1966, Becker quickly set about adapting the screenplay into what would become his debut novel. By the end of the year, Becker had signed a contract to publish *Jakob der Lügner*. Two years later, the novel was published and quickly became a rare example of a bestseller in both the GDR and Federal Republic. The commercial and critical acclaim of the novel meant that *Jakob der Lügner* suddenly became a much sought-after project which drew interest from West German producers. According to Beyer, the West German television station ZDF approached Becker with a view to adapting the book and, wanting to remain loyal to his friend, the author notified Beyer who in turn set about negotiating with DDR-FS (with whom he held a contract following his dismissal from DEFA) to resurrect the project.[30] Although Beyer's account gives chronological coherence to events, it nevertheless fails to explain why Beyer thought the television executives would agree to his proposal.

Biographies of Beyer often portray him as being cast out into the wilderness at the Staatstheater Dresden after his contract with DEFA was terminated. In reality, Beyer only worked in Dresden until 1969 and thereafter he had a contract with DDR-FS where he was active as a television director. Moreover, while not detracting from the fact Beyer was barred from his chosen career for alleged cultural and ideological infringements that he never intended to commit, Dresden was hardly a cultural backwater. During this period in 'exile', he directed four television films and enjoyed access to the DDR-FS management. When outlining his motivation for approaching DEFA, Beyer has described how he 'pointed to the passage in my contract allowing me to work for DEFA at specified intervals and asked for permission. For reasons of loyalty, I suggested that we undertake the project as a co-production between film and television'.[31] However, given that DEFA–DDR-FS co-productions were increasingly common in the 1970s, this was far less unusual than Beyer's account suggests.

Reasons of pragmatism rather than loyalty were most likely to be behind Beyer's decision to approach DDR-FS. Beyer clearly realised that a co-production with DEFA was the quickest way to rehabilitation with the film studio, a fact that did not go unnoticed by the DDR-FS management who complained that Beyer was conducting separate conversations with film and television officials so that he could 'always [be] promised the most favourable terms'.[32] Nor was it a coincidence that Beyer's decision to approach DEFA and DDR-FS coincided with the end of production for Kurt Jung-Alsen's *Die Bilder des Zeugen Schattmann*. Beyer would have been fully aware that an East German DEFA–DDR-FS co-production about Jewish persecution which had permission to shoot in Poland was being made for one very simple reason: his wife, Renate Blume, played the role of Esther Schattmann. Beyer seems to have approached the East German television and film studios buoyed by the news of a DDR-FS production made with the assistance of DEFA which focused on Jewish persecution and which had secured on-location filming.

This re-examination of the production history of *Jakob der Lügner* allows us to establish the parameters of representation in the late 1960s and early 1970s for East German Holocaust film. The film was far less controversial than has been assumed. A complex mix of factors contributed to the cancellation of the project, but the film's subject matter was not one of them. Put simply, a film depicting Jewish persecution without an antifascist resistance narrative was not considered to be controversial. However, this statement requires immediate qualification as the issue of *what* was depicted should always be considered secondary to *how* it is depicted. That is to say, it is important to ask to what extent the film specifically foregrounds Jewish persecution, because when we turn our attention to the complex ways in which the film navigates the characters' Jewish identity, the extent to which we can definitively claim that *Jakob der Lügner* marked a decisive break from previous depictions of the Holocaust becomes more complicated.

The Politics of Identification

Jakob Heym is far from a typical DEFA hero. Not only is the film's protagonist a Jewish victim of National Socialism, he is a character described in the casting notes as 'unremarkable, absolutely not the norm of a cinema hero'.[33] As we have seen in previous chapters, the inclusion of Jewish characters without reference to the antifascist resistance was unusual in East German Holocaust film, although by no means unprecedented: *Ehe im Schatten* and *Lebende Ware* also omitted the figure of the antifascist resister. Furthermore, while Jakob's Jewish identity is significant, we must be careful not to overlook how the Jewish characters are presented. Although Beyer may appear to position Jewish characters as the sole focus of the film and to omit reference to an antifascist hero, the presentation of the Jewish characters and key casting decisions require us to re-examine the centrality of explicitly Jewish victimhood in the film.

Were it not for external markers imposed on the Jewish characters in *Jakob der Lügner*, audiences may well be unaware that the majority of characters were in fact Jewish. The emphasis on the arbitrary othering of the Jewish characters is introduced in the very first scene. Jakob's entry in the film is framed against the dreary greys and browns of the ghetto. As a result, our eyes are immediately drawn to the colour of the yellow star on Jakob's front and back. Before Jakob has even spoken, external symbols have marked him as 'other'. However, over the course of the film, Beyer undermines this ostracism by refusing to depict Jakob as linguistically, culturally or religiously different in any way. Yiddish words are used sparingly and only one character, the orthodox Jew Herschel Schtamm, displays any obvious signs of being religiously observant. Yet even then, his appearance in Eastern European clothing and his wearing of *Payot* are shown to stem from an active choice: his twin brother appears in the same secularized manner as Jakob and the other ghetto prisoners (Figure 7.1).

The secularized presentation of the Jewish characters in *Jakob der Lügner* has come under increased scrutiny in recent years. Alan Corkhill has argued that the 'downplaying of the Jewishness of the ghettodwellers in favour of their deracialized status as members of the universal human family may well have served ideological ends'.[34] Corkhill is correct to point to the film's deliberate strategy of deemphasizing the characters' Jewish identity, but we must nonetheless be careful not to overstate the significance of this presentation of the Jewish characters. With the exception of the opening scene of *Lebende Ware*, East German

Figure 7.1. In the screenplay, Herschel and Roman Schtamm are actually described as twin brothers, although this is not made explicit in the film. © DEFA-Stiftung/Herbert Kroiss.

films set in the Third Reich consistently presented Jewish victims of National Socialism as assimilated Jews. Although the repeated framing of Jewish characters in libraries and studies codified Jews as bourgeois and proponents of traditional, German cultural values, East German film did not present Jews as orthodox in appearance or religious observance. Moreover, while Corkhill is correct to question the extent to which the characters are presented as explicitly Jewish, the character for whom the film's secularizing approach has the most important consequence is not Jakob, but rather his best friend Kowalski.

Jakob may be the titular character of the film, but he is not necessarily the character with whom the audience is primarily encouraged to identify. Although Jakob exhibits none of the physical and moral attributes of the typical East German hero, his best friend Kowalski does (Figure 7.2). In one scene, Jakob faces almost certain death after sneaking into the German officers' lavatory in the hope of gathering scraps of newspaper to provide him with news to share with the eager ghetto prisoners who still believe he is in possession of a radio. When it appears that Jakob will be discovered by a soldier, Kowalski deliber-

Figure 7.2. Erwin Geschonneck's star quality complicates readings of Jewish victimhood in *Jakob der Lügner*. © DEFA-Stiftung/Herbert Kroiss.

ately topples a stack of crates in the railway yard to create a diversion. Kowalski is played by Erwin Geschonneck. Geschonneck actively campaigned for the role of Jakob, but Beyer insisted that he should play the part of Kowalski because it was important that Geschonneck's large physical frame contrasted with the frailty of Brodský's.[35] Kowalski is not just a physically stronger presence on screen, he is also a witty and yet deeply sympathetic character, whose suicide arguably marks the emotional climax of the film.[36]

To an international audience, it may make little difference if Kowalski is presented as the more engaging of the two characters: since Kowalski is also Jewish and presented in the same secularized manner as Jakob, differing points of identification have little bearing on the overall impact of the film. However, within a domestic context the implications of casting Geschonneck had the potential to create a different effect. Erwin Geschonneck had both an exemplary record as an antifascist during the Second World War and was a popular actor in the GDR. Having joined the KPD in 1929, Gechonneck was imprisoned in Sachsenhausen, Dachau and Neuengamme for his communist activities. The East German state's estimation of the actor is clear from the fact that he received the prestigious National Prize five times, an honour only exceeded by the Karl Marx Medal and the Patriotic Order of Merit, the latter of which he received in Silver in 1965 and Gold in 1976.[37] Most importantly, to an East German audience Geschonneck would have been immediately recognisable from his antifascist roles including Heinrich Witting in *Fünf Patronenhülsen*, Bartuscheck in *Leute mit Flügeln* and Krämer in *Nackt unter Wölfen*. This raises the question as to whether Geschonneck was deliberately cast because audiences would recognize him from his antifascist roles, thereby instilling the film with overtones of communist resistance. This certainly accounts for the privileged discussion in reviews of Geschonneck's performance in the film above – and at times instead of – that of Brodský's and several reviews even included stills featuring Geschonneck alone.[38]

Innovation and Conformity

The international success of *Jakob der Lügner* may have been unprecedented, but the film was released in a highly hospitable climate. Worldwide the number of films dealing with the Holocaust doubled between 1960 and 1970.[39] Filmmakers and studios around the world exploited the opportunities presented by the increased public awareness of, and interest in, the crimes of the Third Reich following the trial of Adolf Eichmann in 1961 and the Auschwitz Trials of 1963 to 1965 to produce films about Jewish persecution.

While the sudden increase in films dealing with Jewish persecution certainly brought visibility to an under-discussed event in film, the increase in the number of Holocaust films also led to the circulation of an increasingly restrictive set of visual markers to signify the Holocaust. This prompted the West German film critic, Karsten Witte, to ask, 'What is left for the visual analysis of fascism to discover except the tautological reproduction of the material with which we already started? The supply of images is exhausted. We have already seen them all, but seldom from a new perspective'.[40] The desire to break free from an increasingly fixed set of visual tropes also underpinned Frank Beyer's approach in *Jakob der Lügner*. In an interview in 1975, the director signalled his frustration with the use of antifascism as a 'pretext for depicting chases and shoot outs'.[41] The violence in *Jakob der Lügner* is not, first and foremost, intended to serve as a demonstration of National Socialist violence towards Jews, but rather as a means of exploring the film's primary interest in the role of truth and lies. Indeed, in the film's official programme notes the words 'truth' and 'lie' appear ten times; the word 'Jew' appears twice.[42]

This film's new approach to the National Socialist past comes to the fore in the aforementioned scene in the railway yard in which Kowalski topples a stack of crates to save Jakob. Kowalski is subsequently beaten by the German officer but, in contrast to films such as *Die Bilder des Zeugen Schattmann*, the actual violence depicted on screen is decidedly elliptical in presentation. At the point of attack, the camera remains fixed on the officer in a medium close-up and Kowalski immediately turns his back to the camera. All that is visible is the yellow star on his clothes. The officer stops to run back to the lavatory and the camera returns to Kowalski to show him wiping a cut on his forehead. After Kowalski is beaten, the officer – who is described as 'no longer irate, more regretful' – drops two cigarettes on the ground as a form of atonement for his violent outburst.[43] However, it is not this action of material restitution, but rather Jakob's utterance, 'did I tell you that the Germans are suffering great losses?' that brings a smile to Kowalski's face. In *Jakob der Lügner*, hope is shown to be far more life-affirming than historical fact and truth has a relative quality. In this way, Beyer's reflection that the film's ending is 'tragic and yet not pessimistic' can be seen to apply not only to the final scene, but also to the entire film.[44]

The transformative role of hope is also explored through the film's use of flashbacks. Whereas flashbacks in *Die Bilder des Zeugen Schattmann* provide an authoritative and reliable picture of the past, the temporal fracturing of the narrative in *Jakob der Lügner* is deliberately self-reflexive and designed to cast doubt on the reliability of the past. Beyer presents his characters' recollection of events as precisely that: an act of recall to memory with all the subjective trappings that entails. In *Jakob der Lügner*, memory is framed as the stories individuals and communities tell themselves in order to make sense of the present. The opening scene introduces the idea of the unreliability of memory from the outset: 'The story of *Jakob der Lügner* never happened in this way. Definitely not. But maybe it did happen like this after all'. The extent to which Jakob's memories may be unreliable becomes clear in the flashback sequences. Jakob's memories of life before the ghetto revolve around happy day-to-day episodes with his partner Josefa and Kowalski. Through the flashbacks, we follow the blossoming relationship with Josefa. However, this is undercut in the penultimate flashback in which Josefa presents Jakob with an ultimatum: unless he marries her, she will leave for America with another man. The reliability of the previous flashbacks is thus placed in doubt through Jakob's failure to recognise –

or recall – Josefa's unhappiness in their relationship. In so doing, and in marked contrast to *Die Bilder des Zeugen Schattmann*, flashbacks and memories in *Jakob der Lügner* are shown as subjective and unreliable.

Visually, the film continues the self-reflexive appropriation of Jakob's memory through alternating film stock. Whereas all the ghetto sequences are shot in Kodak Eastman Color which drains the image of colour, the flashback sequences are shot using the hyper-real East German ORWO film stock. The alternation of the film stock creates a visual discord that repeatedly draws attention to the break in narrative and temporal flow. Instead of presenting the past as a reliable narrative for the justification of present-day events, the change of film stock forces the spectator to question the inherent subjectivity of memory. While ORWO film stock may strike the modern-day spectator as highly stylized, it would have appeared extremely familiar to an East German audience as this was how DEFA's children's films were shot. Beyer thus makes a direct call to the audience's own childhood memories where dreams and realities were intermixed with little need for separation. It is unclear whether Jakob's memories are reliable or are, in fact, as fanciful as Lina's projections (Figure 7.3). The opening intertitle, the use of

Figure 7.3. Even in her fanciful daydreams, Lina wears the 'Judenstern'. © DEFA-Stiftung/Herbert Kroiss.

ORWO film stock and the revelation that Josefa was not as content in their relationship as his memories suggest, encourage such scepticism. But the film's message is that, ultimately, it does not matter if they are real or not. Jakob's memories provide as much sustenance to him as Lina's fantasies do to her. In the dire reality of the ghetto, there is only one truth: survival. The hope that escapism can provide, be it through recourse to dreams of princes or the belief in a radio, instils the characters' lives with a belief that demonstrative truth cannot.

DEFA Goes to the Oscars

The international success of *Jakob der Lügner* began in 1974 when Beyer's film played at the London Film Festival. This was followed by screenings in 1975 in the Federal Republic, where it became the first DEFA film to play at the Berlinale and at which Vlastimil Brodský was awarded the Silver Bear for Best Actor. But it was the news in 1976 that the film was to be nominated for an Oscar that marked the most significant breakthrough for East German filmmaking. In a letter dated 9 November 1976, Herbert Bulla of DEFA-Außenhandel informed the Ministry for Culture that 'we have been invited by the Academy of Motion Pictures Arts and Sciences to take part in the forty-ninth competition for the Best Foreign Film'. Although Bulla encouraged the Minister of Culture to utilize the opportunity presented by the nomination because 'the nomination of a film guarantees press conferences and publicity value', economic rather than political concerns underpinned this petition. Of primary importance to Bulla was the fact that 'quite apart from the prestige success, our economic results would also be positively influenced'.[45] Given that DEFA-Außenhandel was the only section of the film studio expected to make a profit, it was in Bulla's interest to ensure that the Ministry for Culture selected a film likely to succeed not just at the Oscars, but at international box offices too. The press conference also seems to have been approached as an opportunity to demonstrate the international compatibility of East German cinema rather than as a stage for political speeches. A handwritten note by Beyer reveals the key words in English and German which the director appears to have anticipated arising at the press conference: whimsical, oddly, Holocaust, to tinge, wry, woebegone, deadpan, persistence, jerry, jerry-built house, slender, remainder.[46] In sharp contrast to the politicization of the press conference for *Professor Mamlock*, there is no indication from Beyer's list of words that the press conference for *Jakob der Lügner* was used as a political platform. Of course, Beyer was hardly viewed as a loyal mouthpiece for the state and it may well have been for this very reason that HV Film suggested sending the head of DEFA-Außenhandel and Erwin Geschonneck whose presence would, HV Film suggested, 'secure an aggressive and propagandistically effective appearance of the GDR in terms of politics'. The SED also envisaged exploiting the opportunity for longer-term aims: the opportunity to make political and commercial inroads in the USA with a DEFA film.[47]

Jakob der Lügner did not win the Academy Award, but it remains one of DEFA's most critically acclaimed and well-known films. Domestically, however, the film proved to be far less successful. When *Jakob der Lügner* played in cinemas, it was seen by just 48,444 spectators in its first month of release (as a point of contrast, *Lebende Ware* recorded ticket sales of 223,057 over the same number of weeks).[48] How do we reconcile the fact that *Jakob der Lügner* is one of the most widely known East German films yet one of DEFA's poorest performing Holocaust films? Certainly, the fact that the film was first broadcast on television would have impacted box office returns. Much to the frustration of Beyer, the film premiered on television on Christmas Eve to provide 'an emotional high point' for DDR-FS during the festive period.[49] On the one hand, Beyer's dissatisfaction appears disingenuous. After all, DDR-FS had co-financed the production and the film was broadcast at the peak time slot of 20:00 which, given the GDR only had two television channels, can hardly be considered symptomatic of an attempt to suppress the film. On the other hand, Beyer's grievances are at least in part justified, especially considering the importance of alternations in the film stock for the film's exploration of memory: the film was broadcast in black and white.

Beyer cited the fact the film premiered on television as the reason behind the film's poor performance by claiming that people had other priorities 'than to concentrate on such a gentle, poetic film' on Christmas Eve.[50] However, this may well have missed the real issue. There were clear discrepancies in how Beyer presented the film in interviews prior to the film's release and how DEFA subsequently marketed it. While international presentations and discussions of the film repeatedly downplayed any overt political or ideological readings, East German reviewers consistently framed *Jakob der Lügner* within a standard East German discourse of the past. A critic for *Neues Deutschland* praised Beyer's film as a production 'dedicated to the antifascist resistance struggle',[51] a reading echoed in Heinz Hoffmann's description of *Jakob der Lügner* as 'a film against fascism'.[52] Even when describing the film as 'the best thing which has been broadcast on television in a long time', Irene Böhme (writing in the weekly newspaper *Sonntag*) framed this accolade within the context of 'the antifascist theme'.[53]

This tone was certainly not countered by DEFA or even by Beyer. *Jakob der Lügner* was released in conjunction with the Month of the Anti-Imperialist Film, a programming decision which clearly encouraged audiences to place the film within a specific East German filmmaking tradition. DEFA's marketing of the film also encouraged cinemas to present the production as an antifascist film. The film's *Einsatzkarte* – a double-sided A5 card designed for cinema managers detailing the plot, cast and crew, suggested taglines and possible marketing strategies – selected 'antifascist film' as its target audience group, foregrounded antifascist films in Beyer's filmography and cited *Jakob der Lügner* as an example of a film to be viewed in conjunction with the 'thirtieth anniversary of liberation from Hitler fascism'. One suggested tagline for the film was even 'an unusual colour film dealing with the major theme of antifascist resistance'.[54] At the same time, Beyer repeatedly sought to distance himself from the very same thematic tradition, often to somewhat contradictory ends. In one of the GDR's leading film magazines, Beyer claimed that although 'the theme of this film ... is not the antifascist resistance fighter', Jakob was 'a resistance fighter and an antifascist, even one of great distinction'.[55] The recently rehabilitated director appeared to have learnt how to appease cultural officials.

Audiences who would normally have been attracted to the very type of antifascist genre films against which *Jakob der Lügner* is positioned would, in all likelihood, have been deterred by the filmmakers' repeated criticism of such stagings of the past. On the other hand, the film's target market – younger spectators and individuals increasingly distanced by the GDR's instrumentalization of the past in films set in the Third Reich – may well have been deterred by how the film was presented in the press and Beyer's contradictory comments, which appeared to signal the film was indeed another conformist retelling of the past. Thus the problem was not the film's tone, nor the decision to premiere it on television, but rather its contradictory marketing as a film which both upheld and broke free from DEFA's antifascist tradition. In trying to appeal to two very different audience groups, the filmmakers may well have missed both. Only with the emergence of a third generation of cinemagoers did the framing of the past on screen and the mode of discussion in the press slowly start to change.

Notes

1. Bulla, 'Letter from Deputy Director Bulla to Rainer Otto'.
2. Otto, 'Letter from Rainer Otto to H.J. Hoffmann'.
3. Jurek Becker was an original signatory to the letter; Beyer added his signature two days later. Armin Mueller-Stahl, who plays Roman Schtamm in the film, also later added his name to the letter in protest.
4. Abteilung Kultur, 'Information über die Nominierung des Films *Jakob der Lügner* für den Internationalen Filmpreis Oscar'.
5. Ibid.
6. Although widely presumed to be set in Poland, Beyer was resolute that *Jakob der Lügner* 'is not set in the Warsaw Ghetto but rather somewhere in the East. It is also rather a "model ghetto" than a concrete place'. Beyer, 'Letter from Frank Beyer to Jauch'.
7. Beyer, *Wenn der Wind sich dreht*, 188.
8. Wischnewski, 'Über Jakob und andere'.
9. Becker, '*Jakob der Lügner*. Exposé'.
10. Becker, '*Jakob der Lügner*. Scenario'.
11. Becker, '*Jakob der Lügner*. Screenplay'. BArch DR 117/323.
12. In 1972, Deutscher Fernsehfunk (DFF) was renamed Fernsehen der DDR (DDR-FS).
13. It is particularly significant that the film was screened in Israel given that diplomatic relations between the two states were never established. Just a few years earlier the Israeli ambassador to the United Nations, Yosef Tekoah, had opposed the admission of the GDR to the United Nations on the grounds that 'the other German state [GDR] has ignored and continues to ignore Germany's historical responsibility for the Holocaust and the moral obligations arising from it'. Cited in Herf, *Undeclared Wars with Israel*, 216.
14. Baron, *Projecting the Holocaust into the Present*, 155.
15. Beyer's own description of the termination of his contract is particularly useful here: 'It was effectively an employment ban [*Berufsverbot*], although the word was scrupulously avoided. It was also not a dismissal which would have had to have been explained. It was a "measure" [*Maßnahme*] . . . It was a question of party discipline'. Beyer, *Wenn der Wind sich dreht*, 153.
16. Becker, '*Jakob der Lügner*. Exposé'; Becker, '*Jakob der Lügner*. Scenario'.
17. Becker, '*Jakob der Lügner*. Screenplay'. BArch DR 117/323.
18. Wischnewski, 'Letter from Klaus Wischnewski to Professor Lothar Berthold'.
19. Mark, 'Letter from Prof. Mark of the Żydowski Instytut Historyczny to DEFA'.
20. Gruppe Heinrich Greif, 'Memorandum'.
21. Gruppe Heinrich Greif, 'Drehbuchabnahme *Jakob der Lügner* am 10.6.1966'.
22. Cited in Niven, *The Buchenwald Child*, 144.
23. Ibid., 128.
24. Cited in Müller, *Stasi–Zensur–Machtdiskurse*, 82–3.
25. Beate Müller has detailed similar tactics, this time by a different Polish film studio (Film Polski) that were employed in the 1970s when production began again. See Müller, *Stasi–Zensur–Machtdiskurse*, 123–5.
26. Althaus, cited in Müller, *Stasi–Zensur–Machtdiskurse*, 88–9.
27. Müller, *Stasi–Zensur–Machtdiskurse*, 90.
28. Baron, *Projecting the Holocaust into the Present*, 155.
29. Beyer, *Wenn der Wind sich dreht*, 187.

30. Ibid., 188. There is no record of this correspondence in Becker's papers at the archives of the Akademie der Künste. While not disputing that ZDF may well have contacted the screenwriter, there is a letter dated 3 May 1971 from CCC Filmkunst GmbH to Aufbau-Verlag expressing an interest in the film rights (CCC Filmkunst GmbH, 'Letter from CCC Filmkunst GmbH to Aufbau-Verlag (Berlin East)'). CCC Film was well-known for its production of films exploring Jewish persecution. A second letter dated 16 February 1972 from Georg Richter at Film- und Fernsehproduktion Georg Richter in Munich to Jurek Becker also enquires about the availability of the film rights (Richter, 'Letter from Georg Richter, Film- und Fernsehproduktion Georg Richter (Munich) to Jurek Becker').
31. Schenk, *Regie*, 72.
32. Ernst Kirst, cited in Müller, *Stasi–Zensur–Machtdiskurse*, 122.
33. DEFA, 'Charakteristik wichtiger Figuren'. Cited in Sander, *Jurek Becker: die Biografie*, 123.
34. Corkhill, 'From Novel to Film to Remake: Jurek Becker's *Jakob der Lügner*', 96.
35. Beyer, *Wenn der Wind sich dreht*, 191–2.
36. In earlier versions of the screenplay, it was Jakob rather than Kowalski who died by suicide.
37. Fellmer, 'The Communist Who Rarely Played a Communist', 41.
38. For example: *Eulenspiegel*, 'Kino-Eule: *Jakob der Lügner*'; Hoffmann, '*Jakob der Lügner*'; Stade, 'Kein Kalender wird anzeigen, wann wir das je vergessen könnten'.
39. Baron, 'Film', 446.
40. Karsten Witte, cited in Kaes, *From Hitler to Heimat*, 22–3.
41. Wischnewski, 'Über Jakob und andere'.
42. Progress Film, '*Jakob der Lügner*'.
43. Becker, '*Jakob der Lügner*. Draft Screenplay'.
44. Richter, 'Frank Beyer: Vom Umgang mit Widersprüchen', 31.
45. The letter continues: 'The nomination alone for the Academy Award (Oscar) would increase the contractual guarantee by US $10,000. The guarantee would rise to $20,000 if our film were to win the prize'. Bulla, 'Letter from Deputy Director Bulla to Rainer Otto'.
46. Beyer, 'Handwritten Notes'.
47. Abteilung Kultur, 'Information über die Nominierung des Films *Jakob der Lügner* für den Internationalen Filmpreis Oscar'.
48. DEFA, 'Besucher- und Einspielergebnisse, Sichttag 15.05.75: Woche 4'.
49. Beyer, *Wenn der Wind sich dreht*, 196.
50. Schenk, *Regie*, 73.
51. *Neues Deutschland*, '*Jakob der Lügner*'.
52. Hoffmann, 'Die schlichte Schönheit einer großen Wahrheit'.
53. Böhme, '*Jakob der Lügner*'.
54. Progress Film, '*Jakob der Lügner*: Einsatzkarte'.
55. Wischnewski, 'Über Jakob und andere'.

PART V

1980–89

The political and financial difficulties that had engulfed DEFA in the late 1970s showed little sign of abating in the 1980s. In 1960, the GDR had 1,369 cinemas which screened over 2.5 million films. By 1980, over a third of these cinemas had closed and the number of film screenings had dropped by over 1.6 million.[1] Over the same period, television ownership had increased from 18.5 to 105 sets per one hundred households[2] and the number of broadcast hours on television had more than doubled from roughly 3,000 hours to 7,700 hours per year.[3] Television continued to provide a source of competition for the film studio, however the rise in television ownership alone does not explain why the number of cinema visits per head of population continued to fall throughout the 1980s. By the 1980s, the source of competition was no longer a question of medium, but rather of country of origin. Although audiences continued to regard television as their preferred source of entertainment, both DEFA and DDR-FS shared a similar source of competition: imported content. Two thirds of all new releases in the GDR in the 1980s were produced in socialist countries (including DEFA productions), but it was the remaining third that consistently attracted the largest audiences.[4] In order to entice audiences back into struggling cinemas, the SED reluctantly agreed to increase the number of Western productions playing in East German cinemas, a move that saw West German imports alone increase from thirty-two films in the 1970s to fifty-two in the 1980s.[5] However, this did little to stem the tide of falling returns and attendance figures continued to fall from an average of 5.4 visits per year in 1970 to 4.8 visits in 1980.[6]

In an attempt to improve the standing of domestic productions, DEFA continued to try to improve the appeal of its output *vis-à-vis* foreign releases and television programming by increasingly relying on *Darsteller-Filme* or 'star vehicle films' featuring actors such as Jutta Wachowiak, Corinna Harfouch, Fred Dürren and Rolf Hoppe.[7] But DEFA's attempts to harness the popular appeal of its stars was frustrated by political prohibitions: in November 1984, the SED decreed that no film which featured an actor who had left, or who had attempted to leave, the GDR could be broadcast on East German television.[8] Given the exodus of stars who left following the Biermann Affair in 1976, much of DEFA's back catalogue became unusable.

Audience apathy was matched by discontent behind the scenes. Young directors in particular were becoming increasingly frustrated with the lack of opportunities at the East German studio. Fearing that the directors would voice their dissatisfaction publicly and form an 'oppositional platform', the state looked for ways to contain their disquiet.[9] The SED leadership's worries stemmed from two primary concerns. Firstly, this younger generation of filmmakers had been exposed to unprecedented levels of contact with the West and its perceived subversive influences. Secondly, this generation's professional mentors had overwhelmingly been directors who had protested against the state after the Biermann Affair.[10] Once again the filmmakers were ultimately left frustrated. Not only did the state steadfastly refuse to reform filmmaking practices, it also increased the presence of the Stasi within DEFA.[11]

Over the course of the 1980s, tensions between filmmakers, DEFA and the Central Committee became increasingly public. In November 1982, *Neues Deutschland* published the so-called 'Vater Brief' ('Father Letter'), a reader's letter purportedly written by a mechanic called Hubert Vater in Erfurt. The letter was published on page two of the newspaper, a position normally reserved for party statements or the editorial.[12] In the letter, Vater called for greater 'pride in what the working class and its party has accomplished' and warned filmmakers of the dangers of 'concerning themselves with small inconsequential issues and forswearing social impact'.[13] Vater was widely believed to be Erich Honecker. The letter was received with a mixture of confusion and consternation from directors who once again were unclear about the nature of their transgression. Konrad Wolf, who at the time was the President of the Academy of Arts, angrily defended filmmakers arguing that they were neither 'sixth formers' [*Unterprimaner*] nor 'in kindergarten' and that they did not deserve 'to be beaten about the head in this way'.[14]

The frustration within DEFA was palpable. Between 1983 and 1985, twenty-five people at the studio applied for visas to leave the GDR and to work in the West.[15] Relations continued to deteriorate in the second half of the decade. In 1988, the 'Working Group for the Next Generation: Committee for Feature Film' composed a manifesto to be read at the Congress of the East German Organization of Film and Television. Describing East German cinema as in a state of 'crisis', this new generation of filmmakers warned that 'undifferentiated internalization of taboos has led to self-censorship, which affects to a greater or lesser degree everyone involved in the collective creative process'.[16] The young filmmakers' desire for greater artistic freedom was inadvertently granted two years later with the collapse of the GDR. This came at an unforeseen price. With the fall of the Berlin Wall and German reunification, DEFA lost its monopoly over domestic filmmaking and, in its place, gained unprecedented levels of international competition. The studio was sold three years later and, although the new owners were required to honour the contracts of DEFA's remaining staff until 1994, East German filmmakers struggled to achieve comparable levels of success – or even the filmmaking opportunities – to those they had enjoyed in the GDR.

DEFA's Final Decade: The Beginning of a New Chapter

Despite the sense of stagnation within the studio and the declining popularity of DEFA's output among audiences, the 1980s also saw an important shift in focus in East German cinema as filmmakers began to explore new subjects and different identities. Women became increasingly prominent leading figures who were no longer defined primarily as mothers, wives or lovers, but rather as complex protagonists who in the face of political, social or personal challenges remain resolute in their chosen course of action. These two dominant trends – an interest in new subject matters and the emergence of female protagonists – also informed the treatment of the National Socialist past during the 1980s in East German film.

The move away from traditional resistance narratives was not met with universal approval and caused considerable disquiet among antifascist veterans' groups in the GDR. In the 1980s, a series of films set in the National Socialist past encountered difficulties during production or after release on the grounds of their purported or actual challenge to dominant narratives. The discussion of the rape of a German woman by a Red Army soldier in Rainer Simon's *Jadup und Boel* (*Jadup and Boel*, 1980) was considered so controversial that the film was banned until 1988. Frank Beyer's *Der Aufenthalt* (*The Turning Point*, 1982) was initially celebrated as a 'testament of the friendship between Poland and the GDR', however, the negative portrayal of Polish civilians and military figures provoked complaints from Polish officials.[17] The SED responded by withdrawing the film from the 1984 Berlin Film Festival. Ulrich Weiß's *Dein unbekannter Bruder* (*Your Unknown Brother*, 1982) explores the theme of loyalty and betrayal within the antifascist resistance. After the film was selected to play at the Cannes Film Festival, the antifascist veteran and Central Committee member Hermann Axen complained about the depiction of the resistance and insisted that the film be withdrawn. Axen's complaints characterized a wider trend in East German cultural politics of the 1980s, namely the influence of the antifascist veterans on cultural engagements with the National Socialist past. Four decades after the end of the war, East German films were still subject to direct political intervention if they were deemed to transgress the parameters of representation.

These examples were by no means isolated instances: they are only an exception insofar as the films were withdrawn after they were finished. A number of projects were cancelled during the production phase. In 1983, Eberhard Görner attempted to adapt Fred Wander's *Der siebente Brunnen* (*The Seventh Well*). The project was envisaged as a DEFA–DDR-FS co-production that would have been released in 1985 to mark the fortieth anniversary of the end of the Second World War. However, the project was cancelled before filming began. According to DEFA's head dramaturge, Rudolf Jürschik, the film was cancelled not only because of the negative and passive depiction of camp prisoners, but also because of a fear within the studio about how veterans within the Committee of Antifascist Resistance Fighters (KdAW) would respond to such a depiction of its members.[18] Similar fates befell Anne Dessau's *Die Kinder vom Bullenhuser Damm* (*The Children of Bullenhuser Damm*) and Hedda Zinner's *Katja* and *Ravensbrücker Ballade* (*Ravensbrück Ballad*).

The two case studies in this section examine the sensitivities around the depiction of the past at a point when new characters, new filmmaking voices and new approaches were shaping a new generation's understandings of the past. Both films are heavily reliant on genre conventions, and Jewish persecution functions as a plot device rather than as a core focus of the plot. Michael Kann's *Stielke, Heinz, fünfzehn* (1987) is a dramatic comedy about a fifteen-year-old member of the Hitler Youth who, after discovering that his father was Jewish, embarks on a coming-of-age odyssey across Germany. Over the course of the film, Heinz attempts to conceal his Jewish identity which leads to a comedy of errors between the National Socialist officers and the blond-haired Jewish teenager. *Die Schauspielerin* (1988) is tonally very different from Kann's *Stielke, Heinz, fünfzehn*. Siegfried Kühn's film explores the romance between the actors Maria Rheine and Mark Löwenthal, who is Jewish. The introduction of the Nuremberg Laws forbids Maria and Mark's relationship. As a result, Maria resolves to change her identity and present herself as Mark's Jewish-German wife, Manja. The film traces the tragic consequences of this decision. *Stielke, Heinz, fünfzehn* and *Die Schauspielerin* were both described as films by directors who did not experience the events first-hand and that were made primarily for audiences who were even further removed from the National Socialist past. In an interview with Michael Kann shortly after the release of *Stielke, Heinz, fünfzehn*, Kann described how a film critic in Leipzig had commented that 'the film failed because it had not followed the tried and tested traditions of the antifascist film in the GDR'. Kann insisted that 'if that alone is the reason, then I am glad we made the film this way'. While he had 'no desire to question that tradition', he argued that 'we are living in a different time, a time of great flux and maybe it is not wrong to renew or replace ways of thinking through attempts to approach a topic differently'.[19] The following two chapters explore the implications of these new engagements to reveal how DEFA's final Holocaust films offer unique insights into behind-the-scenes discussions and public debates about legacies of the past and East German identity in the present.

Notes

1. Staatliche Zentralverwaltung für Statistik, *Statistisches Jahrbuch der Deutschen Demokratischen Republik*, 326.
2. Ibid., 53.
3. Ibid., 59.
4. Hake, *German National Cinema*, 148.
5. Stott, *Crossing the Wall*, 267–72.
6. Feinstein, *Triumph of the Ordinary*, 214.
7. Wiedemann, 'Anmerkungen zu einem Forschungsprojekt', 12.
8. Schittly, *Zwischen Regie und Regime*, 247.
9. Ibid., 245.
10. Ibid., 224.

11. Ibid., 245.
12. Rinke, *Images of Women in East German Cinema*, 53.
13. Vater, 'Was ich mir mehr von unseren Filmemachern wünsche'.
14. Cited in Rinke, *Images of Women in East German Cinema*, 57.
15. Schittly, *Zwischen Regie und Regime*, 243.
16. Ibid., 253.
17. Cited in *Der Spiegel*, 'Kein *Aufenthalt* zur Berlinale'.
18. Görner, '*Der siebente Brunnen* von Fred Wander', 68.
19. Linke, 'Lieber am Anfang als am Ende'.

Chapter 8

SHIFTING IDENTITIES

Michael Kann's *Stielke, Heinz, fünfzehn*

Michael Kann's debut film, *Stielke, Heinz, fünfzehn* (1987) was supposed to signal the renewal of one of the core interests of East German cinema, the antifascist film.[1] Reviewers acknowledged that by the end of the 1980s, East German directors were no longer confronting 'a piece of their own past' when making films about 'DEFA's longest and probably best tradition', but rather were working through 'a history that they have not themselves directly experienced'.[2] For the first time, there was widespread acknowledgement among both film critics and studio officials that the emergence of a younger generation of filmmakers and audiences necessitated a new way of engaging with the past. As one film critic at the time reflected, 'if any work of art today wants to make human behaviour tangible beyond historical factual knowledge . . . and to make corresponding or contradictory behaviour rationally and emotionally understandable', then filmmakers should focus on an 'intensive and socially accurate psychological interpretation of the characters and events portrayed'.[3]

When first presenting the material for *Stielke, Heinz, fünfzehn* to DEFA, the production company Gruppe Johannisthal described Kann's film as 'a film that has every chance of reaching our young main audience in an effective and exciting way and of bringing an important historical subject closer to them'.[4] The film's 'new' and 'original' approach to the studio's antifascist filmmaking tradition was cited as a key reason to approve the film. The studio's eagerness to attract a younger audience was not only driven by the desire to ensure 'continuity in an important thematic field'.[5] Rather, pragmatic reasons also underpinned the need to reach this demographic: at the start of the 1980s, roughly seventy per cent of all cinemagoers were aged between fourteen and twenty-five.[6] In the face of falling audience numbers and revenues, a film that engaged a younger audience could begin to address DEFA's continuing difficulties.

Stielke, Heinz, fünfzehn depicts the adventures of Heinz Stielke, a fifteen-year-old boy who is the model student of the Hitler Youth. Able to outrun his classmates in athletics and quote National Socialist legislation at length, Heinz appears to be the ideal young 'Aryan' male. However, one day Heinz is summoned to the headmaster's office where he is told that he is to be expelled with immediate effect because his father, a fallen Wehrmacht soldier, was in fact Jewish. Unable and unwilling to register the implication of this revelation, Heinz finds refuge in National Socialist physiognomy books which he uses to 'prove' his 'Aryan' heritage. When he returns to school to reveal his findings to his classmates, he is chased away. While hiding from his former classmates, Heinz is caught up in a bombing raid in which his mother is killed. As an orphan, Heinz begins a journey through Germany during which he is repeatedly detained by German officers who, not realising that the athletic, blond boy is in fact half-Jewish, send him to an elite training and education camp for talented National Socialist youth. What is framed by the film as consensual is nonetheless predicated on exploitation and abuse when, after arriving at the camp, Heinz is sexually exploited by Marga, the wife of the training camp commandant. When Marga shifts her attention to a new arrival at the camp, Heinz is ridiculed by the other boys and he decides to flee again in order to escape the taunts of his peers.

While on the run, a chance encounter with a steam engine driver convinces him to enlist for the Reichsarbeitsdienst (Reich Labour Service) in order to serve the German fatherland. On his way to the camp, Heinz meets Gabi who invites him to spend the night at her grandfather's home. Both Gabi and her grandfather are committed antifascists, but Heinz remains indifferent to their alternative image of German patriotism. Nevertheless, moved by the warmth shown to him by Gabi, he resolves to return to her after the war. At the work camp, Heinz befriends Max who, soon thereafter, receives a letter from his father in which he urges his son to abandon German fascism for a more peaceful cause. In an abrupt and entirely unconvincing change of tack, Heinz quickly declares that the pair should abandon the National Socialist cause and once again flee. However, their plans are interrupted by an order from their commander to take part in an attack against a group of civilians. Although Heinz is content simply to abscond mid-operation, Max urges him to help sabotage the action. Their plans end in disaster when Max is inadvertently killed in the chaos that ensues.[7] The film ends with Heinz, still carrying his Reichsarbeitsdienst jacket, running off into the distance to be reunited with Gabi.

Stielke, Heinz, fünfzehn was not the first film to target young audiences when addressing the National Socialist past. In keeping with the emblematic heroes of the 1950s, one of the earliest antifascist children's films, Heiner Carow's *Sie nannten ihn Amigo* (*They Called Him Amigo*, 1958), focuses on the exemplary efforts of the fifteen-year-old Rainer (nicknamed Amigo) to help a communist resistance fighter on the run from the National Socialist authorities. When his complicity is uncovered, Rainer is sent to a concentration camp. The film ends in postwar Berlin as the young protagonist joins the Nationale Volksarmee (National People's Army). The unproblematic trajectory from young resister against the National Socialist regime to loyal soldier in the GDR may have been a recurring feature of the 1950s antifascist film, but with the onset of the 1960s the seamless transmission of antifascist identity became increasingly unstable in films targeting young audiences. The seventeen-year-old protagonist of Joachim Kunert's *Die Abenteuer des Werner Holt* (*The Adventures of Werner Holt*, 1965) is far removed from the heroic resister of the 1950s. Werner is enlisted into the Wehrmacht and he willingly fights against the Red Army. Only after witnessing the execution of his school friend and the massacre of civilians by the SS does Werner re-evaluate his loyalty to the National Socialist cause. Werner's (eventual) conversion to the communist cause may well have placated the East German authorities' concerns about audience identification with a charismatic character whose support of the National Socialist regime is given far more narrative exposition than his renunciation of it. This was not the case for Heiner Carow's *Die Russen kommen* (*The Russians Are Coming*, 1968). In the film, the sixteen-year-old protagonist, Günter, is not only complicit in the murder of a forced labourer, but he never undergoes the typical antifascist conversion which ensured the realignment of perpetrators to the 'right' cause. Rather, the film's 'psychologizing of fascism' led to the decision to ban it in 1968.[8]

The increasing ambivalence of the antifascist hero continued to inform the presentation of young protagonists throughout the 1970s and 1980s. The ten-year-old protagonist of Egon Schlegel's *Die Schüsse der Noah Arche* (1983) is never fully able to reconcile the polyphony of identities – society's National Socialism, his father's communism and his mother's Christianity – accorded to him: 'A Nazi at school, a communist at home?' asks his mother. 'And wisdoms from the Bible?' retorts his father in one scene. When Klaus finally chooses to return to Germany with the Red Army rather than stay in a Christian children's home, he justifies his decision with a notable lack of enthusiasm by conceding that he is duty bound to honour a promise he made to his father. Although it is true that none of these films challenges the core tenets of the antifascist narrative, by the end of the 1980s it was clear that filmmakers no longer rehearsed the core narratives of antifascist identification. Meanwhile, the question of how to engage younger audiences remained fraught with difficulty.

On first viewing, Heinz Stielke is cast in the mould of previous incarnations of teenage protagonists from DEFA's antifascist films of the 1960s and 1970s. Audiences are initially asked to sympathize with a character who unreflectively and uncritically rehearses fascist ideology. Kann embraces the narrative conventions of the adventure film to structure his protagonist's ideological and sexual coming of age. However, typical of other films of the 1970s and 1980s, Heinz's transition to maturity lacks the conviction of DEFA's earlier antifascist films and instead betrays an ideological superficiality that did not go unnoticed by reviewers or film officials. Kann's film was roundly criticized for both relying on 'a past whose rituals and cruelty, data and facts are known only from textbooks'[9] and embedding this within a 'macabre sex story with the sadistic woman camp commandant' in which 'the lurid scenes take on a life of their own and completely suppress everything else'.[10] Where *Stielke, Heinz, fünfzehn* does unquestionably break new ground, however, is in the presentation of a teenage protagonist who is half-Jewish. Kann's film offers a fascinating case study of the generational reconfigurations of the 'staple of GDR filmmaking' as well as uncovering wider societal debates about the challenges of transmitting the central founding myth of the GDR to the first generation of Germans born into the socialist system.[11]

Reinforcing Division

Over the course of the film's production, the studio and director considered over thirty different titles for the film. Within the lists of different titles, we find two dominant themes: identity and journeys.[12] Ultimately, the film never fulfils the expectations set by either of these ideas, but Kann's protagonist certainly had the potential to provide a new and challenging perspective on Jewish victimhood. Kann introduces his young protagonist standing under a portrait of Hitler and reciting the tenets of National Socialist 'Rassenkunde' ('racial science'). However, within the first five minutes of the film, we see Heinz repositioned from a decorated Rottenführer ('Section Leader') to a marginalized 'Mischling' ('half-Jew') when the school's headmaster reveals that Heinz's father was Jewish and orders Heinz to leave the school at once. When Heinz's classmates discover that his father was Jewish, they tear up a photograph of the once-celebrated war hero.[13] The pupils' inability to understand that Heinz's father could be both German and Jewish, and still be a patriotic hero, is central to the film's exploration of Germanness and Jewishness. As Heinz stands before his peers from the Hitler Youth with the torn-up fragments of his uniformed father's portrait at his feet, there is a clear sense that Kann's protagonist has the potential to act as a reconciliatory figure for the overcoming of National Socialist exclusive designations of 'race'. Through his dual identity as patriotic German and Jew, Heinz becomes the one character who could demonstrate to his peers, elders and, crucially, to himself that identity is a polyvalent construct.

The repeated undermining of 'racial' dichotomies appears to signal the film's critical engagement with antisemitic stereotypes whereby the ensuing comedy of errors is designed to hold a mirror up to the fallacy of the exclusive identity constructions forwarded under National Socialism. Having revealed Heinz's Jewish background at the start of the film, Kann then demonstrates how the most ardent advocates of National Socialism – the visiting state official, the wife of the camp commander and the local Gestapo – are unable to discern any difference between the epitome of the Hitler Youth and the ostracized and demonized 'Mischling'. Here, however, the film undermines its own position. Heinz's experience is by no means representative of everyday antisemitism. The very premise of the film lacks credibility. Heinz is told that he is either half-Jewish or quarter-Jewish on account of his father's background. The suggestion that Heinz's father could have become a decorated, high-ranking member of the Wehrmacht and that his Jewish background would only have been discovered posthumously is highly improbable. Furthermore, as the episodic nature of the film continues, Jewish identity increasingly becomes something to be denied and avoided. There are no other Jewish characters in the film who offer an alternative understanding of what it means to identify as, or be identified as, Jewish. Instead, we are offered an exceptional character in a unique scenario. Like Heinz, the film never comes to terms with the Jewish experience or offers any insight into Jews' everyday experience in Germany.

Even if we overlook this factual point in favour of exploring the dramatic potential of such a scenario, the opportunity to provide a biting critique of exclusive constructs of identity is never realized. Having been expelled from school, Heinz returns home and consults his physiognomy books and measures his own head in an attempt to disprove his Jewishness to himself and to others (Figure 8.1). Heinz does not want to be Jewish and, in order to 'prove' he is 'Aryan', he uses National Socialist pseudo-science. His repeated cry of 'I'll prove it to you all' signals the fundamental flaw with Kann's protagonist. Heinz's primary motivation for wanting to be a member of the Hitler Youth is not to survive, but to belong.

It is unclear how the audience is expected to respond at this point. The film's strategy appears to be based upon the simultaneous presentation and rejection of antisemitic tropes. If Heinz is Jewish but does not conform to the antisemitic stereotypes circulating in National Socialist propaganda, then by implication these same stereotypes must be

Figure 8.1. The film's inability to transcend stereotypes ultimately renders its treatment of antisemitism superficial. © DEFA-Stiftung/Herbert Kroiss. Source: Filmmuseum Potsdam.

false. However, the film never achieves full command of this strategy, not least because the consequences of undermining such stereotypes are always related back to the experience of an exceptional individual whose overwhelming response is one of relief rather than enlightenment. The film is not concerned with the consequences of the circulation of antisemitic tropes in textbooks and in schools for anyone other than Heinz. Instead, antisemitism ultimately becomes a plot device that allows the protagonist to move between different settings on his 'odyssey' through Germany.

The audience may accept his Jewish identity and the spurious logic of 'racial science', however Heinz does not. There is no indication that the character ever attempts to grapple with the question of what it means to be Jewish or German, or with the impact of these exclusive designations of identity for the persecution of Jews. His most profound exploration of Jewish and German identity is his questioning of Gabi and Marga about whether they would knowingly enter a relationship with a man who was not 'completely Aryan'. Heinz may embark on a physical journey from his family home across Germany, but the character himself shows little sign of development or maturity. As one critic reflected, Heinz 'learns nothing, suffers nothing, unlearns nothing, does not change' (Figure 8.2).[14]

Figure 8.2. At the end of the film, Heinz runs off into the distance to be reunited with Gabi – still carrying the uniform that he wore when he was inculpated in crimes against civilians. © DEFA-Stiftung/Herbert Kroiss.

Heinz's Subjective Misfortune

One of the central weaknesses underpinning *Stielke, Heinz, fünfzehn* is the director's inability to reconcile empathy for Heinz's crisis of identity with the critical message of the film. This is undoubtedly a deliberate strategy designed to achieve cognitive distance between the young ardent National Socialist and the East German audience. However, this critical distance does not account for the tonal discrepancies in the film's configuration of victimhood. Kann is unable to reconcile two critical impulses: why Heinz faces persecution and how that persecution is interpreted. Kann never seeks to supress Heinz's Jewish identity. After all, the protagonist's attempts to conceal his Jewish background serve as the dramatic impetus for the entire film. However, according to the filmmakers, the reason Heinz is persecuted is not why he is a victim. In their discussion of the film, the filmmakers repeatedly stressed that, first and foremost, Heinz is not a victim on account of his Jewish identity, but rather because of his failure to distance himself from National Socialist ideology. As Kann and the screenwriter Manfred Schmidt argued, 'Stielke fails to comprehend what good fortune he has, that he is thrown out and thus does not become a fascist murderer. He perceives this as a misfortune and even acts against it. That is actually a comical, a grotesque process'.[15] Herein lies one of the key problems in the film, namely its failure to acknowledge the implications of having a Jewish identity in the Third Reich and the concomitant reduction of the persecution Heinz faces to being a 'subjective misfortune'.[16]

There are two core problems with presenting Heinz's persecution as a 'subjective misfortune'. The first relates to Heinz's own understanding of the threat posed by being Jewish. The unsympathetic presentation of Heinz is compounded by the fact that his actions do not stem from the fear of the persecution Jews faced in National Socialist Germany. Rather, his wish to be a member of the Hitler Youth is underpinned by the desire to avoid the rejection that he would face – as he did at school – were his Jewish identity to be revealed. The desire to be a member of the Hitler Youth is more important to Heinz than the implications of being Jewish. As a result of his desire to act as a fully integrated member of the Hitler Youth, Heinz perpetually acts as a perpetrator, but at no point in the film does the audience gain an insight into the reasons compelling Heinz to act in the way he does, other than his superficial desire to belong to the dominant group. Indeed, were he not Jewish, there is little indication that Heinz would have become anything other than a cognisant perpetrator.

Stielke, Heinz, fünfzehn may have been positioned as a comedy, but its superficial and at times derogatory presentation of National Socialist persecution reduces the danger faced by Heinz, and more troublingly by Jews more broadly, to a coming-of-age odyssey. Heinz is placed in an *Erziehungsanstalt* or elite SS training school. Here the film appears to draw upon the aesthetics of a concentration camp within the context of a privileged German elite (Figure 8.3). The boys work in a quarry carrying stone, but are permitted lunch breaks in which they can talk freely among themselves. The boys sleep in barracks, but Heinz is overwhelmingly depicted resting or admiring his appearance in the mirror. Tensions between the boys in the barracks are reduced to teenage rivalry. Most troublingly, the only act of physical persecution depicted on screen by a National Socialist is the sadomasochist whipping of Heinz by the camp commander as Marga looks on with sexual pleasure. The only episode of Jewish persecution takes place off screen and, while the agonized cries of a tortured male clearly affect Heinz, they have no lasting impact on him. Instead, persecution becomes a narrative device for dramatic or comic effect.

DEFA was certainly aware of the film's shortcomings. In their pre-release reports, both DEFA and HV Film heavily criticized the super-

Figure 8.3. In *Stielke, Heinz, fünfzehn*, victimhood is visually appropriated, but narratively absent. © DEFA-Stiftung/Herbert Kroiss.

ficiality of the character of Heinz and his engagement with his Jewish identity. The report from HV Film concluded that:

> the so-called 'hard way to enlightenment' that this boy has to traverse or transcend through suffering remains for me very superficial. His inner struggle with the fact that his father is a Jew is quickly abandoned without the direction of his thinking at least becoming clear; his final decision has a predominantly spontaneous character. There is no indication of a process of awareness apparent to me.[17]

Similarly, the East German studio's foreign distribution department highlighted the protagonist's lack of 'believable, appropriate emotions'[18] to his situation in the film, while a second report from HV Film criticized the 'playful treatment of facts that are of an all too serious nature'.[19] In short, as one East German critic concluded at the time, *Stielke, Heinz, fünfzehn* 'paints a picture that only has surface'.[20]

A New Reading of the Past

When asked about his approach to depicting the Third Reich on screen, Michael Kann was resolute that, 'my generation cannot help but look at the past with our knowledge, with our attitude, of today'.[21] It was this 'attitude' that placed Kann and the producers in conflict with Wolfgang Kellner, whose 1984 novel *Abenteurer wider Willen* ('Unwilling Adventurer') served as the literary basis for the film. At the heart of Kellner's criticism was the filmmakers' justification of their adaptation according to their 'reading' [*Lesart*] of the material and the extent to which National Socialism should function as a dramatic backdrop.[22] While Kellner accepted the director's argument that 'action, strong confrontation, [and] great visual theatre' were needed in order to appeal to a new, young audience,[23] he questioned the reductive treatment of his source text which failed to grapple with the 'complications and multi-layered nature of the times'.[24]

A recurring theme in much of the correspondence between the author and production company is whether changes to the source material were underpinned by different generational approaches to the past. Kellner himself pointed to the fact that 'the filmmakers are of an age that they only know about this period through reflection. And I wrote my book precisely in order somewhat to relativize this reading'.[25] Interestingly, this tension was initially seen as a core motivation for approving the film. In a letter to DEFA, the head of the production company stressed that the material's 'almost lurid beginning' and 'wealth of adventurous action', coupled with a protagonist who would be 'of such interest to young cinemagoers', would be an 'interesting and justified statement of a no-longer quite so young upcoming director [*Nachwuchsregisseur*] on this historical topic'.[26] The importance of adopting a new approach to the National Socialist past was also acknowledged by film officials. Drawing parallels between Kann's approach and the work of East German directors Ulrich Weiß and Karl Heinz Lotz, HV Film's report on the film's scenario highlighted how a new generation of directors was 'making use of other artistic means to get closer to this period and also considering other subjects worth exploring than those that link personal experiences with the fascist period'.[27] This new approach was welcomed by officials at Progress Film who expressed their hope that young audiences would 'feel they are being spoken to through the fate of the young boy'. In so doing, the filmmakers would accomplish one of their key aims, namely 'to keep consciousness alive so that such times are never allowed to repeat themselves'.[28] The criticisms of the film did not centre on the film's aesthetic engagement with the National Socialist past or even the choice of protagonist, but rather they focused on the decision to transform a traditionally antifascist narrative and setting into a 'political adventure film'.[29] Reviewers overwhelmingly considered the film a missed opportunity, a sentiment perhaps best encapsulated in Eleonore Sladeck's review for the *Norddeutsche Zeitung*: 'When a young film debutant like Michael Kann turns to the long-standing theme of DEFA, that makes us curious – curious about the perspective'. But, Sladek concluded, while not wanting to detract from Kann's 'serious efforts at working through history for our teenage generation', the director's approach to the antifascist theme ultimately verges on 'colportage'.[30] Ultimately, in seeking to engage with questions of identity and victimhood in new ways, Kann inadvertently exposes the hollowness of rehearsed narratives of the past.

In films such as *Professor Mamlock* and *Die Bilder des Zeugen Schattmann*, we find the recurring trope of young men decrying the lack of engagement of their fathers' generation. This call to action was evidently designed to stress the importance of political engagement among young people and its transformative potential for the individual and for society as a whole. However, this becomes highly problematic when the active resistance of the younger generation is contrasted with the passivity of their fathers. The protagonists may demonstrate the coexistence of Jewish identity and communist resistance in theory, but in practice this polyvalent identity is rarely extended to other characters. Instead, characters who are presented solely as Jewish are often explicitly condemned for their lack of engagement. In *Professor Mamlock* and *Die Bilder des Zeugen Schattmann*, fathers are an inhibiting presence for their sons' antifascist development.[31] In contrast to their fathers, the sons are able to negotiate their Jewish identity by embracing communism and entering a state of active resistance. This, in turn, exposes the fathers' passivity which, in the absence of any other marker of identity, is inadvertently attributed to their Jewish identity. It is the young men's peers who provide an education in antifascist resistance that allows them to move from a 'victim of fascism' to a 'fighter against fascism'; and it is implicitly these young men who become the founding fathers of the GDR.

Father figures are strikingly absent in *Stielke, Heinz, fünfzehn*. Heinz's father dies before the film begins; the death of Max's father may provide the impetus for the teenage boys to question their role in the attack against civilians, but his words are only conveyed through a beyond-the-grave letter; and the absence of Gabi's parents is never explained. The only male voice other than the National Socialist characters is Gabi's grandfather. If the character of Heinz is designed to appeal to younger audiences by bringing 'an important historical subject closer to them, one which at the same time also contains contemporary significant questions', then Gabi's grandfather is designed to convey the wisdom of the first generation of East Germans.[32] Yet the grandfather remains a strangely peripheral figure throughout the film. He may assert that 'everyone is equal', that anyone who claims that Jews are '*minderwertig*' ('inferior') has 'something to hide' and that 'laws are only valid when they are for the good of the people', but we only learn this through Gabi's repetition of such phrases. Heinz may have been criticized for being 'a featherbrained Nazi who cannot think or express himself independently: he simply parrots', but Gabi's repeated refrain of 'Grandfather says. . .' carries little more reflective insight.[33]

We may be tempted to dismiss *Stielke, Heinz, fünfzehn* as a telling indictment of the superficiality of East German attempts to engage with the specificities of the persecution of Jews. However, while not detracting from the film's manifold shortcomings, Kann's film nonetheless shares many similarities with generational shifts in the depiction of the National Socialist past that were unfolding beyond the GDR's borders. Even a cursory look at cinematic output since the late 1980s reveals the marked increase in films depicting Jewish persecution under National Socialism in which children and teenagers are cast as the principal protagonists in films such as *Au revoir, les enfants* (*Goodbye, Children*, 1987), *A Friendship in Vienna* (1988), *Hitlerjunge Salomon* (*Europa Europa*, 1990) and *Alan & Naomi* (1992). It hardly seems a coincidence that this shift in focus should be accompanied by the coming of age of the first generation which had no direct relationship to, or memories of, the events portrayed on screen.

This nonetheless raises the question as to what the film's targeted message to this generation actually is. Audiences would certainly learn little about the specificities of National Socialist persecution from the film. We could well expect that Heinz's transformation from child to adult would map his ideological awakening from non-cognisant perpetrator to engaged resister. This, in turn, would provide an – albeit highly selective – retelling of older audiences' transition from citizens of a fascist regime to citizens of the socialist GDR, while also providing younger audiences with an idealized model of the power of antifascist conversion. Strikingly, *Stielke, Heinz, fünfzehn* does not follow this model. Rather, the film leaves the distinct impression that Heinz would undoubtedly adopt the socialist mantle with the same ease as he did the National Socialist regime, such is the superficiality of his conversion.

Of course, the choice of an unrepresentative protagonist need not be seen as a weakness of a historical film. As Robert Rosenstone has argued, historical films rely on 'compression' and 'condensation' in order to present complex historical events within the confines of a feature film.[34] This frequently results in the presentation of 'history as a process' whereby 'economics, politics, race, class and gender come together in the lives of individuals and groups'.[35] However, what marks a significant shift not only in *Stielke, Heinz, fünfzehn*, but also in the aforementioned examples, is the lack of functionality ascribed to the protagonist. Heinz is not designed to be a composite character representing several characters' experiences. Indeed, the entire premise of the film is dependent upon his very exceptionality.

Stielke, Heinz, fünfzehn undoubtedly embarks on a 'new' and 'original' path by breaking free from the narratives of the past, but there is a clear sense that the filmmakers fail to find their own voice. Images of antisemitic persecution circulate freely within the film, however they only ever receive a surface-level treatment. The film points to a series of antisemitic tropes and terms that circulated in National Socialist propaganda such as the 'Mischling', 'Rassenkunde', 'Rassenschande' and 'Jewish' physiognomy and employs them as labels rather than as persecutory concepts. They are exposed as specious and baseless when applied to Heinz, but their consequences for Jews living in the Third Reich more broadly are never explored. Similarly, there is no attempt by the filmmakers to use Heinz as a vehicle to raise questions for the spectator in the present or future. Rather, the film concludes with a clear caesura as the young man walks away from the camera to start a new life in the future. The past, meanwhile, is presented as a closed chapter.

Notes

1. Parts of this chapter have previously been published in Ward, 'Who Is Heinz Stielke? Questions of Identity in Michael Kann's *Stielke, Heinz, fünfzehn*' in Stephan Ehrig, Marcel Thomas and David Zell (eds), *The GDR Today: New Interdisciplinary Approaches to East German History, Memory and Culture*. Reprinted with the kind permission of Peter Lang.
2. Kersten, 'Ein untaugliches Objekt'.
3. Baschleben, 'Nur eine abenteuerliche Odyssee wider Willen'.
4. Scheinert, 'Gruppe Johannisthal: Thesen zum Projekt'.
5. DEFA, 'Stellungnahme. *Stielke Heinz, fünfzehn*'.
6. Bisky and Wiedemann, *Der Spielfilm*, 13.
7. It is not entirely clear whether Max is killed or seriously wounded.
8. Museum of Modern Art, '*Die Russen kommen (The Russians Are Coming)*'.
9. Sladeck, '*Stielke, Heinz, fünfzehn*'.
10. *Märkische Union*, 'Wesentliches fehlt'.
11. Brady and Hughes, 'German Cinema', 310.
12. For example, 'Wer bin ich: Stielke' ('Who am I: Stielke'); 'Heinz, Sohn des Johannes' ('Heinz, Son of Johannes'); 'Johannes' Sohn' ('Johannes' Son'); 'Sohn des Vaters Heinz' ('Son of the Father, Heinz'); 'Vaters Sohn' ('Father's Son'); 'Stielke ein deutscher Junge' ('Stielke, a German Boy'); 'Am Anfang das Ende' ('At the Beginning of the End'); 'Odyssee des Windhundes oder Heinz im Glück' ('Odyssey of a Greyhound or Heinz in Luck'); 'Weg mit Stielke' ('Away with Stielke').
13. In a curious and unexplored episode in the film, it is revealed that Heinz's father is killed by partisans. It is unclear how the audience is supposed to respond to the killing of the protagonist's father.
14. *Märkische Union*, 'Wesentliches fehlt'.
15. Linke, 'Wer will Stielke?'.
16. Gruppe Johannisthal, 'Führungskonzeption zum Szenarium *Abenteurer wider Willen* (AT) frei nach dem gleichnamigen Roman von Wolfgang Kellner'.
17. Abteilung Künstlerische Produktion, 'Einschätzung des Szenariums *Stielke, ein deutscher Junge*'.
18. DEFA-Außenhandel, 'Stellungnahme. *Stielke, Heinz, fünfzehn*'.
19. Abteilung Künstlerische Produktion, 'Einschätzung *Stielke, Heinz, fünfzehn*, DEFA Studio für Spielfilme, zur staatlichen Zulassung am 7.11.86'.
20. Sobe, 'Von des Rätsels Lösung keine Spur'.
21. Fiedler, 'Um eigene Erzählweise bemüht'.
22. Kellner, 'Letter from Wolfgang Kellner to Andreas Scheinert', 17 October 1986.
23. Kellner, 'Letter from Wolfgang Kellner to Andreas Scheinert', 11 October 1986.
24. Ibid.
25. Kellner, 'Letter from Wolfgang Kellner to Andreas Scheinert', 20 October 1986.
26. Scheinert, 'Letter from Andreas Scheinert to DEFA'.

27. Abteilung Künstlerische Produktion, 'Einschätzung des Szenariums *Stielke, ein deutscher Junge*'.
28. Progress Film, 'Stellungnahme: *Stielke, Heinz, fünfzehn*'.
29. Gruppe Johannisthal, 'Bestätigung des Filmstoffes'.
30. Sladeck, '*Stielke, Heinz, fünfzehn*'.
31. In *Die Bilder des Zeugen Schattmann*, this also applies to uncles.
32. Scheinert, 'Gruppe Johannisthal: Thesen zum Projekt'.
33. Kellner, 'Letter from Wolfgang Kellner to Andreas Scheinert', 1 February 1986.
34. Rosenstone, *History on Film/Film on History*, 39.
35. Ibid., 48.

Chapter 9

CALENDAR-BASED SHAME?

Siegfried Kühn's *Die Schauspielerin*

1988 marked the fiftieth anniversary of the 1938 November Pogroms. Although the event had been marked in the GDR before, the fiftieth anniversary offered a unique opportunity for the SED to demonstrate its readiness to commemorate Jewish persecution. The SED's preparations began sixteen months in advance when the Central Committee's Working Group for Church Affairs convened to discuss arrangements. All present agreed that this was 'a political event of significance for all of society', not least because of a 'growing international interest both of Jewish circles abroad and of political powers' in 'the existence of Jewish life in the GDR'.[1] A ten-page report was subsequently compiled which outlined a series of cultural, educational and media activities to take place on or around the 9 November 1988. It was against this backdrop that Siegfried Kühn's *Die Schauspielerin* (1988) was released. In the weeks running up to the anniversary, articles, interviews and reviews of *Die Schauspielerin* began to appear in newspapers, magazines and on television. The film was featured on the front cover of one of the GDR's leading film magazines, *Film und Fernsehen*, and a poster campaign in Berlin and the GDR's fourteen district capitals was financed by Progress Film.

Die Schauspielerin focuses on the fictional character of Maria Rheine, a stage actress in the ascendancy in 1930s Germany. Extolled by newspaper critics as 'the ideal of a German woman', Maria gains public and critical attention through a series of prominent stage roles including

Mary in *Maria Stuart* and Johanna in *The Maid of Orleans*. While performing at the theatre, she becomes romantically involved with Mark Löwenthal, a fellow actor and a Jew. After the coming to power of the NSDAP and the subsequent introduction of antisemitic legislation, Maria and Mark's careers move in opposite directions. Maria moves into a luxurious apartment in Munich, while Mark is relegated to living in a small flat in Berlin and only able to act at the Jewish Theatre.[2] Initially, Maria attempts to ignore the political situation by refusing to observe the boycott of Jewish shops or end her relationship with Mark. The introduction of the Nuremberg Laws suddenly designates Maria and Mark's 'mixed' relationship as illegal. Maria decides to take drastic actions to remain with the man she loves: she fakes her own suicide, adopts the identity of Manja Löwenthal and reinvents herself as Mark's Jewish wife. Unable to act on stage as Manja for fear of being recognized, Maria struggles to adapt to her new life and appears on the verge of a nervous breakdown. However, with Mark's encouragement, she decides to act again and the film ends with the pair reunited on stage at the Jewish Theatre.

West German critics were quick to highlight the far from coincidental timing of the film's release. Writing in *Der Tagesspiegel*, Heinz Kersten described the film as part of a state-sponsored 'remembrance campaign' launched by the SED which, in the journalist's view, was at least in part 'also motivated by foreign policy interests'. The timing of the film's release was, according to Kersten, indicative of a type of 'calendar-based shame' evident in both the GDR and the Federal Republic whereby prominent dates led to a sudden, renewed interest in the crimes of National Socialism.[3] In the *Frankfurter Allgemeine Zeitung*, Monika Zimmermann also responded with scepticism about the timing of the film's release. Over sixty per cent of her review, '*Die Schauspielerin* and the Politics of the GDR', is dedicated to arguing that 'perhaps it is no coincidence that the film is being shown just now, because it fits well in the political landscape of the other Germany'. Highlighting the fact that the GDR 'has always understood itself to be an antifascist state and has dismissed any share of responsibility for the period of German history associated with fascist rule', Zimmermann interpreted the state's 'conspicuous striving for a more intense relationship with the Jews' as part of an elaborate plan designed to improve the GDR's standing with the United States. After all, concluded Zimmermann, 'it is an open secret that Erich Honecker entertains the desire to be invited to America during his term of office – and even the GDR seems to know that Jewish influence on politics is stronger there than in their own country where numbers in the Jewish community amount to only a good three hundred'.[4]

The SED's desire to improve relations with the United States was not simply a matter of achieving a much-coveted invitation to the White House; it also urgently hoped to improve its economic relationship with the United States. According to Angelika Timm, a reduction in oil imports from the Soviet Union, difficulties in securing coal and iron ore from Poland and the subsequent need to buy these key resources from Western Europe using hard currency had contributed to an increase in foreign debt throughout the 1970s and into the 1980s.[5] The SED's financial problems were compounded by the decision of its Western creditors to withdraw forty per cent of their deposits from the GDR after the financial crises in Poland and Romania, and the provision of 1.95 billion DM in West German credits did not end the threat of bankruptcy so much as merely postpone it.[6] The SED believed the answer to its financial problems lay in the acquisition of Most Favoured Nation (MFN) status with the United States in the hope that the removal of tax restrictions from East German exports to the United States would significantly bolster the East German economy.

The two major obstacles to realizing these aims were the GDR's human rights record and its failure to pay reparations to Israel.[7] In its pursuit of a negotiated solution, the SED launched a personal offensive aimed at enlisting key foreign figures to act as advocates on the GDR's behalf. A number of these individuals were influential Jewish figures who were perceived to have links to the United States administration.[8] This was most obvious in the sustained pursuit of the President of the World Jewish Congress, Edgar Miles Bronfman who, during a visit to the GDR in 1988, was awarded the Großer Stern der Völkerfreundschaft (Grand Star of Nations' Friendship) in recognition of his 'extraordinary services to the German Democratic Republic, the understanding and friendship of the peoples and the preservation of peace'.[9]

The SED's commemoration of the fiftieth anniversary of the November Pogroms was thus unquestionably part of a broader political and economic strategical plan. However, it would be wrong to place Siegfried Kühn's *Die Schauspielerin* within this state-driven attempt to instrumentalize the past. We may well be tempted to approach a film that places Jewish victimhood at the core of its narrative as further evidence of the cynical exploitation of the National Socialist past, but as Daniela Berghahn argues, *Die Schauspielerin* is 'more than just an interesting example of an opportunistic change of the GDR's politics of memory'.[10] Not only does an explicitly political reading of *Die Schau-*

spielerin misattribute the origins of the film, but it also overlooks the competing political, cultural and commercial interests that shaped the GDR's final film to place Jewish persecution at the heart of the narrative. This chapter begins by re-examining the production context of *Die Schauspielerin* in order to draw out the significance of Kühn's presentation of his strong female protagonist. This lays the foundation for an examination of Jewish victimhood, the ways in which Maria's Jewish and gender identities intersect and the extent to which *Die Schauspielerin* marked a decisive repositioning of the Holocaust on screen in East German cinema.

There is little doubt that the release of *Die Schauspielerin* was carefully managed to coincide with the fiftieth anniversary of the November Pogroms. The premiere took place at Berlin's prestigious Kino International on 21 October 1988 and was described in *Neues Deutschland* as a 'solemn occasion' that formed 'part of a chain of events taking place during these weeks in our country in sombre memory of the antisemitic pogroms organized by the fascists in Germany fifty years ago in November 1938'.[11] Special guests included Hedda Zinner (author of the source novel, *Arrangement mit dem Tod*) and Martin Brandt, the only living survivor of the Jewish Theatre.[12] The premiere was attended by the Deputy Minister of Culture, Horst Pehnert, and the Minister of Church Affairs, Kurt Löffler. The screening of the film was preceded by the documentary short *Das Singen im Dom zu Magdeburg* (*Singing in Magdeburg Cathedral*, 1988) and an exhibition about the Jewish Theatre in Berlin titled 'Theatre in the Shadows' was organized in the cinema foyer.[13]

It is certainly tempting to conclude that *Die Schauspielerin* was DEFA's contribution to the SED's 'remembrance campaign'.[14] As a film which focuses on Jewish persecution in Germany during the Third Reich, *Die Schauspielerin* served as a visible example of the GDR's commitment to confronting Germany's fascist past. Nonetheless, when we examine both the film and its production files, it becomes clear that any such initiatives were driven by DEFA rather than the state. The film was already in pre-production when commemorative plans to mark the November Pogroms were first drafted by the Working Group for Church Affairs and it certainly was not commissioned by the SED as part of the official commemorations. The working group compiled a list of films that were to be screened in conjunction with the state-sponsored commemorative events. By the time the plans were submitted to the Central Committee for approval in March 1988, filming had already been completed for *Die Schauspielerin*. This means that the film could have been added to the list had the Minister or, indeed, the Central Committee, so desired. Yet no such statement appears.[15] Nor is there any mention of the film in the exhibition 'Und lehrt sie: Gedächtnis!' ('And Teach Them: Memory!') held at the Ephraim-Palais in Berlin 'in memory of the fascist November pogroms fifty years ago' despite a section dedicated to 'Film – an ever-present theme'.[16] Six films are singled out to illustrate that 'the antifascist theme and also the suffering and struggle to survive of the Jews in Germany were and are thematic constants of feature film production in that other Germany'. However, no reference is made to *Die Schauspielerin*. Instead, evidence of how Jewish persecution was 'a thematic constant' in East German film ends with a production made in 1974, *Jakob der Lügner*.[17]

Production documents reveal that the decision to approve *Die Schauspielerin* may well have been influenced by quite specific cultural-political problems rather than by any foreign policy offensive initiated by the Central Committee. The earliest document relating to the film is a nine-page report entitled 'Film conception for Hedda Zinner's novel *Arrangement mit dem Tod*' from December 1985. By 1985, there had been two attempts to film a Hedda Zinner text within the space of twelve months, both of which had failed because of perceived political and ideological transgressions of the screenplays. *Katja*, a critique of the doctrinal role of antifascism in the lives of young East Germans, was due to be filmed by Fernsehen der DDR (DDR-FS) in late 1984, but production was suddenly cancelled in September of the same year. Following the cancellation of *Katja*, DDR-FS recommended that the production team develop Zinner's *Ravensbrücker Ballade* (*Ravensbrück Ballad*) for the fortieth anniversary of the end of the Second World War. Again, the project was cancelled in pre-production because of concerns raised by the Committee of Antifascist Resistance Fighters (KdAW) about the film's inclusion of asocial and criminal prisoners in its narrative. A meeting was called between Zinner, the DDR-FS management, a representative of the KdAW, the deputy leader of the Central Committee's Department for Agitation and Zinner's son, John Erpenbeck. The written protocol of the meeting lays bare the tensions between the writer and the KdAW. The KdAW representative worried about what message young people would take away from a film which, he argued, focused too much on criminal prisoners and not enough on political prisoners.[18] In return, Erpenbeck retorted that the KdAW should not become the 'Committee for the Protection of Antifascist Art'.[19]

Here DEFA's decision to accept a screenplay based on Zinner's *Arrangement mit dem Tod* gains another context. Kühn submitted his proposal just ten months after the *Ravensbrücker Ballade* project was cancelled. Given the embarrassment caused by the cancellation of two works in quick succession by one of the GDR's leading authors, *Die Schauspielerin* provided DEFA with a suitable solution. With *Die Schauspielerin*, DEFA could exploit the opportunities offered by the fiftieth anniversary of the November Pogroms with a film that was sufficiently focused on themes of Jewish persecution to be marketable for the occasion, but ideologically innocuous enough to overcome the hurdles faced by previous Zinner adaptations. In fact, one of the most striking features of *Die Schauspielerin* is the extent to which the film not only avoids, but also decisively omits reference to antifascism and even to the Third Reich itself.

From Maria to Manja to Martyr

The presentation of a strong female character who decides to adopt a Jewish identity is designed to frame Maria's 'identity search' as a critique of gender and Jewish stereotypes.[20] Daniela Berghahn has described this as a 'significant departure from gender and racial stereotypes of earlier antifascist films'.[21] In comparison to the presentation of passive female characters in *Ehe im Schatten*, *Sterne*, *Professor Mamolock*, *Das Tal der sieben Monde* and *Die Bilder des Zeugen Schattmann* and the almost complete absence of female characters in *Lebende Ware*, *Jakob der Lügner* and *Stielke, Heinz, fünfzehn*, the focus on a strong woman who behaves with considerable independence and whose actions form the narrative core of the film provides an illuminating point of contrast with earlier DEFA Holocaust films. However, the extent to which *Die Schauspielerin* actually represents a significant reconfiguration of gender stereotypes requires further exploration.

Kühn's filmography has been described by Joshua Feinstein as 'a steady stream of light dramas or romantic comedies concerning relationships and stage-of-life crises among young adults or teenagers'.[22] It is perhaps not surprising, therefore, that Maria should also resemble women found in the *Alltagsfilm* ('film of everyday life') rather than those of the antifascist film. Andrea Rilke has revealed how women in Alltagsfilme in the 1960s were overwhelmingly presented as content workers whose professional achievements would anticipate personal happiness. By the 1970s, there was a gradual shift in depictions of female characters: they were no longer 'heroines constructed as exemplary models of the all-rounded developed socialist personality', but rather were presented as 'rebels who criticize society from a position within'.[23] By the 1980s, the strength and determination of female characters eclipsed their male counterparts. While male figures 'seem[ed] to be tilting at windmills' and 'losing strength, even breaking', female characters emerged emboldened and more confident, even from 'circumstances which are also not favourable to their self-assertion'.[24] The presentation of Maria breaks with depictions of passive femininity in comparison to films such as *Ehe im Schatten*, *Sterne* and *Jakob der Lügner*, however when placed in the context of the depiction of women in DEFA's 1980s output more broadly, it becomes clear that the figure of Maria was not out of place with contemporaneous female protagonists.

This point is important because Kühn's depiction of Maria as a strong woman has a direct influence on the film's depiction of Jewish identity. When the presentation of Maria is considered alongside that of Mark, it becomes clear that Kühn does not so much challenge stereotypically 'feminine' attributes found in films set in the Third Reich as he does displace them. Maria may be a strong and independent character, but traditionally 'feminine' attributes – submissiveness, lack of visibility in the public sphere and reduced screen presence – are instead attributed to Mark. At no stage in the narrative does Mark drive the plot; instead he is continually reacting to decisions taken by Maria. He frequently appears within a domestic setting and is repeatedly called upon to provide emotional support to Maria. The displacement of such 'feminine' attributes is all the more problematic given that Mark is Jewish. Kühn's film may challenge prescribed gender identities, but in so doing, it inadvertently reinforces Jewish stereotypes. By rendering Mark passive in order to emphasize Maria's agency in the plot, Kühn actually upholds the stereotype of the feminized Jew.[25]

To a certain extent, the strong focus on Maria to the detriment of other characters is not entirely unexpected given the deliberate change of title from Zinner's *Arrangement mit dem Tod* ('Arrangement with Death') to *Die Schauspielerin* ('The Actress'). Not only does the film's title clearly announce the centrality of one female character, it also underlines the importance of acting and identity construction to the film's plot. This 'programmatic' change, argued Kühn, was made because 'Maria knows no division between work and private life. . . . She is completely absorbed by her occupation. Occupation as vocation. The theatre is her life and her life cannot go on without theatre'.[26] This point is reinforced in the very opening scene which establishes Maria as an actress accustomed to playing different roles. It also offers an insight into her own understanding of character and identity. After experimenting with different poses and intonations when delivering her lines for Schiller's *Maria Stuart*, Maria sighs and bemoans the fact that she must play the role of Mary rather than Elizabeth. At this point, she understands identity as a straightforward construct with no scope for ambiguity: Mary is a weaker character and her royal cousin Elizabeth is the stronger woman.

As the film progresses, however, Maria's superficial understanding of identity starts to break down. The film is divided into two sections which roughly correspond to Maria's initial introduction to the audience and her decision to become Manja. Each section begins with Maria staring at her reflection in her dressing room mirror as she repeats the words, 'Women are not weak; there are heroic souls among the sex'. Whereas Maria looks into a single mirror in the opening scene, thereby reflecting her own single view of identity, the second time the sequence appears, her image is reflected from three different angles. Suddenly, her identity becomes polyvalent and fractured. Prior to this point, the vast majority of Maria's lines in the film have not been an articulation of her own thoughts, but rather those of the characters she is playing. The decision to reject the identity of Maria not only means the disavowal of her professional life on the stage; rather for the first time in the film, she is forced to play herself while simultaneously learning to be Manja.

A key obstacle for Maria as Manja lies not only in how others perceive her, but also in how she understands her own relationship to Jewishness. In this way, Daniela Berghahn has pointed to Maria's construction of a Jewish identity as 'a performative act through which she makes her role of Manja her new self'.[27] Maria's journey from the 'incarnation of Germanness' to an actress at the Jewish Theatre certainly challenges rigid notions of German and Jewish identities. However, when we examine Maria's process of transformation in closer detail, it becomes clear that the film is not only dependent upon, but often reinforces, Jewish stereotypes. Kühn never makes it clear whether Manja is merely another role for Maria. Maria herself describes Manja as such, telling Mark that, 'I can't even keep my role up in the street. But on stage I can't be any other actress than the one I used to be'. As Maria reflects at the start of the film, 'Sometimes I feel that I don't have any thoughts at all. At least no serious ones. And then I become frightened and think that there is no me. Just the different roles'. Maria recites lines written for fictional characters for much of the film and whether she actually considers the persona of Manja to be any different from playing a character on stage is a question that the film never attempts to answer.[28]

Zinner foresaw this very problem arising from the change of title from *Arrangement mit dem Tod* to *Die Schauspielerin*. At a meeting in November 1986 attended by Zinner, Regine Kühn[29] and the production company's dramaturge, Erika Richter, the author is recorded as having been 'appalled' at the change of title because 'she understands the word "actress" in the sense as if the heroine were being an actress . . . so an actress and nothing else, without responsibility, without real human values'.[30] The filmmakers defended the title by arguing that 'the intention of the film is just the opposite, that she simply stands by her morality, her love, her human responsibility as an actress. What she starts perhaps as just a role, she sees through to the bitter end'. But the report curtly concludes, 'Hedda Zinner would not have her mind changed by our explanation' because 'she sees in this title something negative that is not commensurate with the character and her actions'. The fact that the filmmakers argued that it was not their intention to depict Maria as an unthinking, chameleonic character for whom the decision to adopt a Jewish identity bears no deeper significance than that demanded by a stage role suggests that the depiction of Maria precisely as such is the result of the filmmakers' inability – rather than their unwillingness – to convey a more nuanced portrait. Nevertheless, this problem haunts the film throughout.

The ambiguity surrounding Maria's deeper awareness of the decision she takes in regard to her different 'role' comes to the fore in a scene that takes place shortly after she is celebrated as the 'incarnation of Germanness'. Having told her fellow actor and friend Montegasso that she is struggling to understand the role of Schiller's Johanna in *The Maid of Orleans,* Maria is seen alone in her large apartment in Munich. As she listens to the radio, Maria hears the sound of voices outside. She approaches the window and sees a group of young girls from the Bund Deutscher Mädel (League of German Girls, BDM) singing. Fascinated by the group's young, confident leader, Maria intently watches her and then steps back inside, faces the mirror and adopts the forceful body language of the girl while reciting lines from the play. When she later draws on this for her performance of Joan of Arc on stage, she is met with rapturous applause. The spectator is evidently expected to draw parallels between the BDM leader and 'the fourteen-year-old fanatical believer', Joan of Arc (Figure 9.1).[31] However, the adoption of the gestures of a member of a fascist organization by a woman whose partner is being persecuted by the National Socialists in order to strengthen her own performance on stage is at best problematic.

Kühn described Maria's decision to adopt a Jewish identity as the realization of a 'developmental arc' from 'an exclusively career-orientated actress to a self-aware tragic heroine'.[32] However, the pre-

Figure 9.1. Maria's unreflexive appropriation of the body language of the leader of the Bund Deutscher Mädel appears out of place against the backdrop of antisemitism. © DEFA-Stiftung/Norbert Kuhröber.

sentation of Maria as a tragic hero within the context of a film set in the Third Reich is deeply questionable since it remains unclear whether or not Maria is only pretending to be Jewish. Moreover, the film encourages audiences to overlook Maria's unreflective attitude and see her not only as the film's principal victim at the expense of the other characters, but also as a martyr. This becomes evident through two significant changes made to the source text. Whereas Zinner's Maria appears in twelve plays in *Arrangement mit dem Tod*, the cinematic Maria is predominantly depicted playing the character of Joan of Arc firstly in Schiller's *The Maid of Orleans* and – most notably in the film's final scenes – in George Bernard Shaw's *Saint Joan*. The decision to end the film with Maria reciting lines as Shaw's Joan could be seen as an attempt to break down rigid notions of who was and was not a victim in National Socialist Germany and instead return to more inclusive notions of victimhood. The film closes with a Jewish production of a play about an iconic martyr and it stresses the independence of a woman who is motivated not through organized or political resistance, but rather by personal happiness. As Daniela Berghahn has noted, the pathos of the scene is further heightened by the screenplay's subtle changes to the ending of Shaw's play. The protagonist's point of identification in the film is subtly modified by the decision to change the line, 'but if I go through the fire, I shall go through it to their hearts for ever and ever'.[33] Instead of 'their' hearts, as in Shaw's original play, Maria positions herself with 'my people', by which the audience is clearly intended to infer the Jewish people.[34] For Maria, the final scene is a triumph. She has reconciled herself with the Jewish identity of Manja and has overcome personal and societal prejudice to return to the stage. In so doing, she appears to have achieved personal happiness. However, the audience is aware that the path Maria has chosen will lead to the gas chambers, a point reinforced through the reference to fire in the film's closing line.

This episode was modified from the source text in which the literary Maria changes the lines of a different play, Julius Roderich Benedix's *Das Gefängnis* (*The Prison*). This raises the question as to why Kühn would have chosen to stage Maria's final scene using Shaw's *Saint Joan* when a similar episode using a different play appears in the novel. Although the modification of Shaw's text creates a triumphant conclusion for the film's deconstruction of gender and 'racial' binaries, the decision to align Maria to Joan of Arc also encourages the audience to view her as a martyr. This is particularly problematic given Joan of Arc's iconic status as a Christian martyr who decided to sacrifice herself and in so doing was aware that her actions would lead to her death. Not only is

Maria ostensibly a Jewish character, but to imply that Maria steps on stage with the knowledge of the fate that awaits her in a concentration camp is a distortion not only of Zinner's source text, but also of the realities facing the vast majority of real-life victims under National Socialism. The decision to present Maria in this way is all the more striking given that in Zinner's novel, Maria explicitly rejects the suggestion she is a martyr: '"I am not a martyr", she said, "and what I have done was anything other than exemplary"'.[35] No such statement is found in the film and, instead of highlighting the danger in which Maria's decision places herself and all those around her, Kühn deliberately constructs his protagonist as a tragic hero.

The failure to clarify Maria's own understanding of her decision to adopt the Jewish identity of Manja has further implications for the presentation of Maria as the film's principal victim and as a martyr. Arguably, the pathos for Maria does not primarily stem from the fact that she represents the suffering and probable death that awaits the Jews, but rather because her decision to adopt a Jewish identity will 'needlessly' cost Maria her life. In order for Maria's decision to appear as a sacrifice, her death needs to appear extraordinary. Conversely, the fate of the Jewish characters needs to be presented as an accepted fact or norm against which to measure Maria's sacrifice. As a result, the processes and prejudices underpinning the persecution of the film's Jewish characters are not questioned. Rather, Maria is celebrated for her active sacrifice, while the passive victimhood of the Jewish characters falls into the background.

Revealing Stereotypes

The marginalization of other Jewish characters' experiences and victimhood is particularly acute in relation to the character of Mark. Whereas Maria appears in seventy-one scenes, Mark features in just forty-five.[36] However, the marginalization of Mark and the other Jewish characters is not merely a question of quantifiable screen presence. Rather, Mark remains an underdeveloped character who is objectified from the outset. We must be cautious not to overstate the changes made by the director and screenwriter to the novel given that the filmmakers repeatedly emphasized that they had 'not filmed Hedda Zinner's novel, but rather made a film based on the themes of this book'.[37] Nonetheless, the filmmakers' treatment of the source text is highly revealing, not least because the changes made to Zinner's source text reveal the extent to which the film inadvertently reinforces Jewish stereotypes on screen. On first viewing, Kühn appears deliberately to undermine preconceived notions of Jewishness. In the screenplay, Mark is described as 'a blond, slender young man', while the Jewish extras are described as people 'among whom, however, there are only a few about whom one could say that their face has a clear Jewish appearance [*deutlich jüdischer Einschlag*]. Most look just as Jewish as Mark – that is to say, not at all'.[38] As in *Jakob der Lügner*, visual and cultural signifiers of Jewish identity are conspicuously absent. There is nothing to suggest Mark is Jewish other than the verbal cues of the other characters. Furthermore, by opening the film shortly after the NSDAP comes to power in 1933, Mark is introduced as a German citizen and without the imposed markers of Judaism such as the 'Judenstern'. Rather, we encounter him as a German citizen who, as the plot advances, becomes increasingly ostracized from society on account of his Jewish background. This has the effect of encouraging the audience to view the sudden alterity of Mark as a purely external and factitious construct. This aspect of the screenplay was singled out for praise by DEFA's studio director, Hans-Dieter Mäde, who reported that 'it is essential that he has nothing intrinsically exotically Jewish [*nichts Exotisch-Jüdisches*], but rather appears as a normal modern young German who is suddenly excluded on account of the "legislation" of an inhumane system'.[39]

Kühn may depict his Jewish characters as assimilated victims at the start of the film, but the narrative quickly undermines this through the repeated presentation of Jewish characters standing outside of German society. Although the film may challenge reductive visual stereotypes through Mark, the dialogue often risks rehearsing the stereotype of Jewishness as a non-German identity. Shortly after their romance begins, Mark warns Maria that he faces persecution because of his Jewish identity and tells her, 'It is my bad luck that my mother is a pretty Spanish Jew and my father is just a normal assimilated German Jew'. Given the exclusion of both Maria and Mark's familial background (in contrast to the novel, in which both sets of parents feature prominently), Mark's revelation that he has a foreign parent serves no narrative function in the film other than to risk associating Jewishness with a foreign heritage. Earlier versions of the screenplay also emphasize Mark's discomfort with being forced to adopt an exclusively Jewish identity given how he had previously considered himself as fully integrated into German society rather than into the Jewish Community. In the scenario from August 1986, Mark tells Maria: 'I also don't know why I am supposed to be a Jew. All of a sudden. I have never felt Jewish. If I at least knew, I would have something to profess. There would be some sense in that'.[40] In the film, however, Mark is depicted as being at ease with his place in the Jewish Community and, while he is forced to join the Jewish Theatre to continue acting rather than actively choosing to do so, he does not seem to question his place within it. Furthermore, whereas the literary treatment of the story includes episodes in which Mark faces verbal taunts, has anonymous notes pinned on his dressing room door, is publicly jeered on stage and beaten to the point of having to be admitted to hospital leaving him 'close to a breakdown', the cinematic Mark appears largely desensitized to antisemitism.[41]

The discrepancy between how Mark is presented visually and narratively is echoed in the presentation of Maria as Manja. The decision to present the same character as both a non-Jewish and Jewish woman allows the film to critique the false dichotomy of Germanness and Jewishness. After Maria's decision to fake her own suicide by killing Maria and reinventing herself as Manja in order to circumvent the Nuremberg Laws and pursue a relationship with Mark, Kühn revisits the film's very first scene. The almost shot-for-shot recreation of the opening scene establishes a pivotal point of comparison by reminding the audience that, despite changes in adjectives and nouns attributed to the protagonist through her decision to change from the 'Aryan' Maria to the Jewish Manja, the woman sitting before the mirror is the same person. However, there is a marked change in how others perceive her. In her first act as Manja, she is chastised for using the 'wrong' lavatory. The demarcation of 'Aryan' and Jewish lavatories recalls an earlier scene in which Maria is sitting on a bench clearly marked 'Only for Aryans' and Maria's markedly different treatment by society provides her with a sudden awakening to the level of societal antisemitic prejudice of which she has hitherto been unaware.

The problem here lies in the fact that Kühn remains dependent upon the visual propagation of the very binaries he is trying to undermine in the film's narrative. Narratively, the film attempts to hold a mirror up to the imposition of fictitious labels which suddenly ostracize the 'incarnation of Germanness' from society based on her decision to adopt a new Jewish identity. In order for this sharp point of contrast to function, however, other characters need to recognize Maria (as Manja) as being Jewish. Here, the film's inability to reconcile its narrative and visual presentations of Jewishness comes to the fore. We first encounter Maria as Manja emerging from the smoke at the railway station (Figure 9.2).

Figure 9.2. The depiction of Maria/Manja is incongruous with both character and setting. © DEFA-Stiftung/Norbert Kuhröber.

The scenario describes Maria's walk through the station as having 'the atmosphere of a nightmare' and, dressed from head to toe in black with dark glasses and a veil, Maria's appearance suggests she is mourning the death of her former self.[42]

When Maria enters the lavatory, a disembodied and shrill voice shouts 'Use the last lavatory on the right!', clearly indicating that her new appearance marks her as Jewish in the eyes of the attendant who 'with one look from top to bottom assesses Maria'.[43] The decision to present Manja as an orthodox Jew in appearance appears to have been driven by narrative expediency and the need to facilitate a scene in which Maria is instantly identified as being Jewish by the lavatory assistant. The film's narrative and visual depictions of Jewishness thus often appear to be operating to different ends and, although Maria's narrative trajectory does problematize binary constructs of German and Jewish, the film nevertheless remains dependent upon visual stereotypes to structure this transformation.

Persecution Without Perpetrators

Given the interference of the KdAW in previous attempts to film screenplays dealing with National Socialist persecution highlighted at the start of this chapter, we might expect that DEFA would have been only too receptive to a screenplay which simultaneously presented the studio with a film which could be released in time for the fiftieth anniversary of the November Pogroms, but which did not challenge the hierarchy of victimhood present in East German historiography. However, reports were far more concerned with the dramatic investment in the Jewish characters. The only pre-release report that questioned the ideological suitability of the film's treatment of its subject matter came from HV Film which pointed to the lack of 'ideological political consequence (class issues)'. Nonetheless, the greatest point of concern for HV Film resided in the fact that 'Maria performs the change of identity . . . as she would research a role; moreover she is never really in danger because there is no real social setting'.⁴⁴ Concerns about the film's dramatic and historical treatment of its subject matter were shared by the film's own production company (KAG). In March 1987, the head dramaturge and the leader of Gruppe Babelsberg reviewed the – by then yet to be filmed – screenplay for *Die Schauspielerin*. In their report, Dieter Wolf and Erika Richter outlined a series of changes which were to be made prior to the filming of *Die Schauspielerin*.⁴⁵ The first set of changes included the complete rewrite or removal of two episodes depicting Jewish characters. The first scene to be re-written (and which was later removed entirely) depicted the Jewish Theatre ensemble celebrating a Passover meal in full orthodox dress in the middle of the theatre courtyard. Zinner had been so appalled by the scene and 'emphasis of the exoticism of Jewish customs' that she described it as 'the worst sort of theatre'.⁴⁶ The next scene depicted a traditional Hora dance – a scene which remains in the final film – and was also rewritten in order that it should lose its 'emotionally demonstrative character'. Alongside the rewriting of these two scenes, there was a second pre-condition for the acceptance of the screenplay: the removal of three episodes of antisemitism. The first of the three episodes depicted Maria reciting an antisemitic essay written by her twelve-year-old neighbour that quoted directly from the National Socialist magazine *Der Stürmer*. The second and third episodes revolved around the NSDAP's attempts to mask its antisemitic acts during the 1936 Olympics – such as the painting over of 'only for Aryans' on benches – only to resume its persecutory actions as soon as the international community had left.

The production company revisited the recommended changes two months later. They again stressed the importance that 'all obvious signs of fascist behaviour' in the screenplay be 'eliminated'. Instead of 'demonstrative signs' of antisemitism, the dramaturges called on the filmmakers to follow the 'general principle of the film' and to 'register the everyday world with its signs of the times' which must 'first be discovered by the spectator'.[47] The importance of 'everyday fascism in the Germany of the Nazi regime' signals an important shift in East German Holocaust film.[48] In *Die Schauspielerin*, the film's primary concern does not lie in individual acts of antisemitism, but rather with its societal propagation. While this approach certainly establishes new ground in highlighting the widespread societal acquiescence to antisemitic acts, it is not without its own problems. As was the case with *Ehe im Schatten*, by potentially holding everyone to account, Kühn fails to question the behaviour of any one individual. The question as to who is responsible for the persecution of Maria and, more broadly, of the film's other Jewish characters, remains unanswered. It is telling that the only identifiable 'perpetrators' in the entire film are a young child who, dressed in an SS uniform, playfully pretends to shoot at Maria, and the aforementioned lavatory assistant who is deliberately positioned at the back of the shot (Figure 9.3). *Die Schauspielerin* appears to be a film about persecution that is strangely lacking in persecutors.

Figure 9.3. The antisemitism in *Die Schauspielerin* is so 'everyday' that it is difficult to apply the term perpetrator at all. © DEFA-Stiftung/Norbert Kuhröber.

Breaking with the Past

In keeping with the shifting modes of engagement evident in *Jakob der Lügner* and *Stielke, Heinz, fünfzehn*, *Die Schauspielerin* reflects a desire among the filmmakers to target new audiences. Regine Kühn defended her decision to present Maria as a woman with more in common with the modern-day spectator than with 1930s society by arguing that, 'in the first instance, Maria is supposed to be very close to the everyday outward manner of young people today in order initially to facilitate uninhibited identification'.[49] The decision that the most effective way to market *Die Schauspielerin* to young audiences was to emphasize the parallels with modern-day society instead of rehearsing the antifascist narratives of the previous generation marks a significant shift in presentations of the National Socialist past. This fading ideological imperative is most powerfully encapsulated in a widely circulated interview given by Kühn at the time of the film's release. When asked the seemingly obligatory antifascist question, 'But, for all Maria is a powerful [and] dynamic personality, doesn't she arrive at active antifascist resistance?', Kühn answered in the negative: 'No, that would be a different story. It would be conceivable for Maria to arrive at antifascist resistance if she carried on developing as she does in the time span of my film. But, as I said, that would be a different film'.[50] *Die Schauspielerin* signals that paying lipservice to the GDR's antifascist heritage was no longer a prerequisite for DEFA films.

The removal of an explicit antifascist framework exposed a significant fracture in the transmission of collective memories in the GDR. Kühn's film, which one reviewer described as 'a film of the later generations about a time of which they have no direct experience', provoked considerable debate in the press and within DEFA about younger generations' knowledge of Jewish persecution.[51] The debate revolved around the film's ending and the extent to which audiences could be relied upon to apply their own knowledge of the period to understand what happened to the Jewish Community after the film ends. The director was born in 1935 and Kühn openly stated that 'I only know German fascism from how it is perceived', adding 'of course, I have read a lot about it [and] watched a lot of films about the period'.[52] Given the director conceded that his limited knowledge of National Socialism was acquired from secondary sources, Kühn's attitude to the film's conclusion is particularly surprising. When asked why the film ends when it does, Kühn replied, 'Our modern-day film spectator knows very well what the Nazis did with the Jews, including with the Jewish actors. I am building on the historical and political knowledge of the audience'.[53] However, his views were by no means shared by journalists or even DEFA officials and the question of whether audiences could reasonably be expected to know what happened to the Jewish characters after the film ends was the subject of a fascinating behind-the-scenes discussion at DEFA.

The debate about audience knowledge first began in 1986. At the initial meeting between the filmmakers and Hedda Zinner, the author raised doubts as to whether the majority of the audience would be able to understand the implications of the Jewish actors' dismissal from the Jewish Theatre.[54] Following the meeting, the filmmakers intended to include text at the end of the film announcing the fate of the Jewish characters. Yet by May 1987 when the screenplay was presented to the head dramaturge of Gruppe Babelsberg, the inclusion of text informing the audience about the fate of European Jews under National Socialism 'was unanimously [and] vehemently rejected' because 'there was the unanimous belief that you can take for granted that the fate of the Jews is really well known and that a scrolling text of that sort would destroy the pathos of the final scene'.[55] HV Film was of a different opinion, however, and described the question of whether 'the fate of the Jews as known can really be assumed' as 'a questionable conclusion'.[56] The final film does not contain the rolling text, but the issue remained open as to whether audiences would necessarily understand what happened to the characters beyond the plot. The press notes prepared by Progress Film announce that Kühn's ending was underpinned by a deliberate ambiguity that pointed to both the 'liquidation of the Jewish theatre' and 'the Final Solution'. The notes continue, 'the audience today knows this terrible end and brings this knowledge into an emotionally activating and continuing relationship with Maria-Manja's act of life and love'.[57] Nevertheless, upon release reviewers continued to question whether audiences, in particular younger spectators, would in fact be aware of this wider historical context.[58]

Audiences would certainly have learnt little about National Socialism from *Die Schauspielerin*. Just as Beyer argued that *Jakob der Lügner* was a film that 'has nothing informational, nothing educational in meaning', *Die Schauspielerin* is a film in which, as one reviewer observed, 'historical and political knowledge is assumed'.[59] It could be argued that both audiences' lack of awareness about the fate of the Jewish characters and the lack of contextual depth in the film are indicative of the institutional failures within East German society to discuss Jewish persecution under National Socialism. However, when placed in an international context, the shortcomings of *Die Schauspielerin* appear far less nationally determined and far more symptomatic of broader generational and demographic shifts in cinematic engagements with the National Socialist past. Kühn's film was by no means the only film in the 1980s that reduced the Third Reich to a dramatic backdrop in order to exploit the dramatic tension arising from the demands placed on individuals' lives under National Socialism for a story about star-crossed lovers. *Le Dernier Métro* (*The Last Metro*, 1980), *Forbidden* (1984) and *38 – Auch war das Wien* (*'38 – Vienna Before the Fall*, 1986) are all romances in which non-Jewish women make personal sacrifices for the sake of their Jewish male lovers. The similarities between *Die Schauspielerin* and such Western productions are not only generic: both *Le Dernier Métro* and *38 – Auch war das Wien* portray strong-willed non-Jewish actresses in a relationship with Jewish men of the theatre (a director and writer respectively), while the plot of *Forbidden*, in which an increasingly emasculated Jewish man is overshadowed by a confident and independent non-Jewish woman, anticipates the gender relations of Kühn's film. Furthermore, all three films were criticized for their failure to engage with the causes and effects of antisemitism. Dietrich Kuhlbrodt criticized '*38* for reducing 'historical facts to a few sentences of dialogue',[60] Fernando Croce accused *Le Dernier Métro* of ultimately succumbing to 'fuzzy-centred nostalgia'[61] and David Robinson argued that the characters in *Forbidden* displayed a level of indiscretion 'quite inappropriate to the dangers around them'.[62]

Die Schauspielerin marked one of the most significant developments in East German Holocaust film. The film's target audience was the first generation to be educated and socialized exclusively in the GDR. In their attempts to attract this demographic, the filmmakers explicitly downplayed possible ideological readings. There is no discussion of class or resistance in the film, nor is there any attempt to displace responsibility to the West. It is true that the film does not seek to challenge its audience morally or politically, but by encouraging the spectator to identify with Maria, the film allows antisemitism to be experienced as a personal struggle rather than as a collective action. Attempts by Western journalists at the time of the film's release to frame *Die Schauspielerin* as an ideologically inflected production overlook the content of the film in regard to what is – and just as importantly, what is not – shown. Precisely because of its circumventive depiction of Jewish persecution, *Die Schauspielerin* may well represent one of DEFA's most internationally compatible films of the National Socialist past.

Notes

1. Cited in Mertens, *Davidstern unter Hammer und Zirkel*, 183.
2. The Jewish Theatre was a theatre for Jewish actors and audiences created by the National Socialist state as a distraction to mask state-sponsored antisemitism to the outside world.
3. Kersten, *So viele Träume*, 306–7.
4. Zimmermann, '*Die Schauspielerin* und die Politik der DDR'.
5. Timm, *Jewish Claims Against East Germany*, 14.
6. Steiner, *The Plans That Failed*, 172.
7. Timm, *Jewish Claims Against East Germany*, 106–7.
8. Ammer, 'DDR und Judentum: 50 Jahre nach den Novemberpogromen', 21. See also Timm, 'Der 9. November 1938 in der politischen Kultur der DDR', 261.
9. O'Doherty, *The Portrayal of Jews in GDR Prose Fiction*, 66.
10. Berghahn, 'Resistance of the Heart: Female Suffering and Victimhood in DEFA's Antifascist Films', 174.
11. Knietzsch, 'Tragischer Weg zu menschlicher Größe'.
12. Zinner, *Arrangement mit dem Tod*.
13. *Das Singen im Dom zu Magdeburg* focuses on performances of Jewish and Christian music by the choir of Magdeburg Cathedral and the chief cantor of the West Berlin Jewish Community, Estrongo Nachama.
14. Kersten, *So viele Träume*, 306.
15. A further opportunity arose one week later when the Central Committee's plans were authorized by the Council of Ministers on 6 April 1988, the day after the final version of *Die Schauspielerin* was approved by DEFA.
16. Grabowski and Strohschein, '*Und lehrt sie: Gedächtnis!*', 107.
17. The films were *Ehe im Schatten, Affaire Blum, Sterne, Professor Mamlock, Nackt unter Wölfen* and *Jakob der Lügner*.
18. 'Protokoll der Diskussion zu *Ravensbrücker Ballade* von Hedda Zinner am 21.2.1985 im DDR-Fernsehen', reprinted in Jarmatz, *Ravensbrücker Ballade oder Faschismusbewältigung in der DDR*, 83.
19. Jarmatz, *Ravensbrücker Ballade*, 87.
20. Kühn, 'Regie-Konzeption zu *Die Schauspielerin*'.
21. Berghahn, 'Resistance of the Heart', 174.
22. Feinstein, *The Triumph of the Ordinary*, 249.
23. Rinke, *Images of Women in East German Cinema*, 8.
24. Schieber, 'Anfang vom Ende der Kontinuität des Argwohns 1980 bis 1989', 274.
25. For more on the stereotype of the feminized Jew in film, see Doneson's 'The Jew as a Female Figure in Holocaust Film'.
26. Agde, '*Die Schauspielerin*'.
27. Berghahn, 'Resistance of the Heart', 178.
28. Ibid., 177.
29. *Die Schauspielerin* was directed by Siegfried Kühn with a screenplay by Regine Kühn. Siegfried Kühn will henceforth be referred to as Kühn. Regine Kühn will be referred to using her full name.
30. Richter, 'Protokollnotiz über ein Gespräch zum Exposé *Die Schauspielerin*, das am 25.11.86 zwischen Hedda Zinner, Regine Kühn und mir [Erika Richter] zeitweise in Anwesenheit John Erpenbecks geführt wurde'.
31. This line is spoken by Montegasso in the film.

32. Kühn, 'Regie-Konzeption zu *Die Schauspielerin*'.
33. Shaw, *Bernard Shaw's Plays*, 195.
34. The line used in the film is thus, 'but if I go through the fire, I shall go through it to the hearts of my people for ever and ever'. Whether audiences would actually have noticed this is highly debatable. Berghahn, 'Resistance of the Heart', 181.
35. Zinner, *Arrangement mit dem Tod*, 241.
36. DEFA, 'Rollenauszug'.
37. Agde, '*Die Schauspielerin*'.
38. Kühn, '*Die Schauspielerin*. Screenplay'.
39. Mäde, 'Stellungnahme zum Film *Die Schauspielerin* nach Hedda Zinners Roman *Arrangement mit dem Tod*'.
40. Kühn, '*Die Schauspielerin*. Scenario'.
41. Zinner, *Arrangement mit dem Tod*, 40.
42. Kühn, '*Die Schauspielerin*. Screenplay'.
43. Ibid.
44. Abteilung Künstlerische Produktion, 'Stellungnahme zu *Die Schauspielerin*'.
45. Gruppe Babelsberg, 'Thesen zur Weiterarbeit'.
46. Gruppe Babelsberg, 'Protokollnotiz über ein Gespräch zum Exposé *Die Schauspielerin*'.
47. Gruppe Babelsberg, 'Thesen zur Weiterarbeit'.
48. Abteilung Künstlerische Produktion, 'Einschätzung zu *Die Schauspielerin*, Spielfilm des DEFA-Studios für Spielfilme, zur staatlichen Zulassung am 26.4.1988'.
49. Gruppe Babelsberg, 'Protokollnotiz über ein Gespräch zum Exposé *Die Schauspielerin*'.
50. Agde, '*Die Schauspielerin*'.
51. Voss, 'Wandlung und Verwandlung'.
52. Agde, '*Die Schauspielerin*'.
53. Ibid.
54. Gruppe Babelsberg, 'Protokollnotiz über ein Gespräch zum Exposé *Die Schauspielerin*'.
55. Gruppe Babelsberg, 'Thesen zur Weiterarbeit'.
56. Abteilung Künstlerische Produktion, 'Stellungnahme zu *Die Schauspielerin*'.
57. Progress Film, 'Progress Pressebulletin: *Die Schauspielerin*'.
58. Kruppa, 'Wider verbotene Liebe'.
59. Semkat, 'Geschichte einer Liebe im faschistischen Deutschland'.
60. Kuhlbrodt, '38'.
61. Croce, '*The Last Metro*'.
62. Robinson, 'Cinema: Invention and Skill Blossom out on a Shoestring Budget'.

Conclusion

Can we speak of a set of characteristics that collectively define East German Holocaust film? We must approach this question with caution. We should certainly be wary of treating DEFA's output, let alone the GDR itself, as a homogenous entity. As this book has demonstrated, the cultural and political conditions under which films were made and released shifted not only between decades, but also within the space of years and even months in what have become known as 'freezes' and 'thaws'. This was further complicated by the ongoing influence of first-generation narratives of antifascist heroism and resistance well into the 1980s which continued to inform the commemorative context of discursive legacies of the National Socialist past in the GDR.

It is true that for four decades, DEFA was under state-ownership and subject to the cultural and political directives of the ruling SED party which exercised a direct and indirect influence over all stages of East German filmmaking. But this did not mean that its productions were unambiguous affirmations of state rhetoric. While filmmaking in the GDR was organized according to vertical structures, the film studio, the production companies (KAG) and individual directors often maintained a considerable degree of independence over the subject matter. Nor was the GDR a hermetically sealed state. Both East German filmmakers and, albeit to a lesser extent, audiences were exposed to films from outside the GDR. West German television was available throughout most of the GDR which afforded audiences access to alternative depictions of the past, as did the carefully selected foreign films that played in East German cinemas. East German filmmakers regularly attended international film festivals, not only in socialist countries such as the Soviet Union (Moscow) and Czechoslovakia (Karlovy Vary), but also in Western countries such as France (Cannes), Italy (Venice) and the United Kingdom (Edinburgh). Moreover, in conjunction with

DEFA-Außenhandel, the Deutsche Hochschule für Filmkunst (the German University for Film Art) regularly screened foreign films to its students that had not been approved for general release.[1] Given that DEFA filmmakers invariably received their training at the Deutsche Hochschule für Filmkunst, the extent to which East German filmmakers were conversant with international filmmaking trends should not be underestimated.

This book has traced the conception, production and release of nine films through a detailed analysis of the images and storylines used to present National Socialist Jewish persecution in East German film. If we are looking to locate a readily identifiable set of visual or textual markers, we will be as frustrated with the case of the GDR as we would with any national cinema. Throughout this book, I have cautioned against conflating what is depicted with how it is depicted. In order to understand the significance of East German Holocaust film, we need to move beyond a set of recurring tropes and instead consider how these visual and textual markers of victimhood and perpetration sat alongside, were interwoven through and even challenged dominant modes of remembrance in the GDR. Here we return to the central question of this book: how did East German filmmakers engage with Jewish persecution in a state which privileged communist heroism over Jewish victimhood and German perpetration?

The Holocaust on film was neither taboo nor unwelcome in the GDR. Jewish victimhood and persecution were present and permissible themes throughout the history of the state and studio. There is no evidence that the SED objected to the focus on, or inclusion of, the theme of Jewish persecution, nor is there any suggestion that DEFA sought to pre-empt any negative response from the state to the subject matter through forms of direct or indirect censorship. Even during periods of heightened cultural and political tensions, filmmakers were not only able to place Jewish persecution at the heart of a film, but they could also rely on the support of the studio management and even state ministers to intervene and assert the irrevocability of the Jewish narrative. As we have seen in the cases of *Lebende Ware*, *Jakob der Lügner* and, to a lesser extent, *Sterne*, the unwavering insistence on the inclusion of Jewish persecution was not always true for DEFA's production partners.

Jewish characters are visible victims in the films. It is true that East German films repeatedly draw on the trope of an older Jewish male who is depicted as a bourgeois, educated Jew who upholds traditional German cultural values and displays a high level of fluency with German cultural heritage. This point aside, there is no attempt to codify Jews visually on screen. Instead, Jewish characters are depicted as highly assimilated and their Jewish identity is signalled through a combination of linguistic signifiers in the screenplay and imposed markers of alterity in the narrative. This is particularly effective in *Ehe im Schatten*, *Professor Mamlock*, *Stielke, Heinz, fünfzehn* and *Die Schauspielerin* as the external markers of Jewish identity are introduced during the course of the film. This approach serves to emphasize the extent to which Jewish characters in the films suddenly find themselves excluded from German society and allows the audience to see the characters' ostracism unfold on screen.

Where this approach becomes problematic, however, is in the often implicit suggestion that Jews had the agency to act like non-Jewish Germans and join the antifascist resistance. It must be stressed that the presentation of Jewish victimhood was never contingent upon the inclusion of an antifascist narrative or a communist figure and *Ehe im Schatten*, *Lebende Ware* and *Die Schauspielerin* demonstrate that it was entirely possible to exclude both an individual antifascist hero and indeed any reference to the antifascist resistance more broadly. That is not to say that the lurking spectre of masculine communist resistance was always absent in East German Holocaust films. *Sterne*, *Professor Mamlock*, *Das Tal der sieben Monde* and *Die Bilder des Zeugen Schattmann* all include episodes of communist resistance.[2] Here again, however, we must be careful not to view East German Holocaust film in a cultural vacuum. In her 1978 article, 'The Jew as a Female Figure in Holocaust Film', Judith Doneson points to the recurring narrative codification of 'the Jew as a weak character, somewhat feminine, being protected by a strong [male] Christian-gentile'.[3] The focus of Doneson's article is the impact of romance storylines on the depiction of Jewish identity in Holocaust films, but her argument – in which she specifically mentions *Sterne* – that Jewish characters are repeatedly reduced to passive figures to be rescued and who serve as a 'humanizing force' for the non-Jewish characters has a clear application to the figure of the antifascist resister in East German Holocaust films.[4]

Doneson's article serves to remind us again of the importance of situating East German Holocaust film in its national and international context. As we have seen throughout this book, in order to understand the narrative and visual strategies employed in East German Holocaust films fully, it is necessary to go beyond the borders of the GDR. This is particularly important from the 1970s onwards when a new generation of filmmakers and audiences who had no direct experience of life in the Third Reich began to demand new ways of approaching the past on screen. Here we find similarities between East German and international Holocaust films, above all those from Western countries. The shifting approaches to the Holocaust on film in the GDR are not always attributable to the secondary effects of generational change, however. One of the most surprising findings of this book has been the extent to which Holocaust films were harnessed by the studio and state as a means of showcasing East German filmmaking and identity to the West. This was often accompanied by a deliberate decision to temper – and even elide – an antifascist narrative when marketing the films to Western audiences. Indeed, the decision to submit *Jakob der Lügner* for the category of Best Foreign Language Film at the Oscars shows that films dealing with the National Socialist past could be selected to represent the state even if they did not feature an antifascist character. Such films may have been situated within the antifascist traditions of East German filmmaking at home, but abroad the studio and state saw these films as unmissable opportunities 'to reach a wide public in the USA for the first time' and allow the GDR 'to become politically and commercially active' in the West.[5]

Where we find the explicit depiction of persecution against Jews, the perpetrators are invariably exteriorized. In *Sterne, Das Tal der sieben Monde, Die Bilder des Zeugen Schattmann* and *Stielke, Heinz, fünfzehn* responsibility is discharged vertically to higher ranking individuals. In *Lebende Ware*, responsibility is also geographically displaced through the decision to cast a West German businessman as the primary focus of the crimes. In the remaining films, the persecutors are secondary characters and in a number of instances are not even named. In *Ehe im Schatten*, the only identifiable persecutor is Elisabeth's and Hans' erstwhile friend Blohm, whereas *Die Schauspielerin* only offers two figures who could conceivably be accused of propagating antisemitic prejudice: a young child who chases Maria in the street and an unnamed lavatory assistant who chastises Maria for using the 'wrong' lavatory. While these two films arguably broach the subject of the complicity of 'ordinary Germans', the failure to anchor this in any broader societal context means that the examples of antisemitism appear as exceptional instances rather than being indicative of any broader societal phenomenon.

Within the confines of a state-owned film studio, it may be tempting to attribute examples of divergence, tension and contradiction in the depiction of victims or perpetrators to a deliberate desire to subvert norms of remembrance in the GDR. The core tenets of remembrance culture in the GDR were clear. Commemorative discourses of the National Socialist past were underpinned by the primacy of antifascist resistance and a celebration of antifascist sacrifice. Responsibility for the persecution of Jews was displaced vertically onto high-ranking military and political elites and horizontally onto the Federal Republic. None of the films directly challenges these established frames of reference. However, they do repeatedly allow for the discussion and debate of themes beyond and outside of this dominant discourse.

The most fascinating aspect of East German Holocaust film is the space it created for public and hitherto unseen debates around East German memory discourses. Behind the scenes, we find discussions about the parameters of representation and commemoration that found little outlet in public or political discussions of the past. Production files document the extent to which studio – and even state – officials expressed concerns about the extent to which antifascist conversion narratives were representative of the East German experience (*Sterne*), the need for films to move beyond increasingly clichéd depictions of perpetrators (*Lebende Ware*, *Jakob der Lügner*) and the desire for filmmakers to engage with more everyday manifestations of antisemitism above demonstrative acts of violence (*Die Schauspielerin*). Their reservations about the extent to which third-generation audiences – audiences who, after all, had been educated and socialized exclusively in the GDR – would intuitively understand the centrality of antifascist resistance narratives in *Stielke, Heinz, fünfzehn* and the fate of the Jews in *Die Schauspielerin* offer a remarkable and candid insight into doubts that were not expressed by officials in the public sphere. Yet such discussions were not entirely kept away from the public. The films themselves offered new ways of viewing the past that no amount of paratextual framing could contain. Even films that featured conventional episodes of antifascist resistance such as *Das Tal der sieben Monde* and *Die Bilder des Zeugen Schattmann* include quite remarkable sequences that broach the wartime rape of women and the legitimacy of the Berlin Wall.

The release of East German Holocaust films was often accompanied by extensive discussion in the domestic press about Jewish victimhood and the future of East German commemorative practices. Consequently, these films reveal the extent to which East German Holocaust films were able, and indeed permitted to, open up discussions of alternative experiences encompassing the failure of the antifascist resistance (*Sterne*, *Jakob der Lügner*), ideologically indifferent protagonists (*Stielke, Heinz, fünfzehn*), charismatic perpetrators (*Lebende Ware*), crimes of sexual assault (*Das Tal der sieben Monde*) and the complicity of the wider population in everyday acts of antisemitism (*Ehe im Schatten*,

Professor Mamlock, Die Bilder des Zeugen Schattmann, Die Schauspielerin). The ability of East German Holocaust films to create a unique space for the discussion of Jewish victimhood and East German commemorative practices renders these productions such valuable resources for film scholars and historians alike.

If we are to understand the relationship between the GDR, film and Holocaust memory, we need to move beyond 'top down' models which uphold the position that if the SED failed to acknowledge its shared responsibility for the crimes of the past, then all of its institutions and citizens were also guilty of refusing to engage with the Holocaust. The aim of this book has not been to replace one singular narrative with another, but conversely to complicate our understanding of presentations of Jewish persecution in the GDR. East German filmmakers' treatment of Jewish persecution was complex and contradictory. However, a reluctance to examine these films, not in spite of their tensions, but precisely because of them, risks consigning some of the most important and interesting engagements with the Holocaust on film to the vaults of history.

Notes

1. In 1969, the Deutsche Hochschule für Filmkunst was renamed the Hochschule für Film und Fernsehen der DDR (the University for Film and Television). In 1985, it became the Hochschule für Film und Fernsehen Konrad Wolf (the University for Film and Television Konrad Wolf). In 1990, the name changed to the Hochschule für Film und Fernsehen Potsdam-Babelsberg (the University for Film and Television Potsdam-Babelsberg) and in 2014 it was renamed the Filmuniversität Babelsberg Konrad Wolf (the Film University Babelsberg Konrad Wolf).
2. Here we could also point to the impact of casting Geschonneck as Kowalski in *Jakob der Lügner* and to the figure of Gabi in *Stielke, Heinz, fünfzehn*.
3. Doneson, 'The Jew as a Female Figure in Holocaust Film', 11.
4. Ibid., 13.
5. Abteilung Kultur, 'Information über die Nominierung des Films *Jakob der Lügner* für den Internationalen Filmpreis Oscar'.

Filmography

1–2–3 Corona (Hans Müller, 1948).
8 ½ (Federico Fellini, 1963).
38 – Auch war das Wien (*38 – Vienna Before the Fall*, Wolfgang Glück, 1986).
Affaire Blum (*Blum Affair*, Erich Engel, 1948).
A Friendship in Vienna (Arthur Allan Seidelman, 1988).
Aktion J (Walter Heynowski, 1961).
Alan & Naomi (Sterling Van Wagenen, 1992).
Am Ende der Welt (*At the End of the World*, Hans Kratzert, 1974).
Au revoir, les enfants (*Goodbye, Children*, Louis Malle, 1987).
Berlin um die Ecke (*Berlin Around the Corner*, Gerhard Klein, 1965).
Betrogen bis zum jüngsten Tag (*Duped Till Doomsday*, Kurt Jung-Alsen, 1957).
Chronik eines Mordes (*Chronicle of a Murder*, Joachim Hasler, 1965).
Das Kaninchen bin ich (*The Rabbit is Me*, Kurt Maetzig, 1965).
Das Mädchen von Fanö (*The Girl from Fanö*, Hans Schweikart, 1941).
Das Singen im Dom zu Magdeburg (*Singing in Magdeburg Cathedral*, Peter Rocha, 1988).
Das Tal der sieben Monde (*The Valley of the Seven Moons*, Gottfried Kolditz, 1967).
Dein unbekannter Bruder (*Your Unknown Brother*, Ulrich Weiß, 1982).
Denk bloß nicht, ich heule (*Just Don't Think I'll Cry*, Frank Vogel, 1965).
Der 20 Juli (*The Plot to Assassinate Hitler*, Falk Harnack, 1955).
Der Arzt von Stalingrad (*The Doctor of Stalingrad*, Géza von Radványi, 1958).
Der Aufenthalt (*The Turning Point*, Frank Beyer, 1982).
Der ewige Jude (*The Eternal Jew*, Fritz Hippler, 1940).
Der Fall Gleiwitz (*The Gleiwitz Case*, Gerhard Klein, 1961).
Der Frühling braucht Zeit (*Spring Takes Time*, Günter Stahnke, 1965).
Der Fuchs von Paris (*The Fox of Paris*, Paul May, 1957).
Der lachende Mann – Bekenntnisse eines Mördes (*The Laughing Man*, Walter Heynowski and Gerhard Scheumann, 1966).
Der Prozess wird vertagt (*The Trial is Postponed*, Herbert Ballmann, 1958).
Der Stern von Afrika (*The Star of Africa*, Alfred Weidenmann, 1957).
Der verlorene Engel (*The Lost Angel*, Ralf Kirsten, 1966).
Des Teufels General (*The Devil's General*, Helmut Käutner, 1955).
Die Abenteuer des Werner Holt (*The Adventures of Werner Holt*, Joachim Kunert, 1965).

Die Bilder des Zeugen Schattmann (*The Pictures of Witness Schattmann*, Kurt Jung-Alsen, 1972).
Die goldene Stadt (*The Golden City*, Veit Harlan, 1942).
Die Leiden des jungen Werthers (*The Sorrows of the Young Werther*, Egon Günther, 1976).
Die Mörder sind unter uns (*The Murderers are Among Us*, Wolfgang Staudte, 1946).
Die Russen kommen (*The Russians Are Coming*, Heiner Carow, 1968).
Die Schauspielerin (*The Actress*, Siegfried Kühn, 1988).
Die Schüsse der Arche Noah (*Shots from Noah's Ark*, Egon Schlegel, 1983).
Die Todesmühlen (*Death Mills*, Hanus Burger, 1945).
Die Verlobte (*The Fiancée*, Günter Reisch and Günther Rücker, 1980).
Dr Schlüter (Achim Hübner, 1965).
Ehe im Schatten (*Marriage in the Shadows*, Kurt Maetzig, 1947).
Ein Tagebuch für Anne Frank (*A Diary for Anne Frank*, Joachim Hellwig, 1958).
Ernst Thälmann – Führer seiner Klasse (*Ernst Thälmann – Leader of his Class*, Kurt Maetzig, 1955).
Ernst Thälmann – Sohn seiner Klasse (*Ernst Thälmann – Son of His Class*, Kurt Maetzig, 1954).
Es geschah am 20. Juli (*It Happened on July 20th*, Georg Wilhelm Pabst, 1955).
Forbidden (Anthony Page, 1984).
Fräulein Schmetterling (*Miss Butterfly*, Kurt Barthel, 1966).
Fünf Patronenhülsen (*Five Cartridges*, Frank Beyer, 1960).
Genesung (*Recovery*, Konrad Wolf, 1956).
Hände hoch, oder ich schieße (*Hands Up or I'll Shoot*, Hans-Joachim Kasprzik, 1966).
Hitlerjunge Salomon (*Europa Europa*, Agnieszka Holland, 1990).
Holocaust (Marvin J. Chomsky, 1978).
Hunde, wollt ihr ewig leben? (*Stalingrad: Dogs, Do You Want to Live Forever?*, Frank Wisbar, 1959).
Ich klage an (*I Accuse*, Wolfgang Liebeneiner, 1941).
Ich war neunzehn (*I Was Nineteen*, Konrad Wolf, 1968).
Ich zwing dich zu leben (*I'll Force You to Live*, Ralf Kirsten, 1978).
Immensee (Veit Harlan, 1943).
In jenen Tagen (*In Those Days*, Helmut Käutner, 1947).
Jadup und Boel (*Jadop and Boel*, Rainer Simon, 1980).
Jahrgang 45 (*Born in '45*, Jürgen Böttcher, 1966).
Jakob der Lügner (*Jacob the Liar*, Frank Beyer, 1974).
Jetzt und in der Stunde meines Todes (*Now and in the Hour of my Death*, Konrad Petzold, 1963).
Jud Süss (*Jew Süss*, Veit Harlan, 1940).
Karla (*Carla*, Hermann Zschoche, 1965).
KLK an PTX – Die Rote Kapelle (*KLK Calling PTZ – The Red Orchestra*, Horst E. Brandt, 1970).
Königskinder (*Star-Crossed Lovers*, Frank Beyer, 1962).
Krücke (*Crutch*, Jörg Grünler, 1993).
Lang ist der Weg (*Long Is the Way*, Herbert B. Fredersdorf and Marek Goldstein, 1948).
Lebende Ware (*Living Wares*, Wolfgang Luderer, 1966).
Le Dernier Métro (*The Last Metro*, François Truffaut, 1980).
Leute mit Flügeln (*People with Wings*, Konrad Wolf, 1960).

Lissy (Konrad Wolf, 1957).
Meine Stunde Null (*My Zero Hour*, Joachim Hasler, 1970).
Mich dürstet (*I'm Thirsty*, Karl Paryla, 1956).
Morituri (Eugen York, 1948).
Nackt unter Wölfen (*Naked Among Wolves*, Frank Beyer, 1963).
Nuit et brouillard (*Night and Fog*, Alain Renais, 1955).
Professor Mamlock (Konrad Wolf, 1961).
Rat der Götter (*Council of the Gods*, Kurt Maetzig, 1950).
Razzia (*Raid*, Werner Klingler, 1947).
Ritter des Regens (*Knight of the Rain*, Egon Schlegel and Dieter Roth, 1965).
Rotation (Wolfgang Staudte, 1949).
Shoah (Claude Lanzmann, 1985).
Sie nannten ihn Amigo (*They Called Him Amigo*, Heiner Carow, 1958).
Sonnensucher (*Sun Seekers*, Konrad Wolf, 1958).
Spur der Steine (*Trace of Stones*, Frank Beyer, 1966).
Spur des Falken (*Trail of the Falcon*, Gottfried Kolditz, 1968).
Stärker als die Nacht (*Stronger Than the Night*, Slátan Dudow, 1954).
Sterne (*Stars*, Konrad Wolf, 1959).
Stielke, Heinz, fünfzehn (*Stielke, Heinz, Fifteen*, Michael Kann, 1987).
Straßenbekanntschaft (*Street Acquaintances*, Peter Pewas, 1948).
Wenn du groß bist, lieber Adam (*When You're Older, Dear Adam*, Egon Günther, 1965).
Wo andere schweigen (*Where Others Keep Silent*, Ralf Kirsten, 1984).
Zwischenfall in Benderath (*Incident in Benderath*, Janos Veiczi, 1956).
Zwischen gestern und morgen (*Between Yesterday and Tomorrow*, Harald Braun, 1947).

Bibliography

Archival Material

Abteilung Künstlerische Produktion. 'Einschätzung des Szenariums *Stielke, ein deutscher Junge*', 15 January 1986. BArch DR-Z/24b.

Abteilung Künstlerische Produktion. 'Einschätzung *Stielke, Heinz, fünfzehn*, DEFA Studio für Spielfilme, zur staatlichen Zulassung am 7.11.86', 6 November 1986. BArch DR-Z/24.

Abteilung Künstlerische Produktion. 'Einschätzung zu *Die Schauspielerin*, Spielfilm des DEFA-Studios für Spielfilme, zur staatlichen Zulassung am 26.4.1988', 25 April 1988. BArch DR1-Z/13.

Abteilung Künstlerische Produktion. 'Stellungnahme zu *Die Schauspielerin*', 7 July 1987. BArch DR 1-Z/13b.

Abteilung Kultur. 'Information über die Nominierung des Films *Jakob der Lügner* für den Internationalen Filmpreis Oscar', 16 February 1977. BArch DR1/12861.

Academy of Motion Picture Arts and Sciences. '1949 (22nd) Academy Awards, Reminder List of Eligible Releases'. 1950. Margaret Herrick Library.

Acker-Thies, Gertraude. 'Letter from Acker-Thies to Wolfgang Heinz', 10 July 1965. BArch DR 117/30363.

Auswärtiges Amt. 'Aufzeichnung betr.: XII. internationale Filmfestspiele in Cannes 1959', 8 June 1959. PA AA, B95, Bd. 463.

Auswärtiges Amt. 'Aufzeichnung betr.: Teilnahme der DEFA an den Filmfestspielen in Cannes 1959', 11 November 1958. PA AA, B95, Bd. 635.

Auswärtiges Amt. 'Betr. internationale Filmfestspiele in Cannes 1957', 18 December 1956. PA AA, B95, Bd. 463.

Becker, Jurek. '*Jakob der Lügner*. Draft Screenplay', 5 July 1973. BArch DR 117/3518.

Becker, Jurek. '*Jakob der Lügner*. Exposé', 10 January 1963. BArch DR 117/10502.

Becker, Jurek. '*Jakob der Lügner*. Scenario', 1965. BArch DR 117/12933.

Becker, Jurek. '*Jakob der Lügner*. Screenplay', 15 December 1965. BArch DR 117/323.

Becker, Jurek. '*Jakob der Lügner*. Screenplay', 15 December 1965. BArch DR 117/324.

Beyer, Frank. 'Handwritten Notes', 1976. Filmmuseum Potsdam/Sammlungen/Nachlass Frank Beyer.
Beyer, Frank. 'Letter from Frank Beyer to Jauch', 27 October 1975. Filmmuseum Potsdam/Sammlungen/Nachlass Frank Beyer 9/2003/N024.
Brückner, Willi. 'Aktennotiz der Diskussion des Rohdrehbuches *Sterne*', 18 March 1958. BArch DR 117/26305.
Bulla, Herbert. 'Letter from Deputy Director Bulla to Rainer Otto', 9 November 1976. BArch DR 1-Z/157.
CCC Filmkunst GmbH. 'Letter from CCC Filmkunst GmbH to Aufbau-Verlag (Berlin East)', 3 May 1971. AdK, Berlin, Jurek-Becker-Archiv, Nr. 1756.
DEFA. 'Besetzungsliste *Lebende Ware*', 2 July 1965. DR 117/30363.
DEFA. 'Besetzungsvorschläge *Professor Mamlock*', undated. BArch DR117/30193.
DEFA. 'Besucher- und Einspielergebnisse: Stichtag 8.12.66 = 13. Wochen', 1 February 1967. BArch DR 117/23302.
DEFA. 'Besucher- und Einspielergebnisse: Stichtag 11.05.66 = 13. Wochen', 7 May 1967. BArch DR 117/23317.
DEFA. 'Besucher- und Einspielergebnisse: Stichtag 15.05.75 = Woche 4', 30 May 1975. BArch DR 117/23439.
DEFA. 'Einschätzung zu dem Film *Lebende Ware*', 14 April 1966. BArch DR 117/32894.
DEFA. 'Handwritten Notes. Department Film Production/Außenhandel/Progress', 1966. BArch DR 117/32894.
DEFA. 'Protokoll über die Diskussion bei der Abnahme des Films *Sterne* am 13.1.1959. Sektor Filmabnahme und -kontrolle'. 17 January 1959, BArch DR 1-Z/308.
DEFA. 'Rollenauszug', 1987. Potsdam Filmmuseum/Nachlass Hans Poppe/ 34/2001/1191.
DEFA. 'Stellungnahme. *Stielke Heinz, fünfzehn*', 22 October 1986. BArch DR1-Z/24b.
DEFA. 'Thesen für die Aktivtagung', 19 October 1962. AdK, Berlin, Konrad-Wolf-Archiv, Nr. 2569.
DEFA-Außenhandel. '*Das Tal der sieben Monde*', 1967. BArch FILMSG/1/16673.
DEFA-Außenhandel. 'Letter from DEFA-Außenhandel to Konrad Wolf', 22 August 1960. AdK, Berlin, Konrad-Wolf-Archiv, Nr. 2193.
DEFA-Außenhandel. 'Memorandum', 10 March 1959. AdK, Berlin, Konrad-Wolf-Archiv, Nr. 359.
DEFA-Außenhandel. '*Stars/Etoiles*', 1959. AdK, Berlin, Konrad-Wolf-Archiv, Nr. 360.
DEFA-Außenhandel. 'Stellungnahme. *Stielke, Heinz, fünfzehn*', 6 November 1986. BArch DR1-Z/24b.
Dósai, István. 'Letter from István Dósai, General Director of Hungarofilm, to the KAG Heinrich Greif', 7 August 1965. BArch DR 117/32894.
Europa Filmverleih. '*Sterne*', 1960. Deutsche Kinemathek–Museum für Film und Fernsehen, Schriftgutarchiv, NFPk: Sterne.
Fernsehdienst der DDR. '*Die Bilder des Zeugen Schattmann*', *Fernsehdienst* 23 (1972). Deutsches Rundfunkarchiv/Pressearchiv/Die Bilder des Zeugen Schattmann.
Fernsehen der DDR. 'New Films of GDR Television Import–Export. Film', 1972. BArch FILMSG/1/23056.

Filmbegutachtungskommission für Jugend und Schule Berlin. 'Protokoll über die Begutachtung des Films *Professor Mamlock* am 6.11.1966', November 1966. Deutsche Kinemathek-Museum für Film und Fernsehen, Schriftgutarchiv, Professor Mamlock, 6343.

Filmbegutachtungskommission für Jugend und Schule Berlin. 'Protokoll über die Begutachtung des Films *Sterne* am 21. Juni 1960', June 1960. Deutsche Kinemathek-Museum für Film und Fernsehen, Schriftgutarchiv, Professor Mamlock, 2828.

Filmbüro Shellhaus. 'Letter to DEFA', 4 December 1946. BArch DR 2/631.

Gramercy Publicity. 'American Film Programme for *Marriage in the Shadows*', 1948. AdK, Berlin, Kurt-Maetzig-Archiv, Nr. 10.

Gruppe Babelsberg. 'Protokollnotiz über ein Gespräch zum Exposé *Die Schauspielerin*, das am 25.11.86 zwischen Hedda Zinner, Regine Kühn und mir [Erika Richter] zeitweise in Anwesenheit John Erpenbecks geführt wurde', 8 December 1986. AdK, Berlin, Siegfried-Kühn-Archiv, Nr. 41.

Gruppe Babelsberg. 'Stellungnahme zum Szenarium *Die Schauspielerin*', 31 March 1987. Potsdam Filmarchiv/Nachlass Hans Poppe/NO19/1193.

Gruppe Babelsberg. 'Thesen zur Weiterarbeit', 20 May 1987. BArch DR 1-Z/13b.

Gruppe Heinrich Greif. 'Abnahmediskussion des Drehbuches Professor Mamlock am 27. September 1960', 17 September 1960. BArch DR 117/29879.

Gruppe Heinrich Greif. 'Drehbuchabnahme *Jakob der Lügner* am 10.6.1966', 21 April 1966. BArch DR 117/33399.

Gruppe Heinrich Greif. 'Einschätzung der Gruppe zu dem Drehbuch *Lebende Ware*', 26 June 1965. BArch DR 117/32894.

Gruppe Heinrich Greif. 'Memorandum', 1966. BArch DR 117/33399.

Gruppe Johannisthal. 'Bestätigung des Filmstoffes', 25 June 1985. BArch DR 117/28480.

Gruppe Johannisthal. 'Führungskonzeption zum Szenarium *Abenteurer wider Willen* (AT) frei nach dem gleichnamigen Roman von Wolfgang Kellner', 12 June 1985. BArch DR 117/28480.

Gruppe Roter Kreis. 'Einschätzung. *Das Tal der sieben Monde*', 15 April 1966. BArch DR 117/33869.

Hartwig, Gerhard. 'Ideologische Begründung. *Das Tal der sieben Monde*', 25 April 1966. BArch DR 117/33869.

Kaul, Friedrich Karl. 'Gedächtnis-Protokoll über die Besprechung betreffend den Film mit dem Arbeitstitel *Lebende Ware* am 22. August 1965', 23 August 1965. BArch DR 117/32894.

Kaul, Friedrich Karl. 'Stoffexposé für einen Film mit dem vorläufigen Arbeitstitel *Lebende Ware*', 9 November 1963. BArch DR 117/12259.

Kaul, Friedrich Karl and Walter Jupé. '*Lebende Ware*. Scenario', 17 December 1963. BArch DR 117/14480.

Kellner, Wolfgang. 'Letter from Wolfgang Kellner to Andreas Scheinert', 1 February 1986. BArch DR 117/28480.

Kellner, Wolfgang. Letter from Wolfgang Kellner to Andreas Scheinert', 11 October 1986. BArch DR 117/28480.

Kellner, Wolfgang. 'Letter from Wolfgang Kellner to Andreas Scheinert', 17 October 1986. BArch DR 117/28480.

Kellner, Wolfgang. 'Letter from Wolfgang Kellner to Andreas Scheinert', 20 October 1986. BArch DR 117/28480.

Kühn, Regine. '*Die Schauspielerin*. Screenplay', 10 June 1987. BArch DR 117/2309.
Kühn, Siegfried. 'Regie-Konzeption zu *Die Schauspielerin*', 30 March 1987. Filmmuseum Potsdam/Nachlass Hans Poppe 34/2001/NO19/1192.
Mäde, Hans Dieter. 'Stellungnahme zum Film *Die Schauspielerin* nach Hedda Zinners Roman *Arrangement mit dem Tod*', 8 April 1988. BArch DR 1-Z/13.
Maetzig, Kurt. '*Aber eines Tages*. Screenplay', 1947. AdK, Berlin, Kurt-Maetzig-Archiv, Nr. 5.
Maetzig, Kurt. '*Aber eines Tages*. Screenplay', 1947. BArch DR 117/2634.
Maetzig, Kurt. 'Letter from Kurt Maetzig to Axel Eggebrecht', 2 October 1946. AdK, Kurt-Maetzig-Archiv, Nr. 1312.
Maetzig, Kurt. 'Letter from Kurt Maetzig to Axel Eggebrecht', 17 January 1947. AdK, Berlin, Kurt-Maetzig-Archiv, Nr. 1312.
Maetzig, Kurt. 'Letter from Kurt Maetzig to Ilse Meyer and Lie Friedländer', 3 March 1947. AdK, Berlin, Kurt-Maetzig-Archiv, Nr. 857.
Maetzig, Kurt. 'Letter from Kurt Maetzig to Prof. Dr W. Liebbrandt', 7 March 1947. AdK, Berlin, Kurt-Maetzig-Archiv, Nr. 833.
Maetzig, Kurt. 'Memorandum. Kurt Maetzig to Dr Klaren', 28 February 1947. BArch DR 117/29879.
Maetzig, Kurt. '*Verfolgte Seelen*. Draft Screenplay'. AdK, Berlin, Kurt-Maetzig-Archiv, Nr. 11.
Mark, Bernard. 'Letter from Prof. Mark of the Zydowski Instytut Historyczny to DEFA', 18 February 1966. BArch DR 117/33399.
No Author. '*Lebende Ware*', no date. BArch DR 117/32894.
Otto, Rainer. 'Letter from Rainer Otto to H.J. Hoffmann', 16 November 1976. BArch DR 1-Z/157.
Progress Film. '*Das Tal der sieben Monde*', *Film für Sie*, 1967. BArch FILMSG/1/16673.
Progress Film. '*Das Tal der sieben Monde*: Film Werbung', 1967. BArch FILMSG/1/16673.
Progress Film. '*Jakob der Lügner*: Einsatzkarte', 1975. BArch FILMSG/1/20391.
Progress Film. '*Jakob der Lügner*'. *Film für Sie*. Berlin: Progress Film, 1974.
Progress Film. '*Lebende Ware*'. *Progress Filmprogramm*. Berlin: Progress Film, 1966.
Progress Film. '*Professor Mamlock*', *Progress Filmdienst für Presse und Werbung*, 1961.
Progress Film. 'Progress Pressebulletin: *Die Schauspielerin*', 10 (1988).
Progress Film. 'Progress-Presse-Informationen: *Lebende Ware*. Ein DEFA-Totalvisionsfilm der Gruppe Heinrich Greif', 1966. BArch DR 117/27727.
Progress Film. 'Stellungnahme: *Stielke, Heinz, fünfzehn*', 6 November 1986. BArch DR1-Z/24b.
Progress Film. '*Sterne*. Werbehelfer'. BArch FILMSG/1/16207.
Progress Film. '*Unsere Familie*', 1961. AdK, Berlin, Konrad-Wolf-Archiv, Nr. 450.
Richter, Georg. 'Letter from Georg Richter, Film- und Fernsehproduktion Georg Richter (Munich) to Jurek Becker', 16 February 1972. AdK, Berlin, Jurek-Becker-Archiv, Nr. 2077.
Scheinert, Andreas. 'Gruppe Johannisthal: Thesen zum Projekt', 28 October 1985. BArch DR 117/28480.

Scheinert, Andreas. 'Letter from Andreas Scheinert to DEFA', 15 May 1985. BArch DR 117/28480.
Teichmann, Willi. 'Letter from Production Leader Teichmann to Benz', 11 February 1971. BArch DR 117/25951.
Wagenstein, Angel. '*Sterne*. Draft Screenplay', 17 February 1958. AdK, Berlin, Konrad-Wolf-Archiv, Nr. 382.
Wagenstein, Angel. '*Sterne*. Screenplay', 20 June 1958. AdK, Berlin, Konrad-Wolf-Archiv, Nr. 383.
Wagenstein, Angel. '*Sterne*. Screenplay', 20 June 1958. AdK, Berlin, Konrad-Wolf-Archiv, Nr. 384.
Wilkening, Albert. 'Einschätzung des Filmes *Sterne* durch die Direktion, Dr Wilkening', 3 January 1959. BArch DR 1-Z/308.
Wilkening, Albert. 'Letter from Prof Dr Wilkening to Ernst Hoffmann', 29 June 1961. BArch DR 117/25728.
Wischnewski, Klaus. 'Letter from Klaus Wischnewski', 8 November 1965. BArch DR 117/32894.
Wischnewski, Klaus. 'Letter from Klaus Wischnewski to István Dósai, General Director of Hungarofilm', 27 August 1965. BArch DR 117/32894.
Wischnewski, Klaus. 'Letter from Klaus Wischnewski to Professor Lothar Berthold', 30 November 1965. BArch DR 117/33399.
Wolf, Konrad. 'Letter from Konrad Wolf to Erich Wendt', 4 July 1958. BArch DR 117/33862.
Wolf, Konrad and Karl-Georg Egel. 'Handlungsaufriss (Fahrplan) für den Film', 16 July 1960. BArch DR117/12634.
ZK der SED. 'Maßnahmen zum 50. Jahrestag der faschistischen Pogromnacht', 29 March 1988. BArch DC 20-I/4/6227.

Newspaper and Magazine Articles

Agde, Günter. '*Die Schauspielerin*'. *Thüringer Neueste Nachrichten*, 20 October 1988.
Aux Écoutes de la Finance. 'Aux Écoutes du Cinéma'. 14 July 1950.
Baschleben, Klaus. 'Nur eine abenteuerliche Odyssee wider Willen'. *Nationalzeitung*, 13 March 1987.
Bauernecho. '*Professor Mamlock*'. 25 May 1961.
Beheim-Schwarzbach, Martin. 'Sterne der Sehnsucht, Sterne der Vernichtung'. *Die Welt*, 30 April 1960.
Böhme, Irene. '*Jakob der Lügner*'. *Sonntag*, 12 January 1975.
Croce, Fernando F. '*The Last Metro*'. *Slant Magazine*, 24 March 2009.
Der Neue Weg. 'Gültiges und Routiniertes'. 13 February 1967.
Der Sozialdemokrat. '*Ehe im Schatten*'. 7 October 1947.
Der Spiegel. 'Kein *Aufenthalt* zur Berlinale'. 7 February 1983.
Die Union. 'Ein erregendes Dokument'. 10 September 1966.
Einhorn, Cläre. '*Sterne*'. *Neues Deutschland*, 1 November 1958.
Eulenspiegel. 'Kino-Eule: *Jakob der Lügner*'. 14 February 1975.
Eylau, Hans Ulrich. '*Sterne*'. *Berliner Zeitung*, 2 April 1959.
Fiedler, Klaus M. 'Um eigene Erzählweise bemüht'. *Thüringer Tageblatt*, 24 May 1988.

Filmkritik. 'Sterne', 6 (1960).
Frankfurter Rundschau. 'Unsere tägliche Frage: *Ehe im Schatten*'. 1 December 1949.
Funke, Christoph. 'Frank und Esther – ein Menschenschicksal'. *Der Morgen*, 30 May 1972.
Funke, Christoph. 'Sieg über den Stacheldraht'. *Der Morgen*, 2 April 1959.
Funke, Christoph. '*Sterne* leuchten in vielen Ländern'. *Der Morgen*, 28 May 1959.
Geßner, Herbert. 'Nachbetrachtung zu einem Film'. *Die Weltbühne* 23 (1947).
Guardian. 'Horror and Humanity'. 25 March 1961.
Gustmann, Egbert. '*Lebende Ware*. Aktuelle Vergangenheit'. *Schweriner Volkszeitung*, 12 September 1966.
Hamburger Abendblatt. 'Film guter Gesinnung: *Sterne*'. 18 August 1962.
Hoffmann, Heinz. 'Die schlichte Schönheit einer großen Wahrheit'. *Nationalzeitung*, 29 April 1975.
Hoffmann, Heinz. '*Jakob der Lügner*'. *Thüringische Landeszeitung*, 26 April 1975.
Honecker, Erich. 'Aus dem Bericht des Politbüros an die 11. Tagung des ZK'. *Neues Deutschland*, 16 December 1965.
Honecker, Erich. 'Rede Honeckers zum 40. Jahrestag der DDR'. *Neues Deutschland*, 9 October 1989.
Honecker, Erich. 'Zu aktuellen Fragen bei der Verwirklichung der Beschlüsse unseres VIII Parteitages'. *Neues Deutschland*, 18 December 1971.
Jahn, Marianne. '*Sterne*'. *Die Frau von Heute*, 20 March 1959.
Keller, Aenne. '*Lebende Ware*'. *Zeit im Bild* 17 (1966).
Kersten, Heinz. 'Ein untaugliches Objekt'. *Der Tagesspiegel*, 15 March 1987.
Kersten, Heinz 'Gegenwart blieb unbewältigt'. *Der Tag*, 15 May 1959.
Klaren, Georg. 'Zeitgemäße Filmstoffe: Filme, die wir drehen möchten'. *Die Neue Filmwoche*, October 1946.
Knietzsch, Horst. 'Tragischer Weg zu menschlicher Größe'. *Neues Deutschland*, 20 October 1988.
Kolditz, Gottfried. 'Sonne und Schatten über den Beskiden'. *Schweriner Volkszeitung*, 13 February 1967.
Kruppa, Renate. 'Wider verbotene Liebe'. *Schweriner Volkszeitung*, 18 October 1988.
Kuhlbrodt, Dietrich. '*38*'. *epd Film* 6 (1987).
Lausitzer Rundschau. 'Ein Verbrecher wird angeklagt'. 12 September 1966.
Leibelt, Hans. '*Ehe im Schatten*'. *Neue Zeitung*, 4 October 1947.
Leipziger Volkszeitung. '*Lebende Ware*'. 4 September 1966.
Linke, Marlis. 'Lieber am Anfang als am Ende'. *Sonntag*, 6 November 1988.
Linke, Marlis. 'Wer will Stielke?'. *Filmspiegel* 16 (1988).
Lücke, Hans. 'Konflikte ohne Tiefe'. *BZ am Abend*, 13 February 1967.
Maetzig, Kurt. 'Der Künstler steht nicht außerhalb des Kampfes'. *Neues Deutschland*, 5 January 1966.
Märkische Union. 'Wesentliches fehlt'. 9 March 1987.
Märkische Volksstimme. 'Die Millionen des Kurt Andreas Becher'. 8 June 1966.
Marcorelles, Louis. 'Winners at Cannes'. *The Observer*, 17 May 1959.
Maurin, François. 'Étoiles'. *Dimanche*, 6 March 1960.
Miska, Peter. 'Da fängt eben der Marxismus an'. *Frankfurter Rundschau*, 22 July 1959.

Mitteldeutsche Neueste Nachrichten. 'Der neue Film'. 19 February 1967.
Neue Zeit. 'Bedrohte Liebe in schwerer Zeit'. 10 February 1967.
Neue Zeit. 'Geschäfte mit der Angst'. 16 June 1966.
Neue Zeit. 'Im Netz politischer Intrigen'. 9 July 1960.
Neuer Tag. 'Das Mädchen mit dem Stern'. 27 May 1961.
Neues Deutschland. 'Biermann das Recht auf weiteren Aufenthalt in der DDR entzogen'. 17 November 1976.
Neues Deutschland. 'Botschafter des guten Willens'. 28 December 1959.
Neues Deutschland. '*Ehe im Schatten* in Schweden aufgeführt'. 28 January 1960.
Neues Deutschland. '*Jakob der Lügner*'. 17 April 1975.
Penser, Ruth. '*Lebende Ware*'. *Nationalzeitung*, 16 April 1966.
Rhein-Neckar Zeitung. '*Sterne*'. 10 June 1960.
Robinson, David. 'Cinema: Invention and Skill Blossom out on a Shoestring Budget'. *The Times*, 28 February 1986.
Rümmler, Klaus. 'Ein neuer DEFA-Film: *Lebende Ware*'. *Sächsische Zeitung*, 30 September 1966.
Sächsische Neueste Nachrichten. 'Blick auf die Leinwand: *Lebende Ware*'. 11 September 1966.
Sächsisches Tageblatt. 'Ein Leben kostete 1000 Dollar'. 13 September 1966.
Schirrmeister, Hermann. 'Wird besonders die Jugend fesseln'. *Tribüne*, 10 February 1967.
Semkat, Ute. 'Geschichte einer Liebe im faschistischen Deutschland'. *Volksstimme*, 3 November 1988.
Sladeck, Eleonore. '*Stielke, Heinz, fünfzehn*'. *Norddeutsche Zeitung*, 24 March 1987.
Sobe, Günter. 'Premiere in Babelsberg'. *Berliner Zeitung*, 14 June 1966.
Sobe, Günter. 'Von des Rätsels Lösung keine Spur'. *Berliner Zeitung*, 16 February 1987.
Sonntag. '*Ehe im Schatten*'. 31 January 1960.
Stade, Heinz. 'Kein Kalender wird anzeigen, wann wir das je vergessen könnten'. *Das Volk*, 11 April 1975.
The New York Times. 'Display Ad 31: *Marriage in the Shadows*'. 21 September 1948.
The New York Times. 'The Ten Best Films'. 26 December 1948.
The Sunday Times. 'Stars'. 26 March 1961.
Thüringer Tageblatt. 'Antisemitische Krawalle in Bad Nauheim', 28 November 1958.
Ulbricht, Walter. 'Brief des Genossen Walter Ulbricht an Genossen Prof. Kurt Maetzig'. *Neues Deutschland*, 23 January 1966.
Vater, Hubert. 'Was ich mir mehr von unseren Filmemachern wünsche'. *Neues Deutschland*, 17 November 1981.
Voigt, Jutta. 'Lust auf Leben. *Jakob der Lügner* eröffnet im Monat des antiimperialistischen Films – Gespräch mit Jurek Becher'. *Sonntag*, 20 April 1975.
von Schnitzler, Karl-Eduard. '*Sterne*'. *Filmspiegel* 8 (1959).
Voss, Margit. 'Wandlung und Verwandlung'. *Berliner Zeitung*, 20 October 1988.
Wischnewski, Klaus. 'Über Jakob und andere'. *Film und Fernsehen* 2 (1975).
Wolf, Christa. 'Das haben wir nicht gelernt'. *Wochenpost*, 27 October 1989.
Zeit im Bild. 'Väter und Söhne'. 3 February 1961.
Zimmermann, Monika. '*Die Schauspielerin* und die Politik der DDR'. *Frankfurter Allgemeine Zeitung*, 20 October 1988.

Secondary Literature

Ackermann, Anton. 'Zum 5-jährigen Bestehen der DEFA', in DEFA (ed.), *Auf neuen Wegen: Fünf Jahre fortschrittlicher deutscher Film* (Berlin: Deutscher Filmverlag, 1951), 5–18.

Allan, Seán. 'DEFA's Antifascist Myths and the Construction of National Identity in East German Cinema', in Karen Leeder (ed.), *Rereading East Germany: The Literature and Film of the GDR* (Cambridge: Cambridge University Press, 2016), 52–69.

Allan, Seán. 'Sagt, wie soll man Stalin danken? Kurt Maetzig's *Ehe im Schatten* (1947), *Roman Einer Jungen Ehe* (1952) and the Cultural Politics of Post-War Germany'. *German Life and Letters* 64(2) (2011), 255–71.

Allan, Seán and John Sandford (eds). *DEFA: East German Cinema, 1946–1992*. Providence, RI: Berghahn, 1999.

Altman, Rick. 'A Semantic/Syntactic Approach to Film Genre'. *Cinema Journal* 23(3) (1984), 6–18.

Ameer, Konstanze, Jan Riebe and Ulla Steuber. 'Ausgeblendet? Der Holocaust in Film und Literatur der DDR', Amadeu Antonio Stiftung (2011). Retrieved 1 March 2019 from https://www.amadeu-antonio-stiftung.de/w/files/pdfs/filmbroschuereinternet.pdf.

Ammer, Thomas. 'DDR und Judentum: 50 Jahre nach den Novemberpogromen'. *Deutschland Archiv* 22 (1989).

Barnert, Anne. *Die Antifaschismus-Thematik der DEFA: Eine kultur- und filmhistorische Analyse*. Marburg: Schüren 2008.

Baron, Lawrence. 'Film', in Peter Hayes and John K. Roth (eds), *The Oxford Handbook of Holocaust Studies* (Oxford: Oxford University Press, 2010), 444–60.

Baron, Lawrence. *Projecting the Holocaust into the Present: The Changing Focus of Contemporary Holocaust Cinema*. Lanham, MD: Rowman & Littlefield, 2005.

Berghahn, Daniela. *Hollywood Behind the Wall: The Cinema of East Germany*. Manchester: Manchester University Press, 2005.

Berghahn, Daniela. 'Liars and Traitors: Unheroic Resistance in DEFA's Anti-Fascist Films', in Daniela Berghahn and Alan Bance (eds), *Millennial Essays on Film and Other German Studies* (Oxford: Peter Lang, 2002), 19–36.

Berghahn, Daniela. 'Resistance of the Heart: Female Suffering and Victimhood in DEFA's Antifascist Films', in Paul Cooke and Marc Silberman (eds), *Screening War: Perspectives on German Suffering* (Rochester, N.Y.: Camden House, 2010), 165–86.

Berghahn, Daniela. 'The Forbidden Films: Film Censorship in East German Cinema in the Wake of the Eleventh Plenum', in Diana Holmes and Alison Smith (eds), *100 Years of European Cinema: Entertainment or Ideology?* (Manchester: Manchester University Press, 2000), 40–50.

Beutelschmidt, Thomas. *Kooperation oder Konkurrenz?: das Verhältnis zwischen Film und Fernsehen in der DDR*. Berlin: DEFA Stiftung, 2009.

Beutelschmidt, Thomas. 'No TV Without Film: Production Relations Between the DEFA Studios and Deutscher Fernsehfunk', in Lars Karl and Pavel Skopal (eds), *Cinema in Service of the State: Perspectives on Film in the GDR and Czechoslovakia, 1945–1960* (New York: Berghahn Books, 2015), 125–44.

Beyer, Frank. *Wenn der Wind sich dreht: meine Filme, mein Leben*. Munich: Econ, 2001.

Biess, Frank. *Homecomings: Returning POWs and the Legacies of Defeat in Postwar Germany*. Princeton, NJ: Princeton University Press, 2006.
Bisky, Lothar and Dieter Wiedemann. *Der Spielfilm: Rezeption und Wirkung*. Berlin: Henschel, 1985.
Bongartz, Barbara. *Von Caligari zu Hitler, von Hitler zu Dr. Mabuse?: Eine psychologische Geschichte des deutschen Films von 1946 bis 1960*. Münster: MakS Publikationen, 1992.
Brady, Martin. 'Discussion with Kurt Maetzig', in Seán Allan and John Sandford (eds), *DEFA: East German Cinema, 1946–1992* (Providence, RI: Berghahn Books, 1999), 77–92.
Brady, Martin and Helen Hughes. 'German Cinema', in Wilfried van der Will and Eva Kolinsky (eds), *The Cambridge Companion to Modern German Culture* (Cambridge: Cambridge University Press, 1998), 302–21.
Braham, Randolph L. *The Politics of Genocide*. New York: Columbia University Press, 1981.
Brinks, Jan H. 'Political Antifascism in the German Democratic Republic', *Journal of Contemporary History* 32(2) (1997), 207–17.
Brockmann, Stephen. *A Critical History of German Film*. Rochester, NY: Camden House, 2016.
Brockmann, Stephen. *Nuremberg: The Imaginary Capital*. Rochester, NY: Camden House, 2006.
Byg, Barton. 'DEFA and the Traditions of International Cinema', in Seán Allan and John Sandford (eds), *DEFA: East German Cinema, 1946–1992* (Providence, RI: Berghahn, 1999), 22–41.
Chamberlain, Brewster. *'Todesmühlen*: Ein früher Versuch zur Massen-"Umerziehung" im besetzten Deutschland 1945–1946'. *Vierteljahrshefte für Zeitgeschichte* 29(3) (1981), 420–36.
Clark, Katerina. *The Soviet Novel: History as Ritual*. Bloomington, IN: Indiana University Press, 2000.
Corkhill, Alan. 'From Novel to Film to Remake: Jurek Becker's *Jakob der Lügner*', in Julian Preece, Frank Finlay and Ruth J. Owen (eds), *New German Literature*, (Oxford: Peter Lang, 2007), 93–106.
Corum, James S. *Rearming Germany*. Boston: Brill, 2011.
Coulson, Anthony. 'Paths of Discovery: The Films of Konrad Wolf', in Seán Allan and John Sandford (eds), *DEFA: East German Cinema, 1946–1992* (New York: Berghahn, 1999), 164–82.
Culbert, David. 'American Film Policy in the Re-Education of German Film After 1945', in Nicholas Pronay and Keith Wilson (eds), *The Political Re-Education of Germany and Her Allies After World War II* (London: Croom Helm, 1985), 173–202.
DEFA. *Auf neuen Wegen: Fünf Jahre fortschrittlicher deutscher Film*. Berlin: Deutscher Filmverlag, 1951.
Dietz Verlag. *Kleines Politisches Wörterbuch*. Berlin: Dietz Verlag, 1973.
Dietz Verlag. *Kleines Politisches Wörterbuch*. Berlin: Dietz Verlag, 1988.
Doneson, Judith E. 'The Jew as a Female Figure in Holocaust Film'. *Shoah: A Review of Holocaust Studies and Commemorations* 1(1) (1978), 11–13, 18.
Edel, Peter. *Die Bilder des Zeugen Schattmann*. Berlin: Verlag der Nation, 1969.
Elsaesser, Thomas. *German Cinema: Terror and Trauma. Cultural Memory since 1945*. New York: Routledge, 2014.

Feinstein, Joshua. *The Triumph of the Ordinary: Depictions of Daily Life in the East German Cinema*. Chapel Hill: University of North Carolina Press, 2000.

Fellmer, Claudia. 'The Communist Who Rarely Played a Communist: The Case of DEFA Star Erwin Geschonneck', in Daniela Berghahn and Alan Bence (eds), *Millennial Essays on Film and Other German Studies* (Oxford: Peter Lang, 2002), 41–62.

Fischer, Jörg-Uwe. 'Historische Justizdramen: Der Fernseh-Pitaval des DDR-Fernsehens'. *Rückblick Info* 7(1) (2005), 46–48.

Fisher, Jaimey 'A Late Genre Fade: Utopianism and its Twilight in DEFA's Science Fiction, Literary and Western Films', in Marc Silberman and Henning Wrage (eds), *DEFA at the Crossroads of East German and International Film Culture* (Berlin: De Gruyter, 2014), 177–96.

Gallwitz, Tim. '"Unterhaltung – Erziehung – Mahnung": Die Darstellung von Antisemitismus und Judenverfolgung im deutschen Nachkriegsfilm 1946 bis 1949', in Fritz-Bauer-Institut (ed.), *Beseitigung des jüdischen Einflusses: antisemitische Forschung, Eliten und Karrieren im Nationalsozialismus* (Frankfurt am Main: Campus-Verlag, 1999), 275–304.

Gemünden, Gerd. 'Between Karl May and Karl Marx: The DEFA *Indianerfilme* (1965–1983)'. *Film History* 10(3) (1998), 399–407.

Gerlof. Manuela. *Tonspuren: Erinnerungen an den Holocaust im Hörspiel der DDR*. Berlin: De Gruyter, 2010.

Görner, Eberhard. '*Der siebente Brunnen* von Fred Wander. Die Geschichte eines Filmes, der nicht gedreht wurde', in Walter Grünzweig and Ursula Seeber (eds), *Fred Wander: Leben und Werk* (Bonn: Weidle, 2005), 47–69.

Grabowski, Jörn and Ruth Strohschein. 1998. *‚Und lehrt sie: Gedächtnis'*. Berlin: Staatliche Museen.

Grieder, Peter. *The German Democratic Republic*. Basingstoke: Palgrave Macmillan, 2012.

Hake, Sabine. *German National Cinema*. Second edition. London: Routledge, 2008.

Hake, Sabine. *Popular Cinema of the Third Reich*. Austin, TX: University of Texas Press, 2001.

Hardt, Ursula. *From Caligari to California: Eric Pommer's Life in the International Film Wars*. Providence, RI: Berghahn, 1996.

Heiduschke, Sebastian. *East German Cinema: DEFA and Film History*. Basingstoke: Palgrave Macmillan, 2013.

Heimann, Thomas. *Bilder von Buchenwald: Die Visualisierung des Antifaschismus in der DDR (1945–1990)*. Cologne: Böhlau, 2005.

Heimann, Thomas. *DEFA, Künstler und SED-Kulturpolitik: zum Verhältnis von Kulturpolitik und Filmproduktion in der SBZ/DDR 1945 bis 1959*. Berlin: Vistas, 1994.

Herf, Jeffrey. *Undeclared Wars with Israel: East Germany and the West German Far Left, 1967–1989*. Cambridge: Cambridge University Press, 2015.

Jarmatz, Klaus (ed.). *Ravensbrücker Ballade oder Faschismusbewältigung in der DDR*. Berlin: Aufbau Taschenbuch Verlag, 1992.

Kaes, Anton. *From Hitler to Heimat: The Return of History as Film*. Cambridge, MA: Harvard University Press, 1992.

Kannapin, Detlef. *Antifaschismus im Film der DDR: DEFA-Spielfilme 1945–1955/56*. Cologne: PapyRossa-Verlag, 1997.

Kapczynski, Jennifer M. 'Armchair Warriors: Heroic Postures in the West German War Film', in Paul Cooke and Marc Silberman (eds), *Screening War: Perspectives on German Suffering* (Rochester, NY: Camden House, 2010), 17–35.

Kellner, Wolfgang. *Abenteurer wider Willen*. Berlin: Verlag der Nation, 1984.

Kersten, Heinz. *So viele Träume: DEFA-Film-Kritiken aus drei Jahrzehnten*. Berlin: Vistas, 1996.

Kirschnick, Sylke. *Anne Frank und die DDR: politische Deutungen und persönliche Lesarten des berühmten Tagebuchs*. Berlin: Ch. Links Verlag, 2009.

Kramer, Sven. *Die Shoah im Bild*. Munich: Ed. Text + Kritik, 2003.

Landy, Marcia. *Imitations of Life: A Reader on Film and Television Melodrama*. Detroit: Wayne State University, 1991.

Löb, Ladislaus. *Dealing with Satan: Rezso Kasztner's Daring Rescue of Hungarian Jews*. London: Jonathan Cape, 2008.

Mertens, Lothar. *Davidstern unter Hammer und Zirkel: die jüdischen Gemeinden in der SBZ/DDR und ihre Behandlung durch Partei und Staat 1945–1990*. Hildesheim: Olms, 1997.

Moeller, Robert. *War Stories: The Search for a Usable Past in the Federal Republic of Germany*. Berkeley: University of California Press, 2001.

Möller, Martina. *Rubble, Ruins and Romanticism: Visual Style, Narration and Identity in Post-War German Cinema*. Bielefeld: Transcript Verlag, 2013.

Möller, Thomas and Gabriele Horche. *Die Vergangenheit in der Gegenwart: Konfrontationen mit den Folgen des Holocaust im deutschen Nachkriegsfilm*. Munich: Edition Text + Kritik, 2001.

Morton, Jim. 'The Eleventh Plenum.' *East German Cinema*, August 2013. Retrieved 1 March 2019 from https://eastgermancinema.com/2013/08/24/the-11th-plenum.

Mückenberger, Christiane. 'Die ersten "antifaschistischen" DEFA-Filme der Nachkriegsjahre', in Rainer Waterkamp (ed.), *Nationalsozialismus und Judenverfolgung in DDR-Medien*, Medienberatung Vol. 4 (Bonn: Bundeszentrale für Politische Bildung, 1997), 11–25.

Mückenberger, Christiane. 'Zeit der Hoffnungen: 1946 bis 1949', in Ralf Schenk (ed.), *Das zweite Leben der Filmstadt Babelsberg* (Berlin: Henschel, 1994), 8–49.

Müller, Beate. *Stasi–Zensur–Machtdiskurse: Publikationsgeschichten und Materialien zu Jurek Beckers Werk*. Tübingen: Max Niemeyer Verlag, 2012.

Museum of Modern Art. 'Die Russen kommen (The Russians Are Coming). 1968/87. Directed by Heiner Carow'. Retrieved 1 March 2019 from https://www.moma.org/calendar/events/2501.

Musial, Torsten and Kornelia Knospe. *Kurt Maetzig*. Berlin: Akademie der Künste, 2011.

Musial, Torsten and Nicky Rittmeyer. *Konrad Wolf*. Berlin: Akademie der Künste, 2005.

Nationale Front des Demokratischen Deutschland. *Braunbuch: Kriegs- und Naziverbrecher in der Bundesrepublik: Staat, Wirtschaft, Armee, Verwaltung, Justiz, Wissenschaft*. Berlin: Staatsverlag der Deutschen Demokratischen Republik, 1965.

Neale, Steve. 'Melodrama and Tears'. *Screen* 27 (1986), 6–23.

Niven, Bill. *Hitler and Film: The Führer's Hidden Passion*. New Haven: Yale University Press, 2018.

Niven, Bill. 'Remembering Nazi-Antisemitism in the GDR', in Bill Niven and Chloe Paver (eds), *Memorialization in Germany since 1945* (Basingstoke: Palgrave Macmillan), 205–13.

Niven, Bill. *Representations of Flight and Expulsion in East German Prose Works*. Rochester, NY: Camden House, 2014.

Niven, Bill. *The Buchenwald Child: Truth, Fiction, and Propaganda*. Columbia, SC: Camden House, 2009.

O'Brien, Mary-Elizabeth. *Nazi Cinema as Enchantment: The Politics of Entertainment in the Third Reich*. Rochester, NY: Camden House, 2003.

O'Doherty, Paul. *The Portrayal of Jews in GDR Prose Fiction*. Amsterdam: Rodophi, 1997.

Pieck, Wilhelm. 'An der Wende der deutschen Geschichte', in Henner Barthel (ed.), *Politische Rede in der DDR: eine kritische Dokumentation* (St. Ingbert: Röhrig Universitätsverlag, 1998), 19–22.

Pinkert, Anke. *Film and Memory in East Germany*. Bloomington: Indiana University Press, 2008.

Pleyer, Peter. *Deutscher Nachkriegsfilm 1946–1948*. Münster: Fahle, 1965.

Ragaru, Nadège. 'The Gendered Dimensions of *Zvezdi/Sterne* (1959)', *Eurozine*. Retrieved 1 March 2019 from https://www.eurozine.com/the-gendered-dimensions-of-zvezdisterne-1959.

Rentschler, Eric. 'Germany: The Past That Would Not Go Away', in William Luhr (ed.), *World Cinema since 1945* (New York: Ungar, 1992), 208–51.

Richter, Erika. 'Zwischen Mauerbau und Kahlschlag: 1961 bis 1965', in Ralf Schenk (ed.), *Das zweite Leben der Filmstadt Babelsberg: 1946–1992* (Berlin: Henschelverlag, 1994), 159–211.

Richter, Rolf. 'Frank Beyer: Vom Umgang mit Widersprüchen', in Rolf Richter (ed.), *DEFA-Spielfilm-Regisseure und Ihre Kritiker*. Vol. 2 (Berlin: Henschelverlag Kunst und Gesellschaft, 1983), 11–38.

Rinke, Andrea. *Images of Women in East German Cinema: Socialist Models, Private Dreamers and Rebels*. Lewiston, NY: Edwin Mellen Press, 2006.

Roman, James. *From Daytime to Primetime: The History of American Television Programs*. Westport, CT: Greenwood Press, 2005.

Rosenstone, Robert. *History on Film/Film on History*. Harlow: Pearson, 2006.

Sander, Gilman L. *Jurek Becker: die Biografie*. Berlin: Ullstein, 2002.

Schenk, Ralf. *Regie: Frank Beyer*. Ed. Hentrich: Berlin, 1995.

Schieber, Elke. 'Anfang vom Ende der Kontinuität des Argwohns: 1980 bis 1989', in Ralf Schenk (ed.), *Das zweite Leben der Filmstadt Babelsberg: DEFA-Spielfilme 1946–1992* (Berlin: Henschelverlag, 1994), 264–327.

Schieber, Elke. *Die Bilder des Zeugen Schattmann: Recherche zu einem Fernsehfilm*. Potsdam: Filmmuseum Potsdam, 2007.

Schieber, Elke. 'Im Dämmerlicht der Perestroika 1980 bis 1989', in Günter Jordan and Ralf Schenk (eds), *Schwarzweiß und Farbe: DEFA-Dokumentarfilme 1946–92* (Berlin: Filmmuseum Potsdam, 1996), 180–233.

Schieber, Elke. 'Spuren der Erinnerung', in Barbara Eichinger and Frank Stern (eds), *Film im Sozialismus – die DEFA* (Vienna: Mandelbaum, 2009), 63–78.

Schieber, Elke. *Tangenten: Holocaust und jüdisches Leben im Spiegel audiovisueller Medien der SBZ und der DDR – Eine Dokumentation*. Berlin: Bertz + Fischer Verlag, 2016.

Schittly, Dagmar. *Zwischen Regie und Regime: die Filmpolitik der SED im Spiegel der DEFA-Produktionen*. Berlin: Christoph Links, 2002.
Schleunes, Karl A. *The Twisted Road to Auschwitz: Nazi Policy Toward German Jews, 1933–1939*. Urbana: University of Illinois Press, 1970.
Schmidt, Wolfgang. 'Krieg und Militär im deutschen Nachkriegsfilm', in Bernhard Chiari, Matthias Rogg and Wolfgang Schmidt (eds), *Krieg und Militär im Film des 20. Jahrhunderts* (Munich: Oldenbourg, 2003), 441–52.
Schweikart, Hans. *Es wird schon nicht so schlimm! oder, Nichts geht vorüber!: ein Filmvorschlag*. Berlin: Verbrecher Verlag, 2014.
Shandley, Robert. 'Rubble Canyons: *Die Mörder sind unter uns* and the Western'. *German Quarterly* 74(2) (2001), 132–47.
Shandley, Robert. *Rubble Films. German Cinema in the Shadow of the Third Reich*. Philadelphia: Temple University, 2001.
Shaw, George Bernard. *Bernard Shaw's Plays*. New York: Norton, 1970.
Silberman, Marc. *German Cinema: Texts in Context*. Detroit: Wayne State University Press, 1995.
Smith, James. *Melodrama*. London: Methuen, 1973.
Spieker, Markus. *Hollywood unterm Hakenkreuz: der amerikanische Spielfilm im Dritten Reich*. Trier: Wissenschaftlicher Verlag, 1999.
Staatliche Zentralverwaltung für Statistik. *Statistisches Jahrbuch der Deutschen Demokratischen Republik*. Berlin: Staatsverlag der Deutschen Demokratischen Republik, 1989.
Steiner, André. *The Plans That Failed: An Economic History of the GDR*. New York: Berghahn Books, 2010.
Stott, Rosemary. *Crossing the Wall: The Western Feature Film Import in East Germany*. Oxford: Peter Lang, 2012.
Thiele, Martina. *Publizistische Kontroversen über den Holocaust im Film*. Münster: Lit Cop, 2007.
Thürk, Harry. *Das Tal der sieben Monde*. Berlin: Das Neue Berlin, 1964.
Timm, Angelika. 'Der 9. November 1938 in der politischen Kultur der DDR', in Rolf Steininger (ed.), *Der Umgang mit dem Holocaust: Europa–USA–Israel* (Vienna: Böhlau, 1994), 246–62.
Timm, Angelika. *Hammer, Zirkel, Davidstern: Das gestörte Verhältnis der DDR zu Zionismus und Staat Israel*. Bonn: Bouvier, 1997.
Timm, Angelika. 'Ideology and Realpolitik: East German Attitudes towards Zionism and Israel', in Jeffrey Herf (ed.), *Anti-Semitism and Anti-Zionism in Historical Perspective: Convergence and Divergence* (London: Routledge, 2014), 186–205.
Timm, Angelika. *Jewish Claims Against East Germany: Moral Obligations and Pragmatic Policy*. Budapest: Central European University Press, 1997.
Torner, Evan. 'Gottfried Kolditz (1922–1982)', in Michelle Langford (ed.), *Directory of World Cinema: Germany 2* (Bristol: Intellect, 2013), 18–21.
Torner, Evan. 'The DEFA Indianerfilme: Narrating the Postcolonial through Gojko Mitic', in Seán Allan and Sebastian Heiduschke (eds), *Re-Imagining DEFA: East German Cinema in its National and Transnational Contexts* (New York: Berghahn, 2016), 227–47.
United States Holocaust Memorial Museum. 'Introduction to the Holocaust'. Retrieved 1 March 2019 from https://encyclopedia.ushmm.org/content/en/article/introduction-to-the-holocaust.

van de Knaap, Ewout. 'Enlightening Procedures. *Nacht und Nebel* in Germany', in. Ewout van de Knaap (ed.), *Uncovering the Holocaust. The International Reception of Night and Fog* (London: Wallflower Press, 2006), 46–85.
VEB Bibliographisches Institut. *Meyers Taschenlexikon*. Leipzig: VEB Bibliographisches Institut, Leipzig, 1963.
Verband der Film- und Fernsehschaffenden der DDR (ed.). *Das Thema 'Antifaschismus' in Filmen der DDR für Kino und Fernsehen: Auswahlfilmographie 1946–1984*. Berlin: Verband der Film- und Fernsehschaffenden der DDR, 1985.
Walk, Ines. 'Wolf, Konrad'. *DEFA Stiftung*, October 2009. Retrieved 1 March 2019 from http://www.defa-stiftung.de/wolf-konrad.
Ward, Elizabeth M. 'Screening out the East: The Playing Out of Inter-German Relations at the Cannes Film Festival'. *German Life and Letters* 68(1) (2015), 37–53.
Ward, Elizabeth M. 'Who Is Heinz Stielke? Questions of Identity in Michael Kann's *Stielke, Heinz, fünfzehn*, in Stephan Ehrig, Marcel Thomas and David Zell (eds), *The GDR today: New Interdisciplinary Approaches to East German History, Memory and Culture* (Oxford: Peter Lang, 2018), 43–63.
Ward, Elizabeth M. 'Zur strategischen Aneignung der Anne Frank-Figur in Konrad Wolfs *Professor Mamlock* (1961)', in Peter Seibert, Jana Piper and Alfonso Meoli (eds), *Anne Frank: Mediengeschichten* (Berlin: Metropol Verlag, 2013), 54–62.
Wiedemann, Dieter. 'Anmerkungen zu einem Forschungsprojekt', in Peter Hoff and Dieter Wiedemann (eds), *Der DEFA-Spielfilm in den 80er Jahren: Chancen für die 90er?* (Berlin: Vistas, 1992), 9–15.
Wischnewski, Klaus. 'Träumer und gewöhnliche Leute: 1966 bis 1979', in Ralf Schenk (ed.), *Das zweite Leben der Filmstadt Babelsberg: 1946–1992* (Berlin: Henschelverlag, 1994), 212–63.
Witte, Karsten. 'The Indivisible Legacy of Nazi Cinema'. *New German Critique* 74 (1998), 23–30.
Wolf, Friedrich. *Professor Mamlock: ein Schauspiel*. Leipzig: Reclam, 1976.
Wolfgram, Mark. *Getting History Right: East and West German Collective Memories of the Holocaust and War*. Lewisburg: Bucknell University Press, 2011.
Wulff, Hans J. 'Bundesdeutsche Kriegs- und Militärfilme der 1950er Jahre: eine Filmbiographie', *Medienwissenschaft. Hamburg: Berichte und Papier* 132 (2012), 1–13.
Zinner, Hedda. *Arrangement mit dem Tod*. Berlin: Buchverlag der Morgen, 1984.
zur Nieden, Susanne. '... stärker als der Tod: Bruno Apitz' Roman *Nackt unter Wölfen* und die Holocaust-Rezeption in der DDR', in Manuel Köppen and Klaus Scherpe (eds), *Bilder des Holocaust: Literatur, Film, bildende Kunst* (Cologne: Böhlau, 1997), 97–108.

Index

1–2–3 Corona (1948), 31
8 ½ (1963), 158
38 – Auch war das Wien (38 – Vienna Before the Fall, 1986), 213

Abenteurer wider Willen (1984), 188
Abeßer, Doris, 86
Academy Awards. See Oscars
Ackermann, Anton, 3, 48, 67
Adenauer, Konrad, 60, 152n3
Affaire Blum (Blum Affair, 1948), 8, 20, 24, 214n17
A Friendship in Vienna (1988), 190
Alan & Naomi (1992), 191
Alltagsfilme, 199
Altman, Rick, 26–27, 123
Am Ende der Welt (At the End of the World, 1974), 134
American Motion Picture Export Association, 17
Apitz, Bruno, 93
Arrangement mit dem Tod (Arrangement with Death, 1984), 197–98, 200–1, 204–6
Atrocity films, 18, 37. See also Die Todesmühlen
Aufbaufilme, 9–10, 47
Au revoir, les enfants (Goodbye, Children, 1987), 190
Axen, Hermann, 176

Bahr, Egon, 131
Balthoff, Alfred, 40
Becher, Johannes, 48

Becher, Kurt Andreas, 98–101, 106–8, 113n43
  depiction in Lebende Ware, 98–104, 107–10 (see also Lebende Ware)
Becker, Jurek, 134–35, 136n10, 153, 156–58, 160, 171n3, 172n30. See also Jakob der Lügner
Behn-Grund, Friedl, 28, 41
Bentzien, Hans, 92
Berlin Film Festival, 168, 176
Betrogen bis zum jüngsten Tag (Duped Till Doomsday, 1957), 74n46
Beyer, Frank, 11, 92, 153–56, 158, 160–61, 164–66, 168–70, 171n3, 171n15, 212. See also Jakob der Lügner; Nackt unter Wölfen; Spur der Steine
  consequences of the Eleventh Plenum, 92, 160, 171n15
Biermann, Wolf, 133
Biermann Affair, 133–34, 136n8, 153–54, 174
Blume, Renate, 161
Brandt, Martin, 197
Brandt, Willy, 131
Braunbuch, 100, 112n23
Brodský, Vlastimil, 164–65, 168
Bruk, Franz, 159
Bund Deutscher Mädel (League of German Girls), 202–3
Burg, Ursula, 86

Cannes Film Festival, 70–72, 176, 216
Carow, Heiner, 181

CCC Film, 172n30
Concentration camps, 18, 49–50,
　152n8, 164
　Auschwitz, 112n16, 152n8, 165
　designated National Sites of
　　Admonition and Remembrance,
　　49
　representation in films, 4, 11,
　　18–20, 21n12, 24, 30, 40, 54,
　　58, 64, 66, 69, 93, 98, 102, 104,
　　115–18, 125–26, 128n8, 136, 139,
　　143–51, 158, 165, 181, 187, 205.
　　See also Atrocity films

Das Kaninchen bin ich (The Rabbit is
　Me, 1965), 91
Das Mädchen von Fanö (The Girl from
　Fanö, 1941), 40
Das Singen im Dom zu Magdeburg
　(Singing in Magdeburg Cathedral,
　1988), 197, 214n13
Das Tal der sieben Monde (The Valley
　of the Seven Moons, 1967), 10,
　94–95, 114–29, 199, 218–20
DEFA (Deutsche Film-
　Aktiengesellschaft), 3–4, 5–7,
　9, 12, 13n14, 16, 17, 21n5, 31,
　34, 40, 47–49, 51, 51n3, 54–56,
　62, 64–65, 67, 69–72, 73n29,
　75–76, 84–86, 89–94, 97–99,
　104–7, 110–11, 111n8, 111n12,
　114–16, 120–21, 123, 127, 132–34,
　138, 142, 154, 156, 158–61, 167,
　169–70, 173–76, 179–80, 182,
　187–89, 197–200, 206, 209,
　211–13, 214n15, 216–17, 219.
　See also individual films
　antifascist conversion narrative,
　　9–11, 50–51, 54, 60, 62, 64, 69,
　　81–85, 118–19, 116, 125, 127, 181,
　　186, 191, 220
　antifascist film, 2–4, 10–12, 47, 50,
　　51n3, 69, 75, 91–94, 127, 134,
　　155, 165, 169–70, 175–77, 179–82,
　　189–91, 198–99, 211, 219
　antifascist resistance hero, 3, 5, 7,
　　10–12, 47, 50, 54–56, 64, 68–9,
　　73n29, 75–79, 85, 87, 93–94, 99,
　　114–16, 118–19, 121, 124–28, 136,
　　139–41, 145–47, 150, 155, 159,
　　161–65, 169–70, 176, 181–82,
　　189–90, 211, 216, 218–20
　censorship, 7, 10, 55, 91–92, 95n11,
　　112n30, 132, 176, 181
　collaboration with East German
　　television, 11, 14n24, 132–33,
　　137–38, 156, 160–61, 176, 198
　founding, 16–17, 21n5
　gender, 12, 30–31, 84–85, 118–20,
　　175, 197, 199–201, 213
　generational shifts, 11, 12,
　　75–76, 85, 87, 91–93, 127, 134–35,
　　137–39, 151–52, 170–71, 174–76,
　　179–82, 188–91, 211–13, 218, 220
　marketing strategies, 6, 42, 51, 56,
　　63–64, 70, 73n29, 76, 85–87, 100–
　　1, 108–9, 112n27, 119, 129n15,
　　129n25, 136, 151, 152n10, 170,
　　194, 212, 219–20
　reception abroad, 3, 6, 12, 41–43,
　　45n48, 53–56, 63–64, 70–72,
　　76–77, 98, 121, 152n10, 156, 158,
　　168–69
　shifting levels of output, 47–48, 91,
　　132, 173
　Vater Brief, 174
DEFA-Außenhandel, 6, 51n7, 55–56,
　63, 98, 129n15, 153, 168–69, 188,
　216–17
Dein unbekannter Bruder (Your
　Unknown Brother, 1982), 176
Denazification, 15–16, 18, 37–38, 40,
　113n43
　film industry, 15–16, 21n2, 40
　policy in the Soviet sector, 16–17
　policy in the Western sectors, 15, 17
Der Aufenthalt (The Turning Point,
　1982), 176
Der ewige Jude (The Eternal Jew, 1940),
　19–20

Der Fall Gleiwitz (*The Gleiwitz Case*, 1961), 111n2
Der Prozess wird vertagt (*The Trial is Postponed*, 1958), 50
Der siebente Brunnen (*The Seventh Well*, 1983), 176
Der verlorene Engel (*The Lost Angel*, 1966), 91, 132
Dessau, Anne, 176
Deutsche Hochschule für Filmkunst, 217, 221n1
Deutscher Fernsehfunk (DFF), 132–33, 138, 171n12. See also DEFA: collaboration with East German television; Fernsehen der DDR (DDR-FS); German Democratic Republic: television
Die Abenteuer des Werner Holt (*The Adventures of Werner Holt*, 1965), 111n2, 181
Die Bilder des Zeugen Schattmann (*The Pictures of Witness Schattmann*, 1972), 11, 14n24, 135–36, 137–52, 161, 166–67, 189–90, 193n31, 199, 218–21
Die goldene Stadt (*The Golden City*, 1942), 28
Die Kinder vom Bullenhuser Damm (*The Children of Bullenhuser Damm*), 176
Die Leiden des jungen Werthers (*The Sorrows of the Young Werther*, 1976), 133
Die Mörder sind unter uns (*The Murderers are Among Us*, 1946), 3–4, 8, 17, 19–20, 21n12, 24, 31, 35, 37
Die Russen kommen (*The Russians Are Coming*, 1968), 181
Die Schauspielerin (*The Actress*, 1988), 12, 177, 194–215, 218–21
Die Schüsse der Arche Noah (*Shots from Noah's Arc*, 1983), 2, 181–82
Die Todesmühlen (*Death Mills*, 1945), 18, 37
Die Verlobte (*The Fiancée*, 1980), 133
Dósai, István, 106

Edel, Peter, 137, 149–50, 152n8
Edinburgh Film Festival, 72, 216
Eggebrecht, Axel, 31, 35
Ehe im Schatten (*Marriage in the Shadows*, 1947), 9, 15, 20–21, 23–46, 51, 64, 78, 162, 199–200, 210, 214n17, 218–20
Eichmann, Adolf, 43, 100, 108–10, 165
  depiction in *Lebende Ware*, 98, 100, 104, 108–10, 111n8, 122
Ein Tagebuch für Anne Frank (*A Diary for Anne Frank*, 1958), 86, 88n28
Eleventh Plenum of the SED, 10, 90–94, 95n17, 97, 99, 105, 110, 112n30, 114–17, 119, 121–22, 124, 127–28, 132–34, 156
  Kahlschlag, 91, 97, 156, 159
Engel, Erich, 20
Erdmann, Otto, 28
Ernst Thälmann – Führer seiner Klasse (*Ernst Thälmann – Leader of his Class*, 1955), 50, 91, 127
Ernst Thälmann – Sohn seiner Klasse (*Ernst Thälmann – Son of his Class*, 1954), 2, 50, 91, 127
exhibitions, 1, 49, 197–98

Federal Republic of Germany (FRG)
  criticisms of the German Democratic Republic, 49, 54–55, 70–71; 73n15, 148–49, 171n13, 195, 220
Filmbegutachtungskommission (West Berlin), 77
Filmbewertungsstelle Wiesbaden (FBW), 54–55
  recognition of the GDR, 70–72, 131
  remembrance discourses, 3, 13n13, 60, 125, 195
  television, 5, 13n16, 160, 172n30, 216

war films, 60, 62, 69, 73n23
  See also German Democratic Republic: criticisms of the Federal Republic
Fernsehen der DDR (DDR-FS), 156, 160–61, 169, 171n12, 173, 176, 198. *See also* DEFA: collaboration with East German television; Deutscher Fernsehfunk (DFF); German Democratic Republic: television
Fernsehpitaval, 99
Forbidden (1984), 213
Frank, Anne, 85
  cultural representations in the GDR, 85–87, 88n22
Fünf Patronenhülsen (*Five Cartridges*, 1960), 2, 92, 165

Gegenwartsfilme, 90–91, 199
Genesung (*Recovery*, 1956), 50, 81
George, Heinrich, 21n2
German Democratic Republic. *See also* Federal Republic of Germany: criticisms of the German Democratic Republic; Ministry for Culture; SED
  1953 June uprising, 48
  antifascism, 1–2, 5, 10, 49, 116, 125, 147, 219–20 (*see also* DEFA: antifascist conversion narrative; DEFA: antifascist film; DEFA: antifascist resistance hero; German Democratic Republic: remembrance discourses; *Indianerfilme*)
  Aufbau period, 9–10, 47, 49–50, 51n2, 89–90
  criticisms of the Federal Republic, 1–2, 6, 43, 50, 53–54, 64, 69, 75–77, 88n28, 94, 98–100, 107, 110, 112nn20–23, 123–24, 134, 138–39, 147–49, 219–20 (*see also Braunbuch*)
  criticisms of Zionism, 92–93, 98, 105, 109

cultural 'freezes', 7, 10, 48–49, 90–91, 94, 110–11, 117, 120, 127–28, 134, 216
cultural 'thaws', 7, 11, 48, 89–90, 132–34, 156, 216
demarcation process, 131–32
diplomatic recognition, 70–72, 131 (*see also* Hallstein Doctrine)
Neue Ökonomische System der Planung und Leitung (New Economic System, NÖSPL), 10, 90
rapprochement with the Federal Republic, 131
remembrance discourses, 1–7, 12–13, 43, 49, 57–58, 60, 63–64, 69, 75–76, 79, 87, 92–93, 95n21, 104–7, 110, 119–20, 125, 127, 135–37, 139–40, 151–52, 171n13, 176, 190, 194–98, 211–13, 216–17, 219–21
television, 11, 13n16, 86, 90, 99, 115–56, 132–33, 138, 169, 171n12, 173–74 (*see also* DEFA: collaboration with East German television; Deutscher Fernsehfunk (DFF); Fernsehen der DDR (DDR-FS))
Ghettos
  representation in films, 11, 149, 153–55, 157–58, 162–63, 166–68, 171n6
Globke, Hans, 138, 140, 147, 152n3
Görner, Eberhard, 176
Gottschalk, Joachim, 24, 32, 34, 40, 44n2, 44n24
Gräf, Roland, 7
Gründgens, Gustaf, 21n2
Gyptner, Rudolf, 116

Hager, Kurt, 132, 134
Hallstein Doctrine, 70–72
Harlan, Veit, 15–16, 18, 28, 40
Hasse, Hannjo, 111n8, 122
Heinz, Wolfgang, 86, 97
Hitlerjunge Salomon (*Europa Europa*, 1990), 190

Hitler Youth, 12, 135, 177, 180, 183–84, 186
Holocaust (1978), 4, 13n15, 43
Honecker, Erich, 11, 90, 131–34, 156, 174, 195
HV Film (Hauptverwaltung Film), 48, 67, 105, 153–54, 159, 169, 187–89, 209, 212

Ich klage an (*I Accuse*, 1941), 18, 28, 41
Ich war neunzehn (*I Was Nineteen*, 1968), 81–82, 93, 111n2, 127
Ich zwing dich zu leben (*I'll Force You to Live*, 1978), 134–35
Immensee (1943), 28
Indianerfilme, 116, 120–24
In jenen Tagen (*In Those Days*, 1947), 19, 24, 44n24
Israel, 93, 156, 171n13, 196

Jadup und Boel (*Jadup and Boel*, 1980), 176
Jakob der Lügner (*Jacob the Liar*, 1974), 3, 11, 14n24, 133–36, 153–72, 198–200, 206, 211–12, 214n17, 217, 219–20, 221n2
Jannings, Emil, 21n2
Jud Süss (*Jew Süss*, 1940), 15–16, 18, 28, 40
Jung-Alsen, Kurt, 138. *See also Die Bilder des Zeugen Schattmann*
Jupé, Walter, 99, 105. *See also Lebende Ware*
Jürschik, Rudolf, 176

Kann, Michael, 177, 186, 188. *See also Stielke, Heinz, fünfzehn*
Karlovy Vary Film Festival, 105, 112n30, 216
Kastner, Rudolf, 98, 100, 108–10, 112n14, 113n43
  depiction in *Lebende Ware*, 98, 100, 103–4, 109–10, 112n14
Katja (1984), 176, 198
Kaul, Friedrich Karl, 99, 105, 107, 112n16. *See also Lebende Ware*

Keller, Änne, 99
Kellner, Wolfgang, 188
Kirsten, Ralf, 132, 134
Klaren, Georg, 31
Klinger, Paul, 28, 45n50
KLK an PTX – Die Rote Kapelle (*KLK Calling PTZ – The Red Orchestra*, 1970), 134
Kolditz, Gottfried, 115–16, 121. *See also Das Tal der sieben Monde*
Komitee der Antifaschistischen Widerstandskämpfer (KdAW, Committee of Antifascist Resistance Fighters), 49, 149, 152n8, 175–76, 198, 208
Königskinder (*Star-Crossed Lovers*, 1962), 92
Kristallnacht. *See* November Pogroms
Krücke (*Crutch*, 1993), 13n15
Kühn, Regine, 202, 211, 214n29. *See also Die Schauspielerin*
Kühn, Siegfried, 177, 198–200, 202, 211–12, 214n29. *See also Die Schauspielerin*
Kulturnation, 26, 44n5, 77, 143
Kunert, Joachim, 181
Künstlerische Arbeitsgruppen (KAG, Artistic Working Groups), 89, 92, 95n2, 216
  Gruppe Babelsberg, 202, 209–10, 212
  Gruppe Johannisthal, 179, 188
  Heinrich Greif, 76, 97, 106, 156–59
  Roter Kreis, 119, 121, 124–25

Lang ist der Weg (*Long is the Way*, 1948), 20
Lebende Ware (*Living Wares*, 1966), 10, 93–94, 97–113, 114, 122, 162, 169, 199, 217–20
Le Dernier Métro (*The Last Metro*, 1980), 213
Leute mit Flügeln (*People with Wings*, 1960), 2, 165

Liebeneiner, Wolfgang, 18, 41
Liefers, Karlheinz, 127
Lissy (1957), 50, 81–82
Löffler, Kurt, 197
London Film Festival, 72, 168
Lotz, Karl Heinz, 189
Luderer, Wolfgang, 99, 107. See also *Lebende Ware*
Ludwig, Alice, 28

Mäde, Hans-Dieter, 206
Maetzig, Kurt, 9, 21n5, 31–32, 34–35, 40, 43, 50, 91–92
  consequences of Eleventh Plenum, 91–92
Meine Stunde Null (*My Zero Hour*, 1970), 134
melodrama, 9, 18, 20, 24, 26–32, 34, 40–42
Mich dürstet (*I'm Thirsty*, 1956), 2
Ministry for Culture, 1, 2, 12, 48, 62, 67–68, 70, 72, 89, 92, 105, 112n30, 153–54, 158–59, 168, 197
Morituri (1948), 20, 24
Moscow International Film Festival, 76, 158, 216
Mückenberger, Jochen, 89, 92
Mueller-Stahl, Armin, 136n10, 153, 171n3

Nackt unter Wölfen (*Naked Among Wolves*, 1963), 8, 92–93, 111n2, 158, 165, 214n17
National Socialism
  antisemitic films, 16, 18
  film industry, 15–18, 27–28, 40–42, 44n2
  Führerliste, 16, 21n3
  Gottbegnadeten-Liste, 16, 21n3
  melodrama, 9, 18, 28, 30
Norden, Albert, 49
November Pogroms, 1, 19, 26, 43, 194, 199–99, 209
Nuit et brouillard (*Night and Fog*, 1955), 4

OMGUS (Office of Military Government, United States), 17–18, 23, 37, 44n1
ORWO film stock, 167–68
Oscars, 3, 9, 42, 45n50, 153–54, 156, 168–69, 172n45, 219

Pehnert, Horst, 154, 197
Pieck, Wilhelm, 47
Pommer, Erich, 17
Prager, Willy, 36, 40
Professor Mamlock (1961), 9–10, 50–51, 75–88, 97, 111n2, 140, 168, 189–90, 199, 214n17, 218, 220
  play (1933), 75, 79, 81, 83–84, 86–87, 88n1
  television film (1958), 83–84, 86–87
Progress Film, 6, 48, 56, 63, 112n27, 189, 194, 212. See also DEFA: marketing strategies

Rat der Götter (*Council of Gods*, 1950), 24, 91
Ravensbrücker Ballade (*Ravensbrück Ballad*, 1985), 176, 198
Razzia (*Raid*, 1947), 31
Riefenstahl, Leni, 15
Rodenberg, Hans, 48, 158
Rotation (1949), 50, 127

Schlegel, Egon, 181
Schleif, Wolfgang, 28
Schulze, Horst, 108–9
Schwab, Sepp, 48
Schweikart, Hans, 40
SED (Sozialistische Einheitspartei Deutschlands, Socialist Unity Party of Germany), 1, 2, 9–10, 21, 43, 47–48, 55, 70, 72, 75, 89–91, 95n17, 116, 131–34, 136n8, 149, 153–54, 157–59, 169, 174, 176, 194–98, 216–17, 221
Shoah (1985), 4
Sie nannten ihn Amigo (*They Called Him Amigo*, 1958), 2, 50, 181

Simon, Rainer, 176
Socialist Realism, 116, 159
Söderbaum, Kristina, 40
Sonnensucher (*Sun Seekers*, 1958), 132
Sowjetische Militäradministration in Deutschland (SMAD, Soviet Military Administration in Germany), 3–4, 9, 16–17, 21, 24, 50
Spur der Steine (*Trace of Stones*, 1966), 92, 112n30, 156, 159
Spur des Falken (*Trail of the Falcon*, 1968), 121
Stärker als die Nacht (*Stronger than the Night*, 1954), 2
Sterne (*Stars*, 1959), 9–10, 50–51, 53–74, 76–78, 82–83, 85, 115, 122, 125, 199–200, 214n17, 217–20
Stielke, Heinz, fünfzehn (*Stielke, Heinz, Fifteen*, 1987), 12, 176–77, 179–93, 199, 211, 218–20, 221n2
Straßenbekanntschaft (*Street Acquaintances*, 1948), 31
Székely, Kati, 86

Thürk, Harry, 128n7
Trümmerfilme, 19

Ulbricht, Walter, 11, 51n2, 132

Venice Film Festival, 216
Vereinigung der Verfolgten des Naziregimes (Association of Persecutees of the National Socialist Regime, VVN), 49
Vienna Film Festival, 72
Volkmann, Herbert, 16
von Stolz, Hilde, 28, 40, 44n16

Wagenstein, Angel, 65, 67–68. *See also Sterne*
Wandel, Paul, 48
Wander, Fred, 176
Weiß, Ulrich, 176, 189
Wendt, Erich, 62, 68
Wilkening, Albert, 48, 54–55, 70, 89
Wischnewski, Klaus, 92, 106–8, 121, 157
Witt, Günter, 92
Wo andere schweigen (*Where Others Keep Silent*, 1984), 2
Wolf, Christa, 2, 133
Wolf, Friedrich, 50, 81, 88n13
Wolf, Konrad, 50, 55, 68, 72, 76, 79, 81–82, 93, 174. *See also Professor Mamlock*; *Sterne*
   consequences of Eleventh Plenum, 95n17
Wolff, Meta, 31–32, 44n2, 44n24

Zeller, Wolfgang, 28, 32, 40
Zinner, Hedda, 176, 197–202, 204–5, 209, 212
Zwischenfall in Benderath (*Incident in Benderath*, 1956), 50
Zwischen gestern und morgen (*Between Yesterday and Tomorrow*, 1947), 19

www.ingramcontent.com/pod-product-compliance
Lightning Source LLC
Chambersburg PA
CBHW071337080526
44587CB00017B/2871